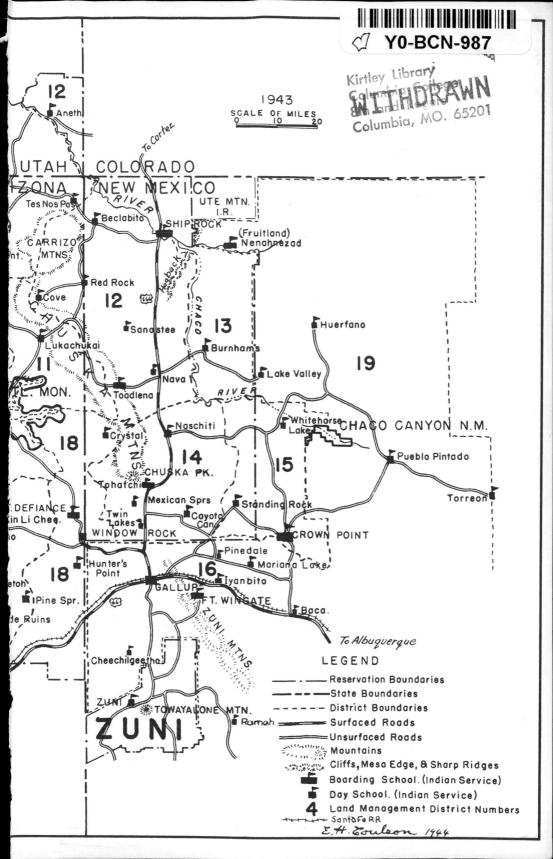

1943
SCALE OF MILES
0   10   20

12
Aneth

To Cortez

UTAH   COLORADO

ZONA   NEW MEXICO

ARIZONA

Tes Nos Pos

UTE MTN. I.R.

Beclabito

SHIP ROCK

RIVER

(Fruitland)
Nenahnezad

CARRIZO MTNS

Red Rock

Cove

12

Sanostee

Cabezon

CHACO

13

Huerfano

Lukachukai

Burnham's

19

MONS

Nava

Lake Valley

L. MON.

Toadlena

RIVER

11

Crystal

Naschiti

Whitehorse Lake

CHACO CANYON N.M.

18

CHUSKA PK.

14

15

Pueblo Pintado

MTNS

Tohatchi

DEFIANCE

Mexican Sprs

Standing Rock

Torreon

Kin Li Chee

Twin Lakes

Cayota Can.

WINDOW ROCK

CROWN POINT

Hunter's Point

Pinedale

Mariana Lake

18

16

Iyanbito

etoh

GALLUP

FT. WINGATE

Baca

Pine Spr.

de Ruins

ZUNI MTNS

To Albuquerque

Cheechilgeetho

LEGEND

ZUNI

TOWAYALONE MTN.

Ramah

ZUNI

────── Reservation Boundaries
── ── ── State Boundaries
─ ─ ─ ─ District Boundaries
═══════ Surfaced Roads
〰〰〰 Unsurfaced Roads
⛰ Mountains
⛰ Cliffs, Mesa Edge, & Sharp Ridges
▆ Boarding School. (Indian Service)
▆ Day School. (Indian Service)
4 Land Management District Numbers
┼┼┼┼┼ Santa Fe RR

E.H. Toulson 1944

CHILDREN OF THE PEOPLE

OFF TO A CEREMONIAL

THE NAVAHO INDIVIDUAL
and his development

CHILDREN
OF THE PEOPLE

By DOROTHEA LEIGHTON
and CLYDE KLUCKHOHN

OCTAGON BOOKS

A DIVISION OF FARRAR, STRAUS AND GIROUX

New York   1974

LIBRARY OF CONGRESS CATALOG CARD NUMBER: 77-96199
ISBN 0-374-94902-6

Printed in U.S.A. by
NOBLE OFFSET PRINTERS, INC.
NEW YORK, N.Y. 10003

TO
FLORENCE ROCKWOOD KLUCKHOHN and
ALEXANDER HAMILTON LEIGHTON

INDIAN EDUCATION RESEARCH STAFF
COMMITTEE ON INDIAN EDUCATION RESEARCH

UNIVERSITY OF CHICAGO
W. Lloyd Warner, *Chairman*
Robert J. Havighurst
Ralph Tyler

OFFICE OF INDIAN AFFAIRS
John Collier, *Chairman*
Willard W. Beatty
Rene d'Harnoncourt
Joseph McCaskill

Laura Thompson, *Coördinator*

NAVAHO PROJECT STAFF

FIELD WORKERS
Helen Bradley
Lisbeth Eubank
Rachel Jordan
Josephine Howard
Clyde Kluckhohn
Dorothea C. Leighton
Alice Leonard
Lillian Lincheze
Bertha Lorenzo
Josephine Murray
Kate Tallsalt
Robert Tallsalt

TEST ANALYSTS
Free Drawings:
    Lisbeth Eubank
    Brooke Mordy

TEST ANALYSTS
Rorschach:
    Dorothea C. Leighton
Thematic Apperception (adapted):
    William E. Henry
    (Under the supervision of
    Robert J. Havighurst)
Emotional Response:
    Jean Hall
    Iva O. Schmidt
Goodenough Draw-A-Man:
    Minna K. Gunther
    Inez E. Pratt
Grace Arthur Point Performance:
    Rhea R. Hilkevitch
Moral Ideology:
    Jeannette Murstine

Roma K. McNickle, *Editor*

ADVISORY COMMITTEE

Grace Arthur
Ruth Benedict
Allison Davis
Fred Eggan
Erik Erikson
Lawrence Frank
A. Irving Hallowell

Bruno Klopfer
Clyde Kluckhohn
Eugene Lerner *
Kurt Lewin
D'Arcy McNickle
Margaret Mead
Scudder Mekeel

* Deceased, September 21, 1944

PREFACE

THIS book was written as a part of the Indian Education Research Project undertaken jointly by the Committee on Human Development of the University of Chicago and the United States Office of Indian Affairs. The immediate objective of the project was to investigate, analyze, and compare the development of personality in five Indian tribes in the context of their total environment — socio-cultural, geographical, and historical — for implications in regard to Indian Service administration. The ultimate aim of the long-range plan of research of which this project is the first step is to evaluate the whole Indian administrative program with special reference to the effect of present policy on Indians as individuals, to indicate the direction toward which this policy is leading, and to suggest how the effectiveness of Indian administration may be increased. It should be made clear, however, that the statements and conclusions are those of the writers and are not necessarily endorsed by the Office of Indian Affairs.

This research has been carried on since 1941 through the coöperative efforts of a large staff drawn from several fields, chiefly anthropology, sociology, psychology, psychiatry, medicine, linguistics, education, and administration. The field program was designed to investigate the development of the personalities of a sample of about a thousand children, six to eighteen years old, selected to represent two or more communities in each of five tribes: Hopi, Navaho, Papago, Sioux, and Zuni. The methods of investigation are described in Chapter 5 of this study. Field data were gathered by or under the supervision of specialists and were analyzed and interpreted by them.

The results of the project are being reported in monographs on the several tribes and in shorter reports on special phases of the work in all the groups. Tribal monographs already published are *The Hopi Way*, by Laura Thompson and Alice Joseph (University of Chicago Press, 1944) and *Warriors without Weapons*, a study of the Pine Ridge Sioux, by Gordon Macgregor (University of Chicago Press, 1946). Studies of the Papago and Zuni tribes are in preparation. The reports on special phases of the work are listed below in the Bibliography, and others are being prepared.

THE NAVAHO STUDY

THE SOURCES of the present book lie partly in the field work carried on by the writers for some years before the Indian Education Research project began, partly in the field work of the project. The published literature has been of little use. Authority for assertions is to be found mainly in the field notes of the writers and of their colleagues who have generously supplied unpublished data. A few facts are drawn from oral statements made in conference by Indian Service personnel. Interpretations were also importantly influenced by these discussions and by criticisms of the book in manuscript.

The Introduction, Chapters 5 to 9, and Conclusion were prepared almost entirely by Dr. Leighton. Dr. Kluckhohn contributed only some of the descriptions of the three communities and editorial and critical suggestions. Chapters 1 to 4 were drafted by Dr. Kluckhohn. Dr. Leighton supervised the whole testing program for the Navahos and did a major share of it herself. Dr. Kluckhohn's direct participation in the testing and interviewing activities of the project was limited to about three weeks' work in the Navaho country (of which only two days were spent at Navaho Mountain and a week at Shiprock) and to advice and conferences with the field staff. He also aided in preparing the pictures used in the Thematic Apperception Test and experimented with giving some of the tests in Navaho to children who had previously been tested in English.

The Navaho, also published by the Harvard University Press, is a companion volume by the same writers. Each book is a separate study, though the two supplement each other. *The Navaho* deals primarily with the situational and cultural context. *Children of The People* deals primarily with the psychological end-product in the individual. While each book stands by itself, two approaches, differently emphasized in the two books, are necessary for the deepest kind of understanding. The Navaho way of life may be learned only by knowing individual Navahos; conversely, Navaho personality may be fully understood only in so far as it is seen in relation to this life-way and other factors of the environment in the widest sense. Realization of Navaho culture is dependent upon acquaintance with personal figures, but equally these personal figures get their definition and organization as individuals only if the student is in a position to contrast each one with the generalized background provided by the culture of The People.

In this volume the accent will be heavily upon childhood and youth. This is done both because the main trends of personality are set early and because the hope of the future rests with the oncoming generation. Social change which is to be most constructive and least destructive must be suitable for the personality foundation created early in life by the treatment children receive in their own families and in the schools.

ACKNOWLEDGMENTS

This book is the product of a coöperative undertaking. Though the writers must bear full responsibility for the form in which all information and ideas finally appear, so many persons have made valuable and indeed indispensable contributions to this study that it is in an important sense a falsification for us to claim authorship.

In the first place, we are naturally dependent upon the Navahos, too numerous to mention, who have — not only during the Indian Education Research program but also during many years of earlier field work — shared their lives and thoughts with us. For the most part they have been patient with our demands upon their time, tolerant of our intrusion into their personal lives, and good-humored about the questions (sometimes stupid or at least meaningless to them). We have done our best to protect them from any embarrassment due to revelation of their identities in any quotations. We hope we have managed to convey some sense of the deep pleasure our personal relationship with them has brought to us. Some of the happiest times we have known have been in the Navaho country, and we count many Navahos among our closest friends. We also trust that our respect for the Navaho way of life and our admiration for many Navaho customs have been apparent in these pages. In short, we hope that the Navahos will feel that this is their book as much as ours — as indeed it is.

Our work would have been infinitely more arduous and less pleasant had it not been for the kindnesses shown us throughout the years by many white traders, ranchers, missionaries, and government employees.

Our obligations to our professional colleagues are also extremely heavy. We are particularly grateful to Flora Bailey, Helen Bradley, Janine Chappat, Malcolm Carr Collier, Margaret Fries, Josephine Murray, and John Landgraf for the aid we have obtained from their

unpublished manuscripts and field notes. We are indebted to the
late Mr. Ben Wetherill, to Dr. Harold Colton, and Dr. Emil Haury
for giving us access to the manuscripts of the late Louisa Wade
Wetherill and allowing us to make quotations from these in Chapter I.

To our associates in the Indian Education Research Project we are
deeply in debt. All of the individuals listed as committee members,
field staff, and consultants helped us by their support and counsel.
Some must be singled out for special mention. Dr. Willard Beatty
readily answered many requests for information and other assistance,
such as the making of the maps. The teachers of the Navajo Service
who coöperated in the research aided us almost as much by the example of their devotion and skill as by the indispensable data they
provided. While many individuals were involved to a lesser extent,
this book could not have been written without the help of the following teachers and interpreters: Rachel Jordan, Lisbeth Eubank, Josephine Howard, Lillian Lincheze, Alice Leonard, Bertha Lorenzo,
and Kate and Robert Tallsalt.

Dr. Laura Thompson, the coördinator of the project, facilitated
our work in all sorts of respects and whatever merit this book may
have owes much to her farsighted intelligence and enthusiasm.
Roma McNickle, the editor, has done far more than an uncom-
monly scrupulous job of editing, for which alone we would have
every reason to be profoundly grateful. She also has generously
assisted in checking proofs. To the Honorable John Collier, former
Commissioner of Indian Affairs, we owe more than can even be suggested by a formal acknowledgment. The whole intellectual and
personal outlook of both of us has been immeasurably affected by
contact with him, and his mind and his spirit provided the creative
force which, more than any other single factor, is responsible for any
good that may be found in this book.

We have to thank many members of the Navajo Service, and
especially Superintendent James M. Stewart, Director of Education
George Boyce, and former Field Representative F. W. LaRouche,
for enthusiastic coöperation and for preparing and assembling useful memoranda. Robert Young prepared a translation into Navaho
of some of the tests. The volume has been greatly enriched by the
photographs and maps provided, respectively, by Milton A. Snow
of the Navajo Service and E. H. Coulson of the Office of Indian

Affairs in Chicago, and by the excellent pictures of Paul J. Woolf.

Dr. Kluckhohn's chapters embody in part the results of researches carried on over a number of years by him which have been supported by the Division of Anthropology and the Peabody Museum of Harvard University, the Social Science Research Council, the American Philosophical Society, the Carnegie Corporation of New York, and the Viking Fund. However, these chapters are not to be considered more than a highly preliminary communication regarding Dr. Kluckhohn's intensive study of the socialization of Navaho children, for war duties have not permitted complete analysis of the data collected. For his original interest in the "culture and personality" field Dr. Kluckhohn is indebted to Professors Edward Sapir and John Dollard. For later guidance, encouragement, and research support he is under the deepest obligations to Professor Ralph Linton.

Dr. Leighton is particularly obligated to Dr. Adolf Meyer, Professor Emeritus of Psychiatry at Johns Hopkins University, for inspiring an interest in studying individuals in their society. This interest was encouraged and facilitated by the Social Science Research Council, by Dr. John C. Whitehorn, Professor of Psychiatry at Johns Hopkins University, and by the John Simon Guggenheim Memorial Foundation.

We must thank Dr. George Boyce, Helen Bradley, Professor Phillips Bradley, Dr. Janine Chappat, Commissioner John Collier, Malcolm Carr Collier, Dr. Elizabeth Colson, Dr. W. W. Hill, Dr. Solon Kimball, Dr. Florence Kluckhohn, Dr. Alexander Leighton, Dr. and Mrs. Adolph Meyer, John M. Roberts, Professor Donald Scott, Superintendent James M. Stewart, Dr. Laura Thompson, Dr. Esther Goldfrank Wittfogel, and Dr. Leland Wyman for reading all or part of the typescript and offering many useful suggestions and criticisms. We are also most grateful to Professor Scott for the interest he took in the publication of this book. Katherine Spencer kindly assisted us with the proof.

Finally, we express our appreciation to Walter Dyk and Harcourt Brace and Company for permission to quote from *Son of Old Man Hat* and to W. W. Hill and the Yale University Press for quotations from *The Agricultural and Hunting Methods of the Navaho Indians*.

DOROTHEA C. LEIGHTON
CLYDE KLUCKHOHN

CONTENTS

PLATES

FIGURES

MAPS

TABLES

A CHILD OF THE PEOPLE

A CHILD of THE PEOPLE

The Navaho Indians call themselves *diné*, "The People."[1] A case can be made for translating this term by "men," or simply "people," but since there are no articles in Navaho, the translation used in this book is formally permissible and is better semantically. A number of interpreters habitually use the English rendering, "The People," and the phrase suggests some things which are central in native feeling. "The People" — like many other societies — feel a strong sense of difference and isolation from the rest of humanity.

Because this is a book about human beings we begin with a document about a real person. When material for this study was being collected, a Navaho girl was asked to write everything she could remember about her life from the time she was born up to the present. She was then eleven years old and in the third grade of a boarding school. Short though her story is, it shows — within the framework of a single human life — many of the factors which are common to and crucial for all the children of The People.

MY LIFE STORY

This is a story about me and my name is Betsy. I am a Navaho girl. I was borned on May twenty-nine the year of nineteen-thirty-one at (the place) they called Ramah.

I am the oldest of the family and I have two sisters alive and one died. The two sisters names are Gretchen and Mary Ann and the one that died was Rita. Besides I got three brothers and their names are Peter and Jonathan and the baby boy is David. My mother is been to school for nine years. She went the same school I am going now. But my father never went to school. Even then he understand English too.

I live in a log house not very far from Ramah. At home I work and help my mother wash dishes also clean the house and help cook. Then I wash clothes with her. It is kind of hard for us to wash clothes because my daddy just hauls water with the wagon. Then I have a horse that I use for riding around. Also I get the horses in when daddy wants to use them. I water them at the Well too. During the summer I just take care of the sheep with my aunt because I have my sheep and goats in her herd. It is always hard to herd sheep when they lambing even then I

---

[1] Spelling and pronunciation of Navaho words is explained in *The Navaho*, Chapter 8.

like it. In the past time when I was three years old I got sick and I had a Navaho Medicine Man his name is Ricardo that sang over me to cure me. I had two different sings by the same Medicine Man then I got better again. Then when I was five years old I went to different sings that they called squaw dances with my mother and daddy around Two Wells. But I never did take a chance in dance because I was a small girl yet.

After when I was seven years old I started to go to school at Ramah this was a public school and I just only went six months there. Then I got sick again so I went to a hospital at Black Rock. There I stay for two weeks then I went home and Doctor told me to stay home for a month because I was weak. But after I got better I never went back to school again because I was left way behind.

Then after I was nine years old I went to this boarding school that I am going went with my niece her name is Susan. Our folks had to pay ten dollar each for our schooling beside that they had to buy our own clothes and shoes. The first year we went we sure got lonesome for our folks. They came to see us all the time too.

When I came back from school my sisters and brothers ask me how I like school? I said I sure like it because they got good things to that. They all wish to go to school over there. When I went second time I took my sister along with me to school. She sure was lonesome for a while then we got over it again like I did. But we sure had a good time too. Last summer we had a white woman come around my place, and she was giving a test to the navaho children. I was the first one to take it, then my sister Gretchen then my brother Peter he took it. But he sure was smart at it and I kind of tease him for that when he gets to school he was not going to be smart at all. But I sure told him wrong too. I was kind of surprise to see him learn things right along, and he sure talk loud too and they told us he is a smart boy at school.

I like to go to school but it is kind of hard for our folks to support us and pay for our schooling too. But then they sure like us to go to school.

This is the end of my story now.

THE THEMES OF BETSY'S STORY

THIS autobiography suggests some of the chief similarities and differences between white Americans and Navahos. For example, Betsy evidently has warm feelings for her parents, is proud of her mother and father and brother, and gets homesick when she leaves them. She is concerned about the cost of her education to her family, but she believes, as they do, that schooling is worth something. When she is at home she helps her mother with the housework. In these ways Betsy is much like many a little white girl that we could find in any community.

In a number of other respects, however, she tells of things that would be very unusual in the life of most white American girls: a father who never went to school; taking care of the sheep; having a "medicine man" sing to cure illness. Perhaps, if we examine her story carefully we shall be able to discover certain themes that will guide us towards an understanding of Betsy's tribe as well as of herself.

THEME I: SICKNESS AND HEALTH

One of the first things Betsy says is, "I have two sisters alive and one died." Later on she mentions twice her own illnesses; for one of them she had two "Sings," while the other interrupted her schooling and sent her to the hospital. Both were evidently major events in her life. Moreover it seems as important to her to state that two sisters are alive as that one has died.

Life and death, sickness and health are matters of much concern to all Navahos, and the prevention of death and sickness and assurance of health are constantly in their minds. Beside the "Sings," which have been developed for times of crisis, numerous everyday duties and restrictions are constantly being observed towards this end. The death of children is so common that it is rather unusual that this family has been able to raise six of its seven, and it would not be surprising if some of them were to die before reaching maturity.

THEME II: THE FAMILY

The family looms very large in Betsy's story. She mentions no one who is not related to her; she specifies each member of the family; she speaks with pride of how long her mother went to school, of her father's ability to speak English without schooling, of her brother's being so smart, of the good times she has with her sister. She evidently associates rather closely also with her aunt, for the aunt takes care of her sheep and in return Betsy helps with the herding.

The Navahos live in small, widely scattered groups, each composed of a few closely related families, although a small number of families live far from all others. They are so busy with their crops and flocks and so far from other groups that weeks may pass without their seeing any outsiders. They depend upon each other for help with the various tasks, and for companionship and advice. If one of them becomes ill, the whole group does everything it can to get him well. If the rain falls on the field of one and not another, the man who harvests a crop will feed his less fortunate relatives, and he will expect the same treatment if his own crops fail. They share very intimately each other's good and bad fortune and emotional ups and downs. It is hard to live so closely and interdependently if opinions and attitudes vary greatly; so their differences are rarely expressed. The children, even more than the adults, are limited in their non-family contacts; unless they go to school their only companions are the other children in the group of close relatives, for whom they develop as strong feelings as if they were all real brothers and sisters.

THEME III: THE CLAN

When Betsy speaks of Susan as her niece, we come upon another aspect of Navaho kinship. To white people a niece is the daughter of one's sister or brother. In this case Susan simply belongs to the same clan as Betsy, and in Navaho the two girls call each other "sister." Since Betsy knows that white people do not call each other "sister" unless they are real sisters, she has used an English term which indicates close relationship but not as close as that of sister. Betsy and Susan feel towards each other much as two white sisters would.

There are many Navaho clans, and every Navaho belongs to one of them. Children automatically become members of the clan of their mother. Outside the family group of close relatives the clan is the strongest tie for a Navaho. Just as one must not marry a real sister or brother, so also one must neither marry nor engage in any flirtatious behavior with a clan sister or brother. When two Navahos meet, each quickly asks the other his clan in order to eliminate the danger of transgressing the rules of conduct and to assure himself of the advantages of a possible clan bond.

This sort of social organization does much to counteract the isolation and helplessness of the individual family groups living at such distances from each other, for it binds each family to many others, not always living near by but ready to be called upon in time of need. Even though a person has never been far from home and has few friends outside the family, he need not feel too timid if he must go to a distant part of the Reservation, for he is almost certain to find someone of his clan upon whom he can count for hospitality and for aid in his mission.

THEME IV: LIFE IS HARD

There are several hints that life is not too easy for this family. Betsy mentions working several times and says nothing about playing; her family lives in a log house rather than one made of lumber; they have a wagon but no automibile; they have to haul their water; even though the school charges them only $10 a year they consider this a large sum of money and have a hard time finding so much.

Navaho economy is an economy of scarcity. It is dependent upon a high, dry country where changes in the weather are about all that can be depended upon. In many places water sources are far apart, and wells cannot be dug or even drilled. Crops may be planted and fail to grow for lack of rain, or be washed out by a flood, or be ruined by a late or early frost. Grass, the main foodstuff for sheep, may dry up under a burning sun. Everybody has to work in order that the family may survive. Children start working as soon as they are able, helping more and more as they grow older. Betsy — and her nine-year-old sister too — were already capable of taking entire care of the house and younger children in their parents' absence. Their reward would be the approval of their relatives and perhaps a gift of lambs or new clothes from the trading post if the family could afford them.

THEME V: SCHOOL

Schooling, and the changes it has brought about in Navaho life, are worth considering in connection with Betsy's tale. Evidently some Navahos, like Betsy's mother, get as much schooling as the average white person. Others, like her father, get none. Her story indicates that English is usually learned at school, which means that those who do not go to school do not speak it as a rule. The problem of communication between white people who speak no Navaho and Navahos who speak no English is a real one, and much confusion arises from it.

Betsy is vague about what she gets in school. She says only that "there are good things to that." She evidently values going to school and doing well in school work, as well as knowing how to speak English. What else she hopes for we cannot tell.

In the boarding schools the children live more comfortably than
they can at home, with beds and bathrooms, ample and varied food,
opportunities for play as well as work. If they stay long enough,
these things become increasingly important to them, and when they
leave they try to acquire such "luxuries" for themselves. Navahos of
the older generations who went to school frequently comment on
how dishes at home have changed from homemade pottery to enam-
elware; how they are now washed instead of being used again and
again without cleaning; how people often have mattresses and even
some bedsteads instead of using sheepskins; how nearly every
"hogan" (house) now has some sort of arrangement for conducting
the smoke from the fire to the outside instead of letting it get to the
smokehole as best it can.

THEME VI: RELIGION

We have already referred briefly to the "Sings" which Betsy mentions. Once she says she was cured by a "medicine man" singing
over her, and again she was taken by her parents to another "Sing"
which included a "squaw dance" in which she was too small to
take part.

These "Sings" are the more dramatic and public aspect of Navaho
religion, about which much has been said in *The Navaho*. They
are ceremonials of varying length and complexity. Prayers and
hymns are spoken and sung, ritual objects are manipulated, and herb
medicines administered. The Navahos borrowed a good deal of the
content of their rites from other Indian tribes but have changed them
so that they have a definitely Navaho flavor. They are used as a
means of dispelling one of the Navahos' chief anxieties — illness —
and it seems certain that they often have a good effect (in both
physical and psychological ways) on the sick person. But treating
illness is by no means the only function of these rites, for they fulfill
somewhat the same need for well Navahos that church attendance
does in white society.

It is hard for most white people to comprehend how all-pervasive
religion is in the lives and thoughts of the Navahos. Except for
things they have learned to do from white people, almost every act
they perform is said to be carried out in the way prescribed by the
Holy People, who are believed to have inhabited the earth before
the Navahos and to have discovered the best means of living on it.

The Holy People gave instructions for social conduct, for planting, for weaving, for making baskets, and for the many different ceremonials, and these instructions are handed down in stories from one generation of Navahos to the next. Everything the Navaho sees as he looks about the countryside reminds him of the Holy People and these stories, and reassures him that, if he does as he should, he will have success, good health, and "good hope." Belief so firmly planted in the very core of a people is, of course, likely to remain there. It is not to be wondered that, although a fair number of Navahos attend mission services and take part in mission activities, are baptized perhaps, and say they believe in Christianity, very few indeed replace their native faith with the new one. Rather they add the new one to what they already have.

It is possible that in the course of years the Navahos may come to live like white people and to think and act more like white people than is now the case. Until that time, in order to understand them, we must learn about their tribal history, their social organization, their way of living and of getting along with each other, their religion and philosophy of life. These matters have been discussed at length in *The Navaho* (see Preface), and material will also be found in numerous other publications.[2] Only with such a background of facts can we hope to grasp Betsy's position with regard to white people and to her own people, the position of the various individual children in this study, and the significance of what the study shows about Navaho psychology.[3]

[2] See Clyde Kluckhohn and Katherine Spencer, *A Bibliography of the Navaho Indians* (New York: J. J. Augustine, 1940) for publications to 1939, and the bibliography in *The Navaho* for later references.

[3] The reader will find more about Betsy in Chapter 9 and Appendix II.

PART I

THE INDIVIDUAL AND
HIS DEVELOPMENT

1.

BECOMING A NAVAHO:

THE FIRST SIX YEARS OF LIFE

BEFORE BIRTH

CHILDREN are highly valued by The People and are almost invariably wanted. Most Navaho women bear a child every two or three years during the whole reproductive period. Contraceptive techniques — use of certain herbs and a ritual which are believed to confer sterility on a woman — are not often applied, and these in most cases only when childbirth has proven peculiarly difficult and dangerous to the mother.

According to Navaho belief, conception results from the union of the male fluid with menstrual blood or other secretions of the female. Most Navahos seem to feel that menstrual blood is the principal basis for the foetus.

A very tiny round thing drops into the woman's uterus. It doesn't start to grow until a month has passed. After two months you can see little spirals on four sides. They grow into the four limbs. Then the baby just keeps growing. But it isn't really alive until its head first sticks out of its mother. Then a wind comes into it — the same thing that will go away as a ghost when the person dies.

During pregnancy the expectant mother leads her usual life. "A woman who is going to have a baby shouldn't lie around. She should keep working and moving around so the baby doesn't get too big inside her," The People say. Women sometimes also take pollen which has been sprinkled over a hummingbird or a taste of the pulverized nest of the bird in the belief that it will help to keep the foetus small.

The People feel that the conduct of the parents while the baby is yet unborn has far-reaching consequences for the child's birth and for his health then and in later life. Both man and wife must avoid tying knots. When one or the other finds it necessary to tie up a goat or harness a team of horses, that person must be most careful to untie the knots later, never leaving it to someone else; otherwise the baby will get tangled up with the cord in the womb. If either the father or the mother looks upon a dry-painting or sees the body-painting ceremony, the child is likely to have a severe illness, although this may not overtake it until adult life. If a parent breaks a pot, the baby's "soft spots" will not close at the proper time, or (according to other informants) the child will stutter or have other speech difficulties. However, these misfortunes may be averted by taking another pot after the baby is born and deliberately breaking it above his head in such a way that the pieces fall together in a pile beneath him. The mother must not turn a blanket on her loom upside down, or the baby will become inverted in the uterus. If she should break wooden weaving tools, the baby will have deformed feet or missing fingers. She must not look at an eclipse, lest her child be born cross-eyed or possibly insane. Countless other taboos could be mentioned, although the particular taboos and the stringency with which they are observed vary considerably from area to area and, of course, from individual to individual.

Shortly before delivery is expected, the ceremonial called Blessing Way is sung over the pregnant woman. In the event of a miscarriage or stillbirth, one of the Evil Way chants is performed over the mother.

There are few preparations for the infant's arrival. It is considered very bad luck to make garments or a cradle before the baby is born. Cloths already on hand in the hogan can be used for swaddling.

THE BIRTH OF THE CHILD

CHILDBIRTH is regarded by The People as a natural function, and many women bear their children, at least after the first, with a minimum of discomfort and difficulty. It is, however, a fable that "primitive" women bear their children without appreciable pain or injury. There is little doubt that they make less fuss about their pains than the average white woman,[1] but they are subject to the same complications and misery. First births in particular are often protracted, and the mother may experience excruciating pain unrelieved by sedatives or anaesthetics.

[1] In comparisons between The People and "White Society," the standard in this and the following chapter is that of middle-class white society. In a number of important respects the differences between the child-rearing habits of the Navahos and those of lower-class white populations are much less great.

Today an increasing number of Navaho women go to Indian Service hospitals for delivery, but they still form a trifling proportion of the total. In the hogan there are no antiseptic precautions, and even elementary hygiene is minimal. Old rags and long-used sheepskins that can then be thrown away without economic loss are preferred to clean or new materials. Hence, infections are common. Maternal mortality is high — an estimated 10 per 1,000 births, as against 4 for Arizona and 2.7 for the United States as a whole. In addition, a number of mothers who survive remain invalids or semi-invalids for the rest of their lives, for even major injuries are left to heal without surgical attention.

When labor pains begin the woman drinks quantities of an herbal concoction which she has also taken about two months previously. Her mother or mother's mother is usually sent for or, if one of these is not available, a sister or some other female relative. Sometimes an older woman who is a semiprofessional midwife is summoned even if she is not a relative. Again, some women give birth without any assistants or with only the help of the husband.

The husband or whatever male relative is at hand brings sand into the hogan and spreads it on the floor west of the center of the hogan. Sometimes this sand is warmed. Upon it women of the household spread old cloths or a sheepskin with the woolly side up. The woman in labor kneels upon this padding. She removes all jewelry and takes down her hair. Over her head a woven red sash is suspended from the roof and sprinkled with pollen. During pains the mother holds onto this sash as high as she can reach and supports herself with it.

If labor does not proceed rapidly, all women in the immediate vicinity (and long-haired men too) untie their hair and let it fall freely over their shoulders. If delivery is really protracted, all horses and other tied animals within a half-mile or so will be released. Someone may be called in to do divination and he may recommend turning the child in the womb or summoning a Singer. A midwife may knead the abdomen, or she and others may hold the woman upside down and shake her. If a Singer is present, he boils a decoction and has the woman drink it. He also sings the song which was sung over Changing Woman when the hero twins were born, and motions the baby out with an eagle feather brush — "to help it out so it won't be hurt."

When labor pains become harder and more rapid, pollen is taken from the buckskin pouch of the mother and rubbed upon her belly. As the final pains approach, one of those assisting kneels in front to receive the baby, and another stands behind with her arms around the mother's abdomen. Pressure is applied to push the baby downward and to aid in expulsion. The father often does this for his wife, especially in the case of later children after he has had some experience. A woman who does not cry out is highly praised, and they rarely let more than a few groans escape.

The woman who receives the baby cuts the cord (formerly, and still sometimes, with a flint knife, but just as likely with a kitchen knife or an old pair of scissors) and ties it, perhaps with a piece of homespun wool or a string picked up from the floor. Unless the baby is already crying or breathing well, it is shaken, massaged on the chest, patted on the back, or held by the feet with the head downwards. It is then tightly wrapped in a woolen blanket or in cotton cloths and a sheepskin and placed near the fire. The head is propped with blankets so it won't get out of shape.

A stone is tied to the placenta end of the cord, or, in some regions, the cord is not cut until the placenta has been expelled. If this does not occur within an hour or so, the mother may be given a cup of yucca suds to which sugar has been added, or a Singer may perform a rite with a feather. As a last resort a midwife will roast a leaf of the prickly pear cactus in the fire until the skin peels off. She will rub the pulp in her hands until the right hand has a heavy, sticky coating and then insert it into the birth canal to bring out the placenta. The afterbirth is carefully disposed of, together with the pelt or cloths upon which birth has occurred, in order to keep them out of the hands of witches. Everything upon which there is any blood may be burned or buried, or it may be bundled up and hidden in the upper branches of a tree in an out-of-the-way place.

The exhausted mother lies down upon sand or boughs that have been warmed (to prevent hemorrhage) and is usually given a tea brewed from juniper or plant leaves. Nowadays, she gets a hearty meal as soon as she wants it, though the old custom was to feed her only cornmeal mush. Some mothers are attending to their household duties within a day or two. The young girl who is having her first child generally does little for three or four days and reclines most of the time, but unless something has gone wrong a confinement of more than five days is a rarity.

MAKING FREE DRAWINGS AT A SHEEP CAMP

ASLEEP, SECURE IN HIS CRADLE

AWAKE, PROPPED UP TO SEE HIS WORL

The woman who has received the baby has also the privilege of bathing it, for which she is given a basket or some other gift. There is often considerable rivalry among female relatives for this post. The bath takes place shortly after delivery but should not be given until the placenta has come. Afterwards the bath water is carefully poured into a hole which has been prepared outdoors. As with the blood incident to birth, the bath water is greatly feared; unless certain precautions have been taken, any contact with it is believed to give the individual a humpback.

After being bathed, the infant is wrapped up in a sheep pelt or white cloths and laid at the left of the mother, towards the north, with its head toward the fire. Its head is anointed with pollen prepared according to directions given by Changing Woman long ago which prescribed that pollen from white and from yellow corn must be shaken over a corn beetle. Next the woman who gave the bath "shapes" the baby. She begins with the nose, putting the thumb up in the mouth and pressing it. "Then the nose will be straight. Otherwise the child will have a short nose." After the nose, the head and the limbs are molded.

The old custom was that for the first four days the baby was fed only with corn pollen suspended in water. Many families purged the new-born by giving it a brew of the inner bark of juniper and pinyon to produce vomiting. Today these practices are followed only in the most conservative families, although there are still many who give the baby nothing but pollen and water until the mother's milk comes freely. Others will give heated goat's milk and water for a few days rather than allow the child to take the mother's watery first milk, which is generally distrusted. If the newborn does not automatically suck the breast, he is gently and skillfully taught.

The ears are often pierced for earrings within the first twenty-four hours. When the umbilical cord dries and the navel is completely healed, the cord is carefully buried in a propitious place. For a girl, this may be under a loom, so that she may become a good weaver. For a boy, the horse corral is an appropriate place. The People say that if the cord is kept in a sack in the hogan, the child will steal. Another practice founded upon beliefs connected with the supernatural is that the hair a baby is born with must be cut off.

The infant is named after four days, or after two weeks, or sometimes after a month or more. In some areas the custom is that the mother has responsibility for the names of daughters and the father for those of sons. But in no case does a parent give his or her own name to the child. Some other person, usually a relative, bestows the name.

If the mother has a sister whom she likes a lot, that sister can give her own name away to the child. Or it can be a grandmother. If it's a boy, the mother's brother or the father's father or maybe the father's brother gives the name usually. The grandfather might say, "I am growing old for my name so I'm giving it to the baby."

The namer does not necessarily give his own name to the child; the name may be that of some dead relative. It is considered of especially good omen to give the name of a person who has lived to a ripe old age or who died of old age, not of sickness.

Only a few members of the immediate family are present at the naming. If the baby is in the cradle, the strings are loosened so that the mother can hold the child up straight. The namer pats the baby a few times and says, "My grandchild (niece, etc.), this will be your name: *baazhnábaa'i* (she came to him in war)."

CRADLE BABIES

WITHIN a few hours after birth the baby is given to the mother or placed near her in its temporary cradle. This relationship of almost constant physical proximity between child and mother is unbroken until weaning. Night and day, wherever the mother goes, whatever she is doing, the baby is either being held by her or is within sight of her eye and almost always within reach of her hand. As soon as she is physically able, the mother herself responds immediately to every manifestation of want or discomfort on the part of her child. Her first response whenever the child cries is to place it to her breast. If this fails to produce quiet, the baby will be cleaned and dried, cuddled, talked to, or sung to. The baby is totally helpless; it can only cry. Wriggling is hardly an outlet for the Navaho baby since it is bound to the cradle board.

THE CRADLE

In the old days (and some of the older children in this study probably passed through this sequence) every Navaho child used four different cradles in succession. For the first twenty to twenty-five days the child was kept in the canopy-cradle which The People call "face-cover." This was very simple. Three arches of willow withes covered with a cloth or skin were put over its head as it lay on the floor, and the baby was thus protected from the sparks of the fire. When the infant began to be taken out of the hogan, a "laced cradle" was made for him. Twigs peeled of their bark were laced together with four strings and placed under the child, with a small blanket for a mattress. This was used for about two months, and then a third type (described below), suitable for carrying the baby on horseback, was made for the next four or five weeks. These first three cradles were discarded after use, but the final type was preserved for all subsequent babies in the family, unless an infant died in it, in which case it served as a coffin.

Today only two cradles are generally used. The first is the "face-cover," which is discarded as soon as the family thinks the newborn has a good chance for survival. Some families consider this test period over when the umbilical cord shrivels up and falls off. Others prefer to wait for some weeks until the baby has definitely outgrown the small cradle.

For a first baby, or when a cradle has been destroyed, the father makes the permanent one. There are two types, corresponding to the third and fourth of the ancient succession. The principal difference between them is that the body of one consists of a single board with a small hole in the lower part to allow for the drainage of urine, while in the other type the board is split in two and then laced together. At the top of either type a narrow padded strip is placed as a head-raise. Over this is arched a wooden bow one and a half to two inches wide, which clears the child's forehead by two to three inches. To the bottom is lashed a footrest. Formerly the cradle was lined with the soft bark of the cliff rose. The infant is wrapped in a number of cloths, sometimes in such a way that the legs are separated and each tightly encased. It is strapped to the cradle by means of a lacing cord which is passed in zigzag fashion between cloth or buckskin loops attached to the sides of the board and is finally fastened through a loop on the footboard. A cloth attached to the top and resting on the bow can be lowered to cover the whole cradle and keep out light, flies, and cold. The reader will perhaps find the illustrations more helpful than more extended description.

Tassels of fringed buckskin in the upper corners of the cradle are seen less and less frequently today, but a turquoise setting or bead

for a boy and a white shell for a girl are still prevalent forms of
decoration. Silver ornaments are also used. Squirrel tails and pouches
of buckskin are usually fastened to the cradle for magical protection.
The pouches contain various plants and pollens, but one of the most
common is pollen which has been shaken over the feathers of a nighthawk. This bird sits quietly on its nest all day long and is not easily
alarmed by noises or movements. The People therefore feel that
pollen which has touched it will cause children to be contented during the daytime and to sleep soundly at night.

The permanent cradle is not made casually, although these days
one sees a few for which boxes or store boards were used. No one
who has been sick for a long time should make a cradle. In years
gone by it was customary to make the carrying board of fir if the
child was a boy and of Engelmann spruce, if it was a girl. (The
tips of the cradle were pointed for a girl, blunt for a boy.) Today
the board is ordinarily made of pine or pinyon, never of juniper, for
The People say that juniper is warlike since when it burns it throws
out sparks. Most fathers select with great care the pine tree from
which the board is to be cut. The tree must not have been struck by
lightning or badly broken or rubbed against by a bear. It should be
tall and straight, likely to live many years, and in a secluded spot
where the chances of its being cut down are not great. The board
should be split off the east side of the pine. Before doing so the
father sprinkles the tree with pollen and says a brief prayer.

In the old days (and, at least in the Navaho Mountain area, within
recent years) the cradle was made and the child was first placed in
the permanent cradle with all or some parts of the following ceremony:

The father [2] (or if he did not have the knowledge, a ceremonial
practitioner) shaved and smoothed the board first with a knife of
white shell and then with one of quartz crystal. As he did this, he
chanted again and again, "I make a smooth cradle for you." After
the board was smoothed, he sang another song, beginning "I have
completed the cradle board." Then he held the head end to the east
and said this prayer: [3]

[2] In some areas it is customary for the father to cut the boards but for the mother to
do the shaping. Sometimes the mother does the whole task.

[3] The following prayers and songs and most of the details of the ceremony are taken
from unpublished notes of the late Louisa Wade Wetherill. Mrs. Wetherill's translations
have been slightly altered on the basis of the texts as she recorded them in Navaho.

> Son of Changing Woman, Go in beauty
> Pollen Boy, Go in beauty
> Everlasting One, Go in beauty.

Pollen was then sprinkled four times on the south side of the board from the foot to the head, the prayer being repeated each time. This completed, pollen was sprinkled once on the center of the board and the following prayer said:

> Spirit of the Pollen Boy
> Voice of the Pollen Boy
> Head of the Pollen Boy
> Go in Beauty.

The back of the board was next sprinkled with pollen and this prayer said:

> Spirit of the Dawn
> Voice of the Dawn
> Head of the Dawn
> Go in Beauty.

Finally the foot of the board was sprinkled with pollen and a last prayer uttered:

> Spirit of the Setting Sun
> Voice of the Setting Sun
> Head of the Setting Sun
> Go in Beauty.

When the cradle was complete in all its parts, the baby was placed in it and laced up. Then the following was chanted:

> I have made a baby board for you, my son (daughter)
> May you grow to a great old age.
> Of the sun's rays have I made the back
> Of black clouds have I made the blanket
> Of rainbow have I made the bow
> Of sunbeams have I made the side loops
> Of lightning have I made the lacings
> Of sun dogs have I made the footboard
> Of dawn have I made the covering
> Of black fog have I made the bed.

Then a line of pollen was sprinkled around the board, commencing in the southeast corner, and this prayer said:

> Dawn Boy, give him many horses
> Dawn Boy, give him many sheep.

Or this longer prayer was sometimes used:

Dawn Boy with your strength let him stand
Dawn Boy let him stand with you
Dawn Boy with the strength of the corn let him stand with you
Let him stand with the strength of the white corn
With the strength of the corn-bird, with the strength of the corn and
    the Dawn
Let him stand
Harvest Fly Boy, Pollen Boy, let him have moccasins like the harvest fly
Let him have leggings like the harvest fly
Let him have a robe like the harvest fly
Let him have a cap like the harvest fly
Let him have feathers like the harvest fly
Let his voice be beautiful like the harvest fly's
Life Pollen Boy, stand before him
Walk before him
Harvest Girl, Harvest Fly Girl, stand behind him
Speech Divinity go back and forth before him
Go with him to his home
On a blanket of pollen let the cradle rest
Let him drink from all the springs of the earth
Let him eat pollen of all the plants of the earth
Let him eat of the pollen of the water
Let him eat of the pollen of the mountains.

The cradle is a strong focus of Navaho sentiments. A young man or woman will point proudly to one still hanging in his parents' hogan and say, "That is the cradle in which I grew up." This pride from individual association is heightened by its mythological background. The first cradles were made for Changing Woman's twins. The earth gave the bottom boards; the hoods were made from a rainbow, the footrests of sunbeams; the side loops were of sheet lightning, and the lacings of zigzag lightning.

The proportion of each day that the baby spends tightly laced to his cradle varies with his age and with the temperament and situation of the mother. If she has older children to assist her in household tasks, she is likely to keep the child out of the cradle for longer intervals than a mother who must do all the work of the household as well as care for the baby. However, since healthy babies sleep most of the time in the early months and do not need to be removed from the cradle for nursing, they can be and often are left there most of the time except when they are bathed or the cloths which serve as diapers are changed.

The hours spent in the cradle tend to diminish as the child grows older. Some families put the baby in the cradle relatively little after he is able to sit up — mainly for traveling and for protection at night — but conservative Navaho opinion tends to condemn this practice. As one old-fashioned mother said: "Babies are kept that way in the cradle to make them straight and strong. Some women let their children lie on sheepskins and roll about, but they are always weak, sick children."

By and large, babies of two months average two hours a day out of the cradle; those of nine months average nearly six. At these times they are held in the mother's arms or lap and occasionally are allowed to lie on a pile of skins or blankets to kick freely. As the baby grows older, he will be permitted to creep about on the floor for brief periods. In addition to these times of full release from the cradle, the child's arms may be freed two or three times a day for varying intervals.

Formerly (and still in conservative families) the final removal of a child from the cradle board was marked with a little ceremony. The child is taken from the board and dressed in its best clothes. The board is placed on the ground and this prayer said:

> Dawn Boy, this is Changing Woman's Son (daughter)
> Let him arise with much wealth, many robes
> Let him arise with many jewels
> This is the earthly son of Changing Woman
> With the strength of the earth
> With earth's black flint shoes for his moccasins
> Let him arise
> Let him be draped with the black flint of the earth
> Let him be draped with the strength of the earth
> Let his hat be made of earth's black flint strength
> Let his bed be covered with earth's black flint strength
> Let the lightning cross over his head.[4]

Then to the accompaniment of a song, the lacing strings are removed and placed in a buckskin bag. The cradle is then deposited in a cove or some other sheltered place to the east of the hogan or hung within the hogan or on a tree to the east. The ground is sprinkled with

[4] This prayer is also from Mrs. Wetherill's notes.

pollen below the cradle and the cradle touched to the pollen. Then another line of pollen is sprinkled on top of the board and a line of white corn meal sprinkled from the head of the board toward the east and a line of yellow corn meal from the foot toward the west.

THE CRADLE AND THE BABY

Since the experience in the cradle is one of the ways in which the Navaho child's development is most obviously different from that of the white child, let us try to see what advantages and disadvantages the practice of cradling seems to afford. The remarks in the following paragraphs apply primarily to the first six months of the Navaho baby's life, but they are partially relevant for at least the whole first year.

During many hours of the day and all of the night, the child's bodily movements are sharply restricted by the cradle. Its position is varied from the horizontal to the upright, but the baby cannot move of its own volition.

Its sensory contacts are also limited by the cradle. It can see well — more than most white babies when its cradle is upright — and of course its hearing and sense of smell are not interfered with. Perhaps the greatest limitation is on the sense of touch. During the many times that the child is moved each day, the hands of the mover do not come in contact with the child, for they grasp the cradle instead. The young baby receives an abundance of stimulation on the face, but its body is handled only during its brief intervals off the cradle board. In turn it has no opportunity to explore its own body because its arms are pinioned. Older babies are given some solid food, teething babies are given bones or other hard objects to gnaw, and occasionally the child will have a small plaything to hold and handle.

Thus the infant may experience a fairly full range of sensory impressions through sight, taste, smell, and hearing and a very limited range of tactile impressions. But, when it is capable of moving its body in response to stimulation from its environment, it is prevented from doing so by the cradle.

The cradle also restricts the baby's response to internal stimuli, such as anger, hunger, or pain. He cannot kick or wriggle about. He can only cry or refuse to suck or swallow.

Perhaps this frustration of desire for bodily movement is not so great as might be expected, for the desire may be lost after repeated frustrations. Perhaps, too, such frustration is no more detrimental to the baby than that which results from the painful outcome of motor activity, such as picking up a hot coal or getting in the way of adults.

Certain aspects of cradling are obviously useful. The cradle board and the thick swaddling provide a measure of protection against harmful insects and snakes. The heavy canopy, which may be raised or lowered slightly, guards the child's eyes against direct rays of the bright sun out of doors; and if, when the mother is traveling on horseback with her baby, the horse should buck or shy and the baby be dropped, the bow provides excellent insurance against head injury. After the child has begun to creep it can be put in the cradle to protect it from getting too close to the fire during occasional moments when all other persons may be out of the hogan. In a crowded hogan where toddlers and older children may be scuffling about, the baby is probably safer in his cradle than on a sheepskin on the floor as the other children sleep.

The cradle is usually placed in an upright position after the child has been nursed. White pediatricians have suggested that this habit may help the baby in digesting his food, much as being held upright helps the white baby to "bubble."

In addition, there are important psychological advantages to cradling. Birth must be an unpleasant experience to the child as well as to the mother. The warmth and complete security of the womb are exchanged for the irregularities of food, alterations in temperature, and other unpredictables of the external world. The abruptness of this transition tends to be cushioned by the cradle. The cradle, like the womb, is a place where movement is restricted, where support is always present, and where changes resulting from movement or from temperature fluctuations are minimized in their effect.

Likewise, the cradle permits babies who could not otherwise sit up unaided to assume for long periods a position other than that of lying down, out of touch with what is going on around them. When the weather is warm or mild, and the family is lounging or eating under the trees outside, for instance, the cradle is usually propped against a tree. This means that the child's face and eyes are on about the same level as those of the adults who are sitting near him. In this, as in several other ways, the Navaho child from the very beginning takes a part in the total society rather than being isolated or segregated from it, "just a baby" as in white families.

Furthermore, at no time is the cradled infant able to interfere physically with the mother or with whatever she is doing. Regardless of her moods, she has little excuse to vent them on him, and the infant has little chance to annoy her. This eliminates a countless number of frustrations for the child and reduces his conflict with the arbitrary emotions of his mother.

Perhaps the best judge of the merits of cradling is the baby himself. There is evidence that during the first six months the protection of the cradle appeals strongly to the infant. Young babies will often cry to be put back into their cradles, and many of them do not sleep satisfactorily anywhere else. After about the sixth month, however, the infant apparently begins to feel the confinement a frustration and will wail to be released.

These considerations suggest some reflections upon the behavior of certain missionaries, teachers, nurses, and other well-meaning whites who, in their zeal to see The People adopt white habits in their entirety and discard their own "backward" ways, urge Navaho mothers to "give up those savage cradles and use cribs like civilized folks." It must never be forgotten that any people's way of life represents their set of solutions to recurrent problems, solutions which they have worked out because of their own special historic experiences and the peculiar conditions of life which they have had to meet.

This was illustrated in the babyhood of Betsy. Her mother had been discouraged by the missionaries from using the cradle, and she carried out their teachings for her first child, Betsy. The other six, however, were kept on a cradle board, because the mother found it much more convenient when she was living like a Navaho and not like a missionary.

A coherent culture represents a very delicate adjustment between people and environment which has been arrived at by countless generations of trial and error. If it be thoughtlessly and undiscriminatingly interfered with, the disruption and the loss to human happiness and human safety may sometimes be incalculable. The use of the cradle board — *under the circumstances of Navaho life* — is an excellent example of this point.

THE BABY'S DAILY ROUTINE

During the first year of life the baby's routines are simple and infinitely repeated. He is bathed in warm water every day or sometimes every other day, depending in part on weather conditions. The cloths that serve as diapers are changed when the baby is bathed and at least once again during the day. Frequency of changing varies greatly. Navaho mothers usually remove only the one cloth that is really soaked and fold the others in such a way that the child's skin comes into contact with only dry materials. A cloth which has been soiled will merely be scraped free of fecal matter and then replaced in the cradle, but usually not as the layer next to the baby's skin.

The baby gets a good deal of affectionate attention. He is, of course, fed and held by the mother. He is also held, touched, and talked to by the father, older brothers and sisters, and indeed all relatives who come and go in the hogan. The relative joggles the cradle a bit and smiles down at the infant, or picks up the cradle and sings a little or makes affectionate noises. All Navahos make a fuss over babies. They receive, from the start, a very great amount of attention and a great deal of facial stimulation by touch. Their faces are patted and their ears are plucked. Their limbs are also stroked when they are out of the cradle, but this occurs far less often.

NURSING

The child is nursed whenever he cries. Only occasionally is there any delay, as when the mother is outside the hogan for a few minutes or is busy with some task which cannot immediately be put aside. The baby himself determines not merely when he wishes to suck but also when he is finished. The mother will not terminate nursing until he has ceased to show interest in the nipples. The willingness of a mother to feed her infant is increased by the fact that she is never more than a few feet from her child in and around her one-room shelter. She sits on the floor and the infant and cradle are easily pulled near her. Since the mother wears a loose blouse and no underwear, the derangement of her clothes is negligible.

A well infant of a few months may nurse only six times during daylight and once or twice during the night. Older children nurse much more frequently. Children close to a year old have been observed to be put to the breast on the average about thirty times during a 24-hour period, and more than sixty such contacts during this interval are by no means unknown. Sometimes a child will be fed three times within fifteen minutes. This is doubtless partly because the mother's supply of milk decreases, and the child sucks only for a short time and does not get much nourishment at any one attempt. Particularly if the mother is undernourished or in indifferent health, the baby will suck fiercely, struggle, and give other evidences of lack of complete satisfaction. An increasing number of Navaho mothers now use a bottle after the first few months for supplementary feedings or as a complete substitute for the breast.

In the later months nursing comes to have secondary or symbolic values. The child gets attention and often obtains freedom from its cradle-prison which gives it a chance to move more freely.

Whether or not the child is taken out of the cradle for nursing depends upon the immediate situation and the mother's personal preference, but the tendency is for older babies to be removed more frequently than younger ones. If the child is in the cradle, a common practice is to lay the board across the lap and let the child turn its head to nurse. When the child is free, it commonly lies on the mother's lap supported by her arm. Older nurslings may suckle standing in front of a kneeling or sitting mother. For infants the mother will often hold the nipple in position between her fingers. Later she will merely pull up her blouse or let the nurser do it and put her hand against its back. Breasts are regularly alternated. Children are very commonly put to sleep by nursing. In this case the mother will lie on one side facing the child and will gently pat him as he nurses. She remains beside him until he falls asleep.

ACQUIRING MOTOR SKILLS

Although fastened within the cradle during part of their waking hours each day, children of The People nevertheless get some chance to explore their bodies and other objects and individuals with their hands, to move all their limbs, to try out their muscular equipment in a variety of ways. Apparently this limited practice is sufficient because there seems to be very little difference between Navaho and white children in the ages at which motor skills are developed. With both there is, of course, considerable individual variation.

Activity immediately after birth is much like that of white babies, except that there is some evidence that hyperactive or "nervous" newborn Navaho babies are much rarer than is this type among white children born in New York City hospitals. At one month an infant's eyes will fix upon a person or an object; it will open its mouth when touched or suck an adult's finger. Between two and three months children begin to smile and to make noises responsively.

The first smile is eagerly watched for. When visitors come to the hogan it is polite to inquire: "Has the baby laughed yet?" When it does so, this is an occasion for rejoicing and for a little ceremony. The baby's hands are held out straight by the mother, and some member of the family (usually a brother or sister) puts a pinch of salt with bread and meat upon them. "If you don't do this to the baby, he won't feel very good, he won't be very healthy. If you do that, he'll be healthy from that day on. He will sit up right away and pretty soon he'll start walking without any trouble." The person who sees the baby smile first should give a present (with salt) to all other members of the family. The father or mother will kill a sheep and distribute this among relatives along with a bit of salt for each piece. While many Navahos do not follow these customs in every detail, the vast majority still mark the first smile in some manner.

The People say that a child sits up when it has two teeth, and generally a baby will sit with support at four months and alone at about five months. By this time children will also reach for things, put their feet in their mouths, pass objects from hand to hand. As they acquire teeth they have the same need for things to chew on as do white children. Creeping or scooting on the buttocks may start at seven months, but the average date is a little later. At eight or nine months babies will stand when supported under the arms, and some will raise themselves to a standing position. At about ten or eleven months they will walk when led, and the first independent steps usually come from two to four months later. These signs of development are aided and encouraged, but the child is under much less pressure to hurry up and walk than white children, and the Navaho mother counts it no disgrace that the child takes his time to grow up.

White people are likely to assume that remaining so much tied to a board must delay the development of walking. On the other hand, a white pediatrician (Margaret Fries) suggests that the custom of propping the cradled child in an upright position before he can crawl or even sit may facilitate walking. She points out that the apparatus of balance and vision are then on the same plane as when the child is walking. His legs are kept constantly extended with feet flexed against the footboard in the position for standing.

It is not certain that Navaho children learn to walk later, on the average, than white children. One set of figures indicates that they do, another the reverse. The fact that the Navahos as a rule make no effort to remember birthdays exactly and are characteristically vague or inaccurate about all dates makes precise comparison difficult. In any case, any difference which may exist is almost certainly not due to the cradle board, for a careful study of two series of Hopi children, one reared on the cradle board and the other off, showed that the average age for the onset of walking in the two series was almost identical.[5] Among The People, as among white people, the range of individual variation is very great. It seems to be mainly a matter of different biological equipment which determines different speeds with which the completion of nerve development takes place. A certain degree of completion of nerve development is essential to the ability to make complicated coördinated movements like walking. Usually the healthy child, either white or Navaho, living in a reasonably secure atmosphere, will begin to creep and to walk as soon as these physiological processes have attained the right stage, and no amount of coaxing or teaching will make a child walk before this.

Navaho babies will respond to words before they utter them. The first word is most often *shimá* (my mother), *shizhé'é* (my father), *mósí* (cat), or *łééchaa'í* (dog). A few words are sometimes learned before independent walking begins, but the beginnings of real speech normally come after the youngster has begun to toddle about freely. Some Navaho words have shortened forms which babies use.

Before the child is able to state its wants verbally, it can gain the attention of others only by crying or fidgeting. Still, something is always done when the child manifests discomfort or demands attention in this way. If the baby's crying is unduly incessant or prolonged, a ceremonial practitioner may even be called in to give treatment. The Navaho recipe "Feed a child whenever it cries, day or night" may seem to white people to be bad for the baby as well as inconvenient for the mother, but the psychological consequences are probably highly beneficial. Among all human beings many of the most deeply rooted aspects of a personality take their form in the

[5] For an account of this study, see Wayne Dennis, *The Hopi Child*, listed on p. 267.

first year of life. They are the more tenacious because they are unverbalized. The basic "unvoiced" attitudes grow out of the interaction between the baby's manifestations of his wants and needs and the responses which surrounding individuals make to them.

To see what this means in this case, let us contrast certain typical experiences of the white child and of the Navaho child in their early days. To the white child, whose feeding and other routines are rigidly scheduled, the mother or nurse (and these are representatives for the entire world of other persons) must appear incalculable. He finds that there are rules of behavior which are above and beyond his needs or wishes. No matter how hard he cries, he does not get his bottle until the clock says he should. He must develop a feeling that each individual is alone in life.

To the Navaho baby, on the other hand, other persons must appear warmer and more dependable, for every time he cries, something is done for him. Every step he takes toward social participation is rewarded. The easier tempo of Navaho life and the fact that the daily tasks of housekeeping are carried on mainly within a single room make it possible for parents and brothers and sisters to give much more constant encouragement to early attempts at creeping, walking, and talking. Few indeed are the moments of its waking hours when the child is alone or isolated from the social scene. This practice may be connected with the fact that in adult life everybody counts (unanimous decisions at meetings; playing down of obvious and outstanding leadership).

TODDLERS

LEARNING to walk usually coincides with complete abandonment of the cradle, although sometimes this has been quite a little earlier. The period when the child is taking its first steps is a time of maximum attention from others. Everyone around takes turns in leading the child. The admiring audience murmurs encouragement and approval.

The toddler runs about exploring his world. He grabs cats and dogs who are so unwary as to permit themselves to be caught. Parents seldom discourage a child's cruelties to animals. They will often join in the laughter of the other children at a dog's yelp when it is kicked or has its tail pulled by a baby. This is a means of turning aggression from other people and toward animals. It is hard on the animals but may have useful results so far as interpersonal relations are concerned. On the other hand, it may also have the effect of training the child to take out his irritations on those less strong than himself.

The child runs from person to person and is petted by each in turn or consoled if it has met with some small accident. The father will take a toddler who wakes fretful from a nap in the heat and soothe him in his arms. Any older person rushes to the child when he screams after a fall or a slight burn or an ant bite. At the same time, the Navaho method is generally to let learning occur through such minor injuries but not to rub the lesson in by further punishment. After the safety of the cradle is gone, the child's principal protection is the presence of elders. But their backs must sometimes be turned, and children learn the realities of fire, knives, and sharp claws through experience. Navahos spend comparatively little time in verbal warnings, in imaginatively enlarging upon such dangers and their consequences. White practice probably tends to make some children unduly fearful and dependent. Navaho practice tends to make children better able to look after themselves, so far as the external world is concerned.

The positive side of child training in this period is mainly a matter of constant encouragement in the acquisition of language and of other skills. Someone is always talking to the baby, giving him words to imitate, telling him especially the proper kinship terms with which to address his various relatives, praising him whenever his random babblings happen to hit a meaningful sound combination.

All training in the first two or three years of life is delayed, gradual, and gentle. Not until he can talk and understand is pressure put on a child to learn Navaho conventions of excretion.

Training in Navaho modesty also starts about this time. Relatives are forever snatching down the skirts of little girls and admonishing them not to expose themselves. Less attention is directed to little boys in this respect at present, for until they learn sphincter control they are dressed in pants that are open through the crotch to facilitate excretion, and thus make constant exposure of the genitals inevitable.

No fuss is made about food or sleep. The child sleeps when and where he chooses. He eats (of what is available) what he pleases

BIG SISTER LOOKS AFTER THE TODDLER

ANIMALS TAKE THE PLACE OF TOYS

and when. "The baby knows what is best for him," Navahos say. Nursing — in the sense of free access to the breast — continues almost always until the child is at least eighteen months old and usually past two years. However, from about six months other food and drink are offered. The toddler will eat some of all the dishes prepared for the rest of the family, but these are never forced upon him. Nor is anything denied. Infants usually have considerable fondness for coffee and tea. This horrifies white observers but coffee and tea have the advantage of being boiled and thus probably are more pure than other fluids as far as germs are concerned. Navaho coffee and tea are also very weak.

According to present conceptions of child psychologists and psychiatrists, the Navaho infant has exceptionally favorable opportunities for developing a secure and confident adult personality. There is no sudden and harsh attempt to compel him to control his eliminative activities. Older persons are almost always quite tolerant of displays of aggression and little temper tantrums. When a two-year-old has something taken from him or fails to get what he wants, he will scream, arch his back, brace himself, and be quite inconsolable until his elders give in (which they often do) or somehow distract him. If a baby or young child holds its breath so long that it begins to get stiff, cold water will be thrown in its face. A child at this age is almost never cuffed or even spoken to harshly.

White observers often comment that The People "spoil" their younger children. They do *indulge* them, but they do not "spoil" them in the original sense of the word, that is, to deform or ruin the character. The "spoiled" child is the one who is petted one moment and neglected or beaten the next — regardless of his behavior. The Navaho toddler is given self-confidence by being made to feel that he is constantly loved and valued. Also, the behavior of the Navaho adults toward children is characteristically consistent.

LIFE BECOMES HARD: WEANING AND FIRST RESPONSIBILITIES

EXCEPT for ill health, the Navaho child's troubles may be said to begin only at the weaning period. Weaning, however, is late, and it is also gradual. In cases where the next baby does not come for some time or at all, the child may often be said to wean itself. As its taste for other types of nourishment increases, as the mother's from the mother, the child's dependency on nursing gradually diminishes. But so long as there is no rival younger child the youngster still has free access to its mother's breast. It is very common indeed to see children two years old (and even children of three) continue to suckle. Generally, however, relatives begin to make fun of children past two if they persist in nursing, and many children will eventually stop under this slight pressure.

When weaning is more urgent because of the advent of a new baby, other measures may be taken. The mother may go off alone for a visit of some days or a week with relatives. In certain areas she may even smear the juice of the chili pepper or some other bad-tasting material upon her nipples. But the usual practice is to make the process as gentle as possible. For a month the mother will reduce gradually the number of times per day the child comes to the breast. She will do this by giving plausible excuses for separation during a longer and longer part of each day, saying that she must go to the trading store or work in the field and that the baby may not come with her because it is too hot or too rainy or too cold, etc. She will also have candy, oranges, and other delicacies on hand and will offer these as an alternative to sucking. Finally, after such a transitional period, she will go off completely for a few days or a week. This separation hits some children very hard.

To the child, weaning means less and less of the mother's attention. Deprivation of the breast is merely one sign of a general loss. For the weaned child is no longer allowed to sleep every night by the mother's side. His sleeping place is now under the blanket which also covers the two or three other children nearest him in age. The mother surrenders to these older children most of the care of the weaned baby. Crying is less immediately responded to and less fully tolerated. A weaned baby who gets in the mother's way may be rather roughly jerked aside. Moreover, the mother starts to make demands of him. Soon, performance of simple chores, such as bringing in sticks of wood for the fire or snow to be melted for water, comes to be expected. Neglect of these, or getting into mischief, will bring a harsh scolding or a cuff or, a little later, a mild switching (on the legs, not on the buttocks).

Serious demands for bladder and bowel control usually coincide with weaning or come shortly thereafter. In other words, the conflict between the child and its parents over this matter is postponed until the child is well past a year old. If he starts to urinate inside the hogan he is told to go outside, and an older child will often gently lead him out. At first elimination is permitted just outside the door; later the child is expected to go away into the bushes. He is not punished for lapses or accidents but encouraged to act like his elders.

It is important to realize that bowel control is not expected of the Navaho child until he is old enough to direct his own movements and merely accompany an elder at night and in the morning. The mother or an older sister takes the child out when she herself goes to defecate and tells the little one to imitate her position and her actions. After a time, the youngster who continues to wet or soil himself is unmercifully teased by all present. However, in the normal case, these functions soon come to be taken for granted. There is none of the obsessive daily questioning as to whether a bowel movement has occurred which is so marked a feature of recent American family life. The Navaho mother pays no attention to these matters unless there is a moderately serious illness. The child's feces are not regularly examined. Moreover, little feeling of disgust for urine or feces is inculcated. There is no exaggerated emphasis upon the unpleasantness of odors or consistency of excreta. The child is not thoroughly washed each time it soils itself. A little girl of four will scrape out the "diapers" of her young brother in a perfectly matter-of-fact manner.

Boys appear to find weaning a more upsetting experience than do girls.[6] At least their temper tantrums are more frequent, more sustained, and more intense. They bite and slap other people (especially their mothers), kick and scream. Why boys should be more affected by weaning than girls can be only guessed at, at present. One guess is that there is a connection with sex experiences. From the very beginning Navahos take sexuality as natural and permitted. They do not interfere with the toddler's exploration of the genital region or with so-called "infantile masturbation" (though the cradle inhibits this earlier). Not only are children allowed to manipulate their own genitals freely but the mother herself may stroke the naked genitals of a nursing child with her hand. Some observations indicate that she does this more often with boys than with girls. This practice and the differing structure of the external sex organs may cause boys to react more strongly than girls to the cessation of nursing.

[6] Cf. Dennis' study of Hopi children, listed on p. 267.

When another baby is born, weaning means really sudden and complete dispossession at the hands of a rival. It means that the weaned child comes into the almost complete charge of an older sibling, grandmother, or some other relative who imposes more restrictions than the mother ever did and who does not offer the compensation of nursing. That Navahos themselves recognize such displacement as a cause of discomfort to the child is shown by a good deal of folklore.

It's easy to wean babies. The child knows a new baby is coming — he can tell from the taste of the milk, and so he doesn't like it any more. . . . A woman who is expecting a new baby mustn't go into a corn field with her youngest child. This is because only happy people with nice thoughts should go there or the corn won't ripen right. A child is always mean and fussy before its younger brother or sister comes.

One of W. W. Hill's informants stressed this attitude of the child in describing why a baby should not be taken into a field by its mother if she is pregnant with another child.

A child, before its mother gives birth to a second child, will act childish and cry all the time. If such a woman went into the fields the roots of the corn and the tendrils of the vines would act just as the child and would make no effort to grow.[7]

Children who have recently been weaned seem to find the sight of the new baby at the mother's breast a disturbing experience. They will commonly run over to the mother on every such occasion and try to get her to pet them or show some affection. But she will often cuff them away, and this experience is also new and highly upsetting. All overt expressions of sibling rivalry are strenuously discouraged. Probably the upset is aggravated by their being continually cautioned not to step on the new baby, not to scuff dust in its face, etc. The baby is always the king in every family, but each king — save the very last child in the series — must come to know the meaning of dethronement. The People, like ourselves, make the most fuss over "the baby." This may be the first basis for that sibling rivalry which the observer notes in both Navaho and white cultures. The forms are not identical — the mixed feelings which Navaho brothers and sisters have for each other are influenced by Navaho

[7] For source, see p. 267.

social organization and economic arrangements, but the psychological core in the two cases is similar.

Children who happen to be the last in the family, or whose following brother or sister dies very soon after birth leaving them the youngest again, undergo life experiences in this period which are different in important respects from those of the average child. Preliminary analyses of materials which the authors have collected indicate, in fact, that adult Navahos who were actually or psychologically "last-born" have a personality structure which differs consistently from that of other Navahos. They tend to be more stable, more secure, less suspicious, generally "happier." It must be realized that the number who are "'psychologically" last-born is large, for the infant mortality rate is very high.

In short, at the weaning period the Navaho child comes to learn effectively that the world around him makes demands and imposes restrictions, in addition to giving reassurances and rewards. Although The People continue to allow great latitude with respect to many activities which are severely regulated by white parents (such as eating and sleeping), the Navaho weaned child must face keenly felt deprivations. Latterly he has been accustomed to nurse as much for comfort as for nourishment. Now this solace is denied him even when he is tired, angry, cross, or frightened. No longer is everything done for him with hardly any effort on his part; instead he must learn to feed, wash, and dress himself. To be sure, these activities do not have the same significance for Navaho children as for white. The etiquette of eating is simple, to say the least. Washing is a matter of hands and face and an occasional yucca suds shampoo of the hair. Except for removing and putting on shoes, dressing takes place more nearly weekly than daily. Nevertheless, life must have a very different quality for the nursing than for the weaned child. Upon the nursing child almost the only restrictions imposed are those which the cradle places upon movement, and even this restriction usually is terminated while the child still nurses. The weaned child, however, finds that no longer are almost all his responses rewarded, no longer does his mother devote herself mainly to his pleasure. After the child really begins to talk, he finds that all responses and rewards are made much more selectively by his elders —he has to do the right thing for attention and praise.

On the other hand, it must not be forgotten that the number of older persons who are available to respond to the child is usually large. One of the most common sights in an extended Navaho family is that of a toddler (especially one who has been recently weaned and feels himself somewhat rejected by his mother) running from one woman in the group to another and receiving some sign of affection from each.

If the initial experiences with the mother have been good (which is usually the case), it seems to be one or more of the older brothers and sisters who bears the brunt of the hostility generated at the period of weaning. Expression of hostility toward the new baby would be an unforgivable sin in a society where children are so highly valued. Conscious or unconscious (emotional) rejection of a child by the mother seems very rare; reciprocally, hatred for a mother — even at the unconscious level — is seldom evidenced. But the freshly weaned child and the older sister (or brother) who has the care of him and bears much of the disciplinary responsibility for him take out a good deal on each other. Certainly the younger child (whose whole expectations have been unhinged by weaning) deflects most of its "meanness" onto one or more older sisters or brothers — especially the one who has him in charge. The older children, in turn, appear sometimes to displace against "run-about" youngsters some of the animosity which they suppressed when a baby actually dethroned them.

A fifth-grade girl wrote the following somewhat nostalgic account of her early years:

When I was born, they wrap me up and put me in the cradle. When I am tired my mother always unties me out of my cradle. She wraps me up with my little quilt. It was smooth, with a little rabbit on the edge of it.

Then I get big and can crawl, and I had two small teeth come so I can eat and help myself a little. But I just go to sleep for a while, then I wake up again. When my mother starts to cook dinner for my father, I have to cry louder and louder. Sometimes I scream so my mother has to rock me back and forth so my eyes go smaller and smaller. I go to sleep; mother doesn't have any trouble to cook dinner.

I did not know that I have a brother and sister, but I know my mother because she always holds me in her arms. My father he sings me to sleep. One chill evening my mother put me on the sheepskin at night. When I got cold I cried. When my mother did not hear me, I had to hit her on the face to wake her up. She just went back to sleep again. Then I cried and cried. My voice got so weak I could not cry any more so I went back to sleep.

THE CHILD'S PICTURE OF THE WORLD

OVER and above the learning of acceptable behavior, which takes place during the first six years of life, learning of a less tangible but equally important kind proceeds. It is sometimes forgotten that a child's education does not consist solely in the acquiring of skills or knowledge. If the child is to be at home in his society, he must also understand and accept the system of values by which life events take on meaning for those around him. Probably by the time the Navaho child is six months old typically Navaho conceptions of life have begun to permeate and to attain a sway which will last forever.

Certainly the lesson that life is hard has been learned in the first few years. Nurses in government hospitals report that even four- and five-year-olds will secrete crusts of bread from their trays. They have learned the meaning of hunger and the realism of having something on hand for the next meal. They also know in their own persons what it means to be sick, and often very sick. What with a diet which no longer has even the advantages of being a trial-and-error adaptation over many generations to the special conditions of Navaho life, with no skills for combatting the diseases introduced by Europeans, with drafty hogans, wet clothing, and other inadequate protections, it is hardly surprising that the children of The People are frequently ill. The fact that an estimated 57 per cent of Navaho deaths for 1941 were children under six speaks for itself. According to official figures, the proportion of deaths of children under two years of age to total deaths is five times greater for Navahos than for the United States as a whole.

During his early years the Navaho child has been much less sheltered from the fact of death than are most white children. The following experience is typical.

I remember when I was six or seven going everywhere with my grandmother. One time we went to a pond so my grandmother could wash wool. She built a fire. She had two stones and she rubbed them together and made sparks. Then she went to the pond and there was something the matter with her and she fell in and a water snake bit her. And I was very scared. I had my moccasins off but I ran as fast as I could to my grandfather and told him and we went back and met my grandmother and helped her home. We put her to bed but she never got well. She died. The snake bite made her sick.

From watching and listening to his elders, the child has begun to get a picture of the supernatural world as potentially menacing. His parents and grandparents (who must previously have seemed almost omnipotent, so successfully could they gratify every need save sometimes the removal of bodily pain) are now seen to confess their impotence to handle various matters in rational ways and to resort to prayers, songs, and ceremonials. When he has learned to understand speech, he hears the whispers about witchcraft and discovers that there are certain fellow tribesmen whom his family suspect and fear. One experience of early childhood which may be of special importance occurs during toilet training. When the toddler goes with mother or with older sister to defecate or urinate, he must notice a certain uneasiness which they manifest by their careful concealment of the waste matter. The mother is now revealed not as omnipotent but as herself very uneasy and afraid, though helpful in that she is teaching the child one way of protecting himself. This experience has another aspect which may be of some importance. In white society children learn bodily cleanliness primarily to please the parents and thus gain approval and other rewards from them. Perhaps the Navaho child feels that this hygiene is a form of *self*-protection. If so, the consequences for character formation which the psychoanalysts have claimed for these disciplines must be quite different among The People.

The child naturally comes to feel that the important thing in life is to be safe. In terms of the supernatural world, this means being careful to do certain things and being equally careful not to do others. In terms of the human world it means carefully following out his share of the expected reciprocities with his relatives. The youngster is *not* urged to strive for individual achievement. There is no promise of personal success for the able and hard-working or the good and the righteous. On the other hand, a sense of worthlessness is never drummed into a child so that his whole subsequent life is a struggle to justify himself. Perhaps in the white world too it is mainly security that people are seeking, but in recent American society the principal recipe for safety is to become "a success."

The Navaho tendency throughout is to depend as much upon magical acts and precautions as upon personal ability and effort for both security and "success." Certainly they feel that the right magic will do at least as much as moral exhortation to help their child become fearless or hardy or a leader. When a young father was asked a few years ago what hopes he had for his baby boy, he replied that he wanted him to "become a leader of the people." When he was asked how he planned to train him in this direction, his answer was:

When the baby is older we catch some birds, maybe a bluebird, and we hold it on a buckskin. Then we put corn pollen all over its feathers and we shake it onto the buckskin. Then we let the bird go and we give some of that pollen to the baby to eat. That makes the baby a leader, both boy or girl, and makes them healthy. [Do you need a medicine man for that?] No, anyone who knows the song.

In some of the more remote districts the same kind of thing is done with a bear. The bear is roped, and pollen is shaken off from the fur onto a buckskin. This pollen is believed to make the child brave. "If that boy is standing here and a man is over there, he will go right up to him and not be afraid. It is that way when he grows up." Another way of making the child "strong" is to rub a live toad on the chest of a five- or six-year-old.

A person will behave in one way or another later on in life in accordance not only with his "reflexes" but also with the needs and values he has derived from his cultural group. White people sometimes forget that no one is born with a "need" for the latest type of radio or the most expensive kind of automobile or a better house than his neighbor — it is not biologically "natural" that he should want such things — and yet such "needs" in white society sometimes appear to drive people harder even than primary biological appetites such as sex.

Just exactly when each aspect of the Navaho view of life is, as it were, "built in" to the child remains, in detail, rather mysterious — because scientists have not yet discovered the right observations to make, the right questions to ask of the Navaho, and how to interpret collected data. But the tests to be described in later chapters make it very plain that these conceptions have somehow become deeply engrained by the time the child goes to school. He has learned to respect the inviolabilities which the Navaho scheme of things imposes upon "private property" and upon other persons. But these are subtly different from those in the white pattern — so much so that teachers sometimes fall into the error of assuming that a Navaho child has no inhibitions about stealing or about displaying aggression. Part of the difference is that the inhibitions are less built up within the child himself. The Navahos depend less upon "conscience" and more upon the "shaming" which comes from the actual or potential presence of other people. Hence stealing is emphasized less than getting caught. Navaho parents do not taboo agression "in principle." Children are often allowed to display aggression — even, indeed, against their parents — without any very serious consequences.

Many objects and events have also acquired secondary or symbolic values so that the meaning of the same occurrence is quite different to the Navaho child and to its white teacher. Again, we cannot say just how these symbolisms are taught. "Taught" is, in a way, the wrong word because systematic, conscious instruction belongs mainly to the after-six period. We can only remind ourselves that, in any society, doing the same as others do, having the reactions which they exhibit, is generally rewarded. Small nuances of behavior on the part of elders encourage small children to perform just those responses which are most likely to be rewarded by the society at large. At least from the time when walking and talking begin, the child is gradually induced — and sometimes, in effect, forced — to develop more complex modes of response which ultimately prove gratifying. The way in which the child is taught the Navaho pattern of behavior and the necessity for conforming to it requires considerably more study before it can be described in detail. But the observations of the writers indicate that Navaho parents and other elders are not so permissive to the small child as casual observers sometimes think. Between weaning and six years the child has experienced a good deal of restriction. White men who go into a Navaho hogan and see a crawler put into its mouth a lump of dirt from the floor or a cup which the dog has just licked, or see a four-year-old sticking a nail through a cat's ear commonly get the impression that the words "No" and "Don't" are never used to Navaho children. This is far from being the case. *T'adoo* (equivalent to "stop that") is one of the most frequently heard sounds where small children are present. Probably there are *fewer* "don't's" than among white men. This is partly because there are fewer prohibitions put upon biological impulses, partly because Navaho life is simpler and there are fewer objects which the child can destroy or be harmed by, and partly because there are no taboos on "dirt" or "germs." On the other hand, the number of "superstitious" taboos which are enforced upon the child are much more numerous. In other words, the number of interferences and prohibitions to the child's activity in the form "I don't want you to do that" is relatively small, but the number in the form "Such and such will happen to you if you do that" is fairly high. If parents are not ultimately responsible for denials and restrictions, then it is useless for a child to try to coax or cajole them. One hears many straightforward requests and even demands from children to their elders but little wheedling; plenty of crying but comparatively little whining. The emphasis upon "reality training" is further evidenced by the fact that conscious deception of children by parents is exceedingly rare.

THE CHILD AT SIX

ALTHOUGH commonly unwashed and uncombed, the average Navaho child of six is found to be winsome by most white observers. Lively, curious, relatively free and easy with his familiars, he is apt to be silent, shy, and diffident with strangers. He has been taught to believe that one is safer with relatives than anywhere else. Whereas children of a year or less will accept friendly overtures from any visitor, Navaho or white, older ones often cry at the appearance of a new face, especially if it be white. This response seems to appear only after conditioning through speech has taken place. If a group of children from, for example, four to ten happen to be left alone at home, they will almost invariably run off to hide in the brush if they hear horses or an automobile approach. Nor will they emerge unless some one of the arrivals is a known and trusted figure.

The child of six already has a sound, matter-of-fact orientation to practical affairs and feels quite a keen sense of responsibility in his tasks. He has not recaptured the joyous spontaneity of his nursing years. He is still readjusting his personality to the demands which followed the indulgence of his infancy but has not achieved the integration which permits a new epoch of carefreeness a few years later.

2.

BECOMING A NAVAHO:
LATER CHILDHOOD

THE MAIN lines of communication in Navaho society are between relatives. Therefore it is natural that the first and most important lessons which the child learns about human relationships are the approved ways of dealing with various classes of relatives. As his horizons expand he carries this pattern over into the larger world.

"HIS SISTERS AND HIS COUSINS AND HIS AUNTS"

THE Navaho child learns early that he can expect certain relatives to follow a prescribed way of behaving toward him. He finds that his mother's brothers will scold him severely or punish him, but that he can get away with playing tricks upon them or making broad jokes about their sex life or disparaging their ability as hunters. He is taught, as he grows older, that toward all the persons whom he calls "my sister" he must be respectful and practice certain avoidances; he must be restrained in any joking and never deal in humor of a sexual connotation; decorum must be observed in face-to-face speech, which in conservative families still involves the use of a special set of personal pronouns. He likewise notes that his elders preserve the same type of respect-avoidance relationship with their relatives by marriage and again follow different linguistic usages from those they employ with their blood relatives.

Two "brothers" or two "sisters" [1] present a solid front to the rest of the world but may tease each other privately. Joking between them takes the form of accusations of laziness, slurs upon personal appearance, epithets of "slave" or "Ute." On the other hand, the youngster comes to expect an exchange of vulgar jokes with anyone whom he calls "my cross cousin" (a child of his mother's brother or

---

[1] Quotation marks indicate that these terms are used in the Navaho sense; that is, not only biological brothers and sisters are meant, but also those members of the extended family or clan relatives who are called by the same Navaho word. (See *The Navaho*, Chapter 3.)

of his father's sister). With the father's parents there is reciprocal
repartee about sex of a somewhat subtler nature. With the mother's
parents joking is more restrained.

We need not follow out all the details of these patterns. Indeed they are breaking down in their specificity, although they
are still important in daily life in most areas. The important
thing is that there is a definite way to behave towards all persons addressed by the same kinship term. This limited set of
patterns for social life, acquired in childhood, is later used to
bridge excursions into the wider social environment. The ways
in which a Navaho adult deals with all individuals who come
into his life tend to represent modifications of these master designs for interpersonal relations. He wants to classify each new
acquaintance with one or another of these relatives and to treat
him accordingly. One of his difficulties in adjusting to white men
is that they do not fit into this system.

Naturally, the "set" which a child develops in dealing with individuals of a given sex, generation, and type of kinship connection
depends not only upon the cultural patterns he is taught but upon
his own personal experience with real people of these categories and
the differing degrees of pleasure or frustration they have brought.
And the composition of the circle of persons surrounding different
Navaho children varies enormously. This variation is both as between different children and as between different periods in the life
of the same child. The child who grows up in a large extended
family has a constant supply of playmates alike of its own age and
older and younger. The children of an isolated biological family
have to depend on each other for companionship most of the time,
regardless of age differences, because the nearest neighbors are probably some miles away. This does not mean — as it does for nine
months of the year among white people — that children below school
age have no older playmates during a good share of the day, for few
indeed are the Navaho families where all the eligible children attend
school.

However, even if the youngster is a member of a big extended
family group, one should not picture him as constantly surrounded
by all the individuals who make up this unit. On the contrary,
ceremonials and a few other occasions are almost the only times
when one can expect to find everybody around the home. On most

occasions some members will be at the main hogan, others at the hogan near the planted fields, still others off working for wages or trading. The child may be away for weeks in a sheep camp with a grandmother and one or two other children. Most Navaho youngsters experience considerable periods of real loneliness while herding. If the child is at the family's main residence, only a few people may be there because the greater number have gone to a "squaw dance" or on a pinyon-gathering trip. It is significant that the reward most frequently promised children for performing household chores is: "If you do that, I'll take you somewhere."

The composition of the group also alters from time to time through death and divorce. In white society, in spite of increasing divorce rates, it is still rather exceptional for a child not to go through at least the first years of his life with the same parents. The expectancy for Navaho children is of quite a different sort. Maternal mortality is high. Early fatherhood coincides with one of the peaks in the tuberculosis death curve. Hence an appreciable number of children lose both parents. Others lose only the mother, but the father, when he marries again, surrenders his children by his first marriage to his first wife's people. Families who have more children than they can support may give one or more for adoption to relatives who are better off or have lost their own children or do not have enough help in herding and other work. The proportion of the children of The People who have been wholly or partially reared by grandparents, sisters of the mother, or other relatives is, to white people, surprisingly high. Figures on 1,000 cases from the Ramah region show that only four children out of ten lived from birth to marriage with their own parents.

The experiences of two children, which are recounted below, could be duplicated with hundreds of others.

A twelfth-grade girl wrote:

My mother died when I was only three years old. I still remember when she was very sick I would go up to her bed and try to lift her up but nothing doing. Finally the last day for her to live my grandmother came and she told her to take care of me after she die. But my other grandmother told her "No" that she was the one who raised my mother, she can't let me go to live with my real grandmother. As the year went by I stayed with my grandmother and I really had a hard time because of one of my aunty. She would not let me play when her children are

playing outside. I would have to stay in and help her with the things
that she wants done before the day was over.[2]

A fifth-grade boy's account was:

When I was four years old my father went away because my mother
was very sick. But pretty soon she got well and lived on. But I worried
about my father because he never came back to my mother, he is still
away now. He just buys me clothes and other things.

Then when I came to be five years old my mother married another
man. He was with her for one year and a half. This is how he went
away — early in the morning he got up. He said, "I am going to the
trading post in Cameron." So my mother gave him a bag and he went
off. All day we waited for him, but he didn't come home all that time.
He didn't come back, so we live together happy. Sometimes we went
without food. That year I didn't come to school. In the summer we came
back to my grandmother.

While relatives as a group are tremendously important, there is
less likelihood than among white men that any particular relative
will have overweening significance. Take the case of the father, for
example. The child's loss of a father through divorce is almost certainly less disturbing than in white society. First of all, there is less
sentimental attachment on the grounds of blood relationship. Moreover, the mother's new husband often speedily becomes for all emotional purposes an adequate substitute father, who is rarely jealous
of the first husband and still less of his children.

Remember that, in any case, a Navaho father's role may be compared in some ways with that of the white father who is a sailor or
who commutes early in the morning and late at night and is at home
with the child only on some week ends, for most Navaho fathers
habitually spend much time away from the residence of their wives.
If the fathers are ceremonial practitioners, they will be called away
often and sometimes for periods of as long as nine or ten days. The
data indicate that a successful Singer spends at least 120 days out of
every year at the homes of his patients. On these visits he is seldom
accompanied by his wife and children, particularly when any child
is still very small. Even if the husband does neither divination nor
singing, he has many more reasons than has the average white father

[2] This and most of the other quotations from children used in this chapter are from
autobiographies written by pupils at the Shiprock and Tuba City government schools
in 1943.

for being apart from his family. Sheepherding, hunting and trading trips, and journeys for salt all take the father away from home for short or long periods. In addition, increasing numbers of Navahos in young adult life and early middle age work for white men on the railroad, on various jobs for the government, and even in distant cities such as Los Angeles and Kansas City. Often circumstances necessitate leaving the family at home. Whatever the father's occupation, he is expected to pay his own mother's family repeated and sometimes protracted visits.

Even when the father is at home most of the time, he does not perform all of the functions associated with fatherhood in white society. While he certainly does act as instructor and even as a disciplinarian, he tends much more to be an affectionate and playful companion than a stern parent. In the more conservative sections of Navaho society much of the "disciplinary" task is taken over by the mother's brothers and also the grandparents. Thus the training and affection expected from a white father are parceled out among a large number of male relatives rather than concentrated in a single person.

The same pattern holds among brothers and sisters. In an extended family group the child may well have not merely three or four but fifteen or more persons whom he calls "my older brother." And the Navaho child calls not one but a number of women "my mother." Once the worst emotional shock of the weaning process is over, the mother's sisters often become almost completely adequate substitutes for the real mother. Indeed there are cases where it appears that a young man or woman actually feels closer to one of these secondary mothers. Navaho mothers are sometimes a trifle stern with their own children but feel freer to indulge their sisters' children.

What does all this mean in terms of the dynamics of personal relations? It means that the Navaho child's emotional energy tends to be spread over a much wider surface than is the case with white children. He is not likely to have the same degree of intense emotional investment in a very few persons. Naturally, the reverse is equally true. The mother is devoted to her own children, but her feeling toward them grades off almost imperceptibly into that for her sisters' children. Her eggs are not all in one basket, emotionally speaking. Hence she is less likely than the white mother to be possessive and to demand that loyalties be centered completely upon her. The child, after he has reached the toddling stage, finds ready and immediate succor and comfort in one of his secondary mothers whenever he feels that his own has been cross or has temporarily rejected him.

This diffuse character of Navaho social organization and of the emotional structure of Navaho society is perhaps the keynote of the whole system. Such a situation in childhood leads to and reinforces general Navaho social organization where, again, authority is highly diffuse. Just as the child's psychological security is never completely centered upon a single father or a single mother, so also no single individual is ever the sole pivot of the adult authority system. Authority is felt to be "the relatives" or "other people" or "the court," rather than "father" or "Mr. Mustache" or "the judge." Similarly, the fact that there are so many broken marriages and the notion that "any woman will do" must be contrasted with the white tendency toward concentration of love both in childhood and in adult life.

THE EXPANDING WORLD

UNTIL the child is five or six he spends most of his time at home. There are occasional visitors, but most of the faces are familiar to the youngster. Then he begins to be taken more often to the trading store and to ceremonials and other gatherings. So far as possible, new people are placed within the kinship system. Behavior patterns toward clan (and linked-clan) relatives are the same in principle but attenuated in practice. However, when a child meets an older person of the same clan he immediately feels a degree of ease with and attraction toward the adult, because the clansman automatically assumes his place in the child's world, a high place in sentimental terms. The youngster expects — and receives — warmth and reassurance, gifts, praise, and other rewards. The same, to a lesser degree, may be said for "relatives" through the father's clan.

Toward nonrelatives reserve is the rule. They are described and referred to by residence, as "the man who lives on the edge of the canyon" or "the wife of the man who lives at Tall Mountain." Or, they may be fitted into the system of known positions as "father-in-law of so-and-so" or "clan kin of so-and-so" (naming perhaps one of the speaker's relatives by marriage).

CHILD TRAINING: NAVAHO STYLE

How are Navaho children taught what to do and what not to do?
How do The People induce their children to subordinate their impulses to the expectations of others?

THE GENERAL PATTERN

Some patterns of good behavior are carefully verbalized. When
the whole family gathers round the fire at night (particularly in the
winter) while one or more of the elders recites a myth or a folk tale
or an anecdote of his parents or grandparents, the narrator or any
older person present will take occasion to point the moral for daily
life. Children are expected not only to be present but to listen at-
tentively. One boy in his teens said, "If I went to sleep, my grandfather would pull my hair and shake my head. I had to listen to
those stories." That this is a systematic program is indicated by the
fact that when one asks adults about the activities of children, they
have a standard reply: "In the daytime they play, but at night they
listen when the old people tell their stories."

Other types of positive instruction will be considered presently,
but let us now see how Navahos eliminate behavior or habits which
are considered objectionable. Reality training is important as it must
be among all peoples who survive. The following anecdote, with
some substitutions in content, has a very familiar ring to whites.

My mother came out of the hogan, and at that moment the coyote
caught the puppy and carried him off. Then I cried more than ever, and
my mother was going after the coyote as hard as she could, screaming
and hollering running. She was gone quite awhile. When she came back
she said, "I couldn't find the puppy anywhere. The coyote has carried
him away. . . . It's your own fault. I told you not to go far from the
hogan. You've given the coyote your puppy. If you'd minded me you'd
have your little dog with you right now. If it hadn't been for the puppy
the coyote would have gotten you and carried you away. You mustn't go
far away; you must stay close to the hogan all the time, because you know
coyotes are around here. If you go far from the hogan he'll get you and
carry you away." [3]

Notice, however, that the mother does not say that the little boy
was "bad" because he was disobedient. She points out to him what

[3] For source, see p. 267.

the advantages of obedience would have been, the value in taking advice and instruction from more experienced persons. She does end with a threat, but not a threat of something *she* will do if he does not obey; it is rather a statement that there are dangerous beings and forces in the world round about and that if one does not pay due regard to these realities one will suffer very unpleasant consequences.

Naturally, not all Navaho children are instructed, disciplined, and trained in precisely the same way. There are important differences among mothers, fathers, and other elders. To some extent, also, there tend to be family patterns that prevail regardless of whether or not any particular family member is present. In some families cruel teasing is frequent. In others teasing is almost entirely restricted to rather impersonal observance of the standardized jokes between certain classes of relatives. In still others teasing follows these traditional lines but takes on a more personal quality and is in fact used as a way of bringing slightly recalcitrant youngsters into line.

In spite of these divergences, one can still point to trends which sharply distinguish the Navaho way of training children from that used by white men. Very striking is the extent to which even seven- and eight-year-old Navahos respond passively to reprimand. The youngster who is accused of something almost never "talks back." He turns his head the other way and says nothing. Again, while one occasionally hears direct threats on the part of a parent ("I'll throw you in that water down at the dam if you aren't good"), the overwhelming tendency is to refer discipline, or the authority for it, to some individual or agency outside of the immediate family circle. Neither parents nor grandparents nor older brothers or sisters habitually assume full responsibility in the eyes of the child. Responsibility is placed either on supernatural agencies or on human beings in general.

Children are told that if they don't behave the big gray yeibichai will carry them off and eat them. This fear is driven home by threats made by the masked figures at the initiation ceremony. (See *The Navaho*, Chapter 6.) In two of the autobiographies of school children we find evidence of this: "The first time I saw the yeibichai I was scared. I thought they eat the children, and I cried." "I never have seen the yeibichai. I am scared to see them. My father said the yeibichai can whip me, that is why I am scared to see them." Insubordinate children are publicly named and terrified at the initiation ceremony. It is to be noted that among The People supernatural sanctions are mainly at the everyday level rather than at that of projected immortality.

There are other bugaboos. In hogans in out-of-the-way places one still sees "owls" (made of rushes and sticks) hung up. At night one can easily get the illusion that the "owl" is real, and the child is warned that it will take him off. This threat is the more sinister because of the association of owls with ghosts and witches. Children are also scared by tales of ghosts and witches.

Supernatural agencies may be said to provide the ultimate sanctions for all behavior, of children and adults alike, but the effective sanctions of daily life are provided still more by gossip and ridicule. Parents sometimes say flatly that a youngster is "naughty" or call him a dunce or a fool, but they have an insistent propensity for referring the child to what "people" will say. One of the most noticeable peculiarities of Navaho conversation is the tendency to evade personal responsibility for a statement. Any long narrative is full of such qualifications as "he says," "that one says," and especially "they say."

The mother, instead of complaining "If you act like that you'll disgrace me," points out "If you act like that people will make fun of you." Rather than setting themselves up as rewarding and punishing surrogates, parents utilize this essentially impersonal "shame" mechanism. This is meaningful to the child, for he experiences not merely the disapproval of his elders but also the most intangible ridicule of other children when he fails to conform.

Never have the writers known a Navaho parent to demand socially acceptable behavior as the condition of parental love and protection or to say to a child "If you do that, mother won't love you any more." There are occasionally conditional statements "If you act like this we won't take you to the trading store this afternoon." Physical punishment is rare, slight, and usually spontaneous. The amount and frequency varies greatly between families. If one can trust the reminiscences of elders, it was commoner one, two, or three generations ago than it is now. Remarks of this sort are often heard: "Long ago they whipped children if they lost sheep or let them into the fields. They would whip old folks, too, if they lost sheep. But nowadays they just scold them. They used to throw them naked into the snow, too. My parents used to grab me by the ears if I didn't mind. [Question] Yes, they did that to girls and boys both." One seldom hears threats of physical punishment. Indeed parents mostly refrain from saying "*I* will punish you" and prefer "If you do thus and so, such and such an unpleasant thing will happen to you." The implication is, of course, that these unpleasant happenings are not only not promoted by the parents, but that they are indeed beyond their control — part of the inevitable texture of human relations and of the nature of the supernatural world.

The whole conception of punishment is less personal among Navahos than among whites. Even in adult life there is little tendency to be vindictive toward those who bring about court sentences. Accuser and accused will often joke and talk in friendly fashion with each other while the trial is going on. The reciprocal of this is that accusers are less self-righteous. A wife will report her husband for beating her but will then help pay his fine or meet him as he is released from jail. This kind of behavior occurs in white society now and then, but it is typical for The People. The foundations for these attitudes are found in childhood training. Only rarely does one hear the utterances on the part of Navaho parents which are so usual among white parents: "Do it because I say it is right," "do it because I say so," "do it because I am your father and children must obey their parents." It is interesting to note in autobiographies that old men and women will often attribute their survival or happiness or success to having followed the *advice* of their parents. They seldom say "I got along all right because I *obeyed* my parents." There is a difference.

Training in specific skills may come from father, mother, mother's brother, grandparents, "aunts," depending upon the sex of learner and teacher, the time the adult has to spare, and his familiarity with the particular skill. "General discipline" comes perhaps more from the mother than any other person, partly because the father is away so much and the mother's brother is present only intermittently, whereas the mother must be constantly on hand to prepare food (or see that it is prepared) and to keep the fundamental routines of the hogan running. Verbal instruction in "morals" (in the widest sense) seems to come mainly from the father. At least in a number of autobiographies of adults the narrators say time without number

that such and such a standard was "what my father taught me."
One fifth-grade girl strikes the same note and gives a very good picture of how the introduction into responsibilities and skills feels to
the child:

> Father is the one who taught me to do the right thing, but my mother
> taught me how to boil coffee, tea, and how to fry bread, meat, teach me
> how to milk the goat. In winter she teaches me how to do things, and
> how to feed the baby sheep. I get punished when I do bad things and do
> not do what my father tells me to do. Sometimes I go out and play with
> the children. My mother has to go out and call me in. There was a pile
> of wool all ready to card. So I got to work and carded all day. It was
> hard work. It was hot in the hogan. When we had done this we put our
> work away until morning, when we start to work again. When we got
> tired we rest for a while. If I card my fingers too, they get sore and hurt.

SEX TRAINING

In a one-room dwelling the "facts of life" are not very long a secret.
Children also get a good deal of sex education through sheep herding, partly from watching the animals, partly from the opportunities
which isolation offers for exhibitionism and experiment.

The general attitude of Navahos toward sex activities of children
is permissive and matter of fact. Most cautions given are highly
practical. "Stay away from lewd women or they'll give you a disease." "Don't give yourself to a man or you'll have a baby and then
a good man won't marry you." "Keep away from that girl or you'll
get yourself and all of us into trouble. They'll try to make you
marry her and we don't want to be tied up with that family." The
only places where admonitions have a strongly affective quality is
with reference to incest and modesty. "Will you be like a coyote
and marry your sister?" "You must be getting crazy — you danced
with your [clan] sister in the 'squaw dance.'" "People who touch
their sisters are getting ready to jump into the fire." Youngsters are
also conditioned into a strong sensitivity against exposure of their
sexual organs, even before close relatives of the same sex. After
puberty especially they are told, "When you have to urinate, you
want to do it by yourself. You don't want your grandfather or your
brother to see you. If you do this before people, you'll burn yourself, they say."

Most mothers will prepare their daughters for menstruation by talking with them when they reach the age of about ten. Shortly before or after the first menses, one or more older female relatives will give the girl advice about heterosexual experience. Boys also receive a talk from their mother's brother or their father. Mothers will sometimes strongly enjoin their sons against too early entrance into relations with the other sex, even going so far as a half-serious, half-playful threat of loss of the sex organ.

"BEHAVIOR PROBLEMS"

Many types of behavior among children which give white men concern are no source of worry to The People. Thumb-sucking is rare, but children under ten will often chew a finger or a fist when they are embarrassed or ill at ease. This is simply ignored. Navaho youngsters pout and cry when corrected, just as white children do, but they are not preached at. The treatment is that of indifference or, occasionally, of ridicule. Three things, however, are a cause of concern: left-handedness, bed-wetting, and walking or talking during sleep.

It is characteristic of Navaho child training that no attempt is made to correct left-handedness until the matter can be explained to the youngster. Then his left hand is tied in front or in back and left there for a number of days, or perhaps encased in a mitten instead, and an explanation is made:

It doesn't look good for a woman to weave left-handed or to spin or card that way. People would talk about it.

The old people say that a man should handle the arrow on his right side and that it is bad if he is left-handed. Pollen must be sprinkled with the right hand. When you get married, you'll have to pick up the pollen from the four directions with your right hand — the left won't do. You know how people talk about that Singer because his boy is left-handed. They say, "What is the matter with that boy? Maybe something is the matter with his father. It shouldn't have gone that way."

If a child past four or five continues to wet his bedding very frequently even when the family have seen to it that he urinated just before going to sleep, a magical rite is resorted to. The child stands naked with his legs spread over a burning nest of the phoebe which commonly builds its nests in the hogan. The nest of a swallow or of a nighthawk may also be used. This helps because birds don't wet their nests. If enuresis persists past the age of puberty, then Blessing

Way is the remedy. "If you don't have this, the person, or his brother or sister, will die because it is a dead person who makes water all the time."

Walking and talking in sleep are of concern to the inhabitants of a one-room hogan because they may affect many or all of the people sleeping close to one another. Disturbances of sleep, like bed-wetting, are treated by magical means. Let an English-speaking Navaho tell about it in his own words:

If there are some children in the hogan who talk in their sleep or walk around, they put charcoal on their little fingers. [What does that do?] Well, the spirit is afraid of black, he goes away. The spirit is big and black. You would call it a devil. You can't see him. It is like the wind, you can't see it either. He comes at night and gets into you. If you have those dreams over again, they get some special weeds and put them on a flat stone in the middle of the hogan and burn them to charcoal. Then they take some fat from a buffalo, coyote, and other animals and grease the child all over his body. Then they put the charcoal all over the body and you sleep like that for one night or generally four. When that black spirit comes again, he is afraid and goes away.

TRAINING IN HARDIHOOD

Even though the practices about to be described are not always followed in detail today, some of the children in the Ramah and Navaho Mountain areas have gone through these disciplines, and almost all of their parents did. "Then they didn't grow old so soon. Nowadays people grow old too soon." As of 1936 six out of ten families in the Ramah area still made their children roll in the snow. In any case, the ideas back of these exercises in hardihood linger in the consciousness of The People, and it is impossible to grasp their "philosophy of education" without this background.

Youngsters (primarily boys) were wakened before daylight and told to get out and run. In winter they were also expected to roll naked in the snow, to shake snow-laden branches over their naked shoulders, to run with pieces of ice in their mouths, to break the crust of ice upon a pool or stream and plunge in. This training began at about eight and continued for a year or so after puberty. It was made plain that this was not punishment or arbitrary cruelty on the part of elders but was in the interest of the participants. "The oldest men said if you get up early and start running you'll be living until you're past ninety." "Racing is good. It makes you strong. You will live long and be around for a long while." Boys not infrequently went through these exercises on their own initiative. Indeed they still do. In the winter of 1945–46 children in more than one family in the Ramah area were observed to organize and carry out with great enthusiasm early morning races through the snow.

Morning racing and rolling in the snow in winter was sometimes followed (usually only after the age of eleven or twelve) by long runs in the noonday summer sun. These runs, like the early morning ones, were always made in a sunwise direction. Just before puberty boys began to take purgatives and emetics, followed by sweatbaths.

Practice in running was often justified on the ground that if one was captured by the enemy one had "a long ways to come back." Older men today claim immunity from weather because they rolled in the snow as youngsters: "When you get wet then you don't shiver. Like the last time I was here, I got in that rain and when I got home I had to dry all my clothes by the fire but I didn't get cold." The same speaker told pridefully (in 1933) how his nephews and other young relatives were voluntarily continuing these disciplines.

Well, two or three boys get together and they say, "We will not sleep for two days and two nights." And they try to keep awake. They never go three days because if they do they will fall asleep and if they are on their horse they will fall off. [Do they go without any food?] No, but lots of times they don't eat. The hardest is to cut a hole in the ice and go into that water, and then carry your arms full of ice to your hogan. Then the boys burn themselves. Maybe you have seen a Navaho with scars. They take the inside stem of that plant with the yellow flowers [sunflower] and they powder it on their hand, maybe in the shape of a little star. Sometimes they put three or four on the back of their hand or on their arms or legs or forehead. Then they take some hot charcoal and the plant burns and makes a sore place. It is very sore for two or three days, then it heals up and leaves the mark.

RESPONSIBILITIES AND SKILLS

Training in hardihood is disappearing, but the present-day program in the hogans for youngsters of the same ages has a less drastic effect in the same direction. Children are severely rebuked and even whipped if they take shelter during a storm while out herding and lose track of the sheep. Neglect or abuse of livestock is the least forgivable of childhood misdemeanors. When children first begin to help with the herding at six or seven, they tend to ride and chase the sheep and goats and otherwise disturb and distract them from feeding. Harsh scoldings break them of these habits quite quickly, but a young herder will go to sleep or play with other children so that animals wander off or get killed by coyotes. When their loss is discovered, the culprit is dressed down properly, and an effort is made to shame him into more responsible conduct. Particularly common are remarks like this: "Are you just lazy and shiftless or do you have some girl out there, my son?" The growth of a sense of responsibility is facilitated by the custom of setting aside each year a sheep or two which, with their increase, belong to the child himself. The young herder feels, then, that he isn't just doing a job for his father and mother — he is also looking after his own property. His own interests become involved in his learning to care properly for the flocks. Present rigid limitations on the number of sheep permitted each family are interfering with this practice. Youngsters cannot build up new herds of their own.

As in the post-weaning period the child learns that he cannot indefinitely continue to have his own way, so between five and eight he has to acquire a sense of responsibility. Every society has to teach its members that they cannot always indulge themselves and that they have duties toward others. The difference lies in when, and how, and by whom the youngster is disciplined. White society's training in some types of self-restraint (for example, toilet training) and in surrender to standards in the fixing of which the child has had no part (e.g., scheduled feeding) comes early. The Navaho child is "beaten down" later — after he is sure of the fundamental affection of his relatives. Also, there are more limits upon the personal punishments and even the scoldings which may be imposed. For instance, when a Navaho woman who lived at some distance from her son's family was paying them a visit and heard her daughter-in-law scold two of the children until they cried, she said, "You mustn't talk to your children that way. It makes them sick. Even if they did lose two sheep, it is bad to talk that way. I am going to take my grandchildren back home with me if you won't promise to treat them nicely." (Nor was this, by Navaho lights, a case of the meddling mother-in-law.)

The period from six through the early teens is a time for learning skills as well as for developing responsible behavior. Besides the chores of chopping and bringing in firewood, emptying ashes, hauling water, husking corn, etc., instruction in more specialized tasks begins.

From about the age of eight on, children of the two sexes tend to be separated a good deal of the time. Each group is trained in certain skills by their elders of the same sex. (This fits with ideas which have many other expressions. For example, Navaho folk say that boys look like their father or their father's parents, girls like their mother or her family. Little girls, from cradle age on, dress as exact replicas of their mothers. Boys imitate their fathers in every detail of costume.) Girls learn to cook and to tend children under the supervision of their mothers and other women relatives. They begin to card and spin at about ten and to weave a little later. Interest and aptitude are reinforced by such remarks as, "She is a good little weaver." Youngsters of both sexes get instruction and experience in animal husbandry and in planting and weeding crops. Fathers teach their sons the care of horses, agriculture, house-building, leather work, and other male skills. Apprenticeship as a silversmith, however, seldom begins in any very serious sense until the late teens, though a smith will naturally use his younger sons to assist him in various nontechnical chores. Navaho children seem to have considerable skill in most types of handiwork and to show aesthetic gifts in painting and the like. Kuipers found that Navaho youngsters manifested greater sensitivity to geometric design than the average white child of the same age.

An eleventh-grade girl remembers her childhood training thus:

In the summer time when daddy works on the farm, my brother and I we used to go around with daddy where ever he goes. I was very interested in every thing my daddy does. I used to don't like to stay at home with mother, because she sometimes asks me to card the wool and wash the dishes, etc. I did all these things in 1927 when I was five years old. In 1928 I kind of got interested in all the things that my mother does. When she puts up a loom to start a rug, I used to watch and try to learn how she puts in all those yarn. When she gets up to rest or to cook, I would get in there and try to do what she did, but I make mistakes, and she would get after me.

Children in their early teens sometimes work very hard indeed. This is particularly true when families are small or when older members are incapacitated by illness or are shiftless or drunken. While, on the whole, there are less often "favorite children" among the Navahos than among white people, and Navaho parents ordinarily are very scrupulous in apportioning tasks, trips, clothes, and other rewards equally, still the phenomenon of the family drudge is not unknown. This is often an adopted child, a "poor relation." There is also a tendency for each child in turn to occupy this position for a few years. The writers have frequently noticed that the youngest unmarried sub-adult in a family group gets a disproportionate share of the dirty work for a time. In various life histories it is striking that the subject indicates resentment over what he feels as exploitation by one or more of his elders at some period in his youth. The mother is almost never specified, the father seldom, but older brothers and sisters rather frequently. Often the maternal uncle or some more distant relative is mentioned; sometimes the reference is vague and generalized. Probably such experiences contribute to the suspiciousness with which many adult Navahos view figures of authority.

AMUSEMENT

Navaho childhood diversions are almost wholly simple and unorganized. Children chase each other around. There is much good-humored scuffling. In occasional quarrels they will jeer and make faces at each other much as white children do. They climb trees or on top of buildings. They twirl (apparently aimlessly — but endlessly) around a post. Now and then one sees a tug-of-war, which is an old-time diversion of adults. These days they have fun with swings made of discarded tires or with carts made of store boxes. Parties of children go off to water tanks or irrigation ditches. They play with dogs and cats — roughly and often cruelly. Boys practice roping trees or domestic animals or their brothers and sisters. They will bat at rocks with sticks. Girls fashion dolls from cloths and wood or pine twigs. In winter (sometimes in summer too, today) children make cat's cradles in string. Star constellations are favorite figures, but certain animals, the lightnings, the double hogan, and others also require considerable skill. The People value this diversion highly as an innocent occupation and also as a useful device for teaching children to concentrate. Apart from dolls and roping there is little sex-typing of amusements in the pre-adolescent period.

Three school children wrote of their earlier play as follows:

The children I like to play with was my brothers and sister. We used to play with rocks. We used to build a little house. The best thing we like was to ride on rams. That's what we like to do.

.   .   .   .   .

When I was three years of age I used to play with tin cans, line them up on the other end of the board and the other end I stand on it, and jump up and down to let the cans fall off the board. It was fun to me. Another one that I liked was dolls. Mother used to make doll for me to play with, my little brothers and sisters we play family. One of us had to be the father and another one be the mother.

.   .   .   .   .

The children that I play with was my brother and sister. We always play in the ditch [pit] where my father puts corn in the fall. When the corn is ready to put away, we hunt up cans and play with them. We put a rock in the cans and shake them and sing. I asked my brother to get some water from home. He went over there, and when he asked his mother if he could take some water out and play with it outside, his mother said, "Where are you going with the water?" Then he told her that I want some water and told her all about what we were going to do with that water.

Soon he came back with nothing in his hand. "Where is the water?" I said. He said, "My mother wants you children to come home." So we get up and start home. When we got near the hogan I got a little bit scared. I said, "Maybe my mother is going to spank us." When the children went in I was standing by the door listening to what my mother said to the children. She asked my brother, "Where is your brother?" My brother did not say anything for a long time. Then he said, "He is standing by the door."

My mother said, "Come in. What are you standing by the door for?" So I do not say any word, I just go in and stand behind the stove again. Then my mother told me to go herd the sheep.

A man in his thirties described his play while herding sheep as a boy:

We took a round stone (about as big as your fist) in each hand. I threw a stone about over there [roughly 25 yards]. Then we would bet who could hit it. We bet maybe a knife or a bandanna. He tried to hit my stone. Then I threw. If it hit it then I won. If I missed, then he would throw his other stone. We took turns that way. We had races. Sometimes we would make sticks out of oak trees. We used to get an oak stick and dig under the ground so we could get the root on it. Then the stick was bent at the bottom and we had a small ball made of buckskin. We buried this in the ground and then we struck at it with our sticks, first one of us, then the other. When it came out one of us would try to keep it by knocking it along. The other boy would try to knock it the other way. . . . We played with bows and arrows. One boy would shoot his arrow. Then the other boy would shoot as near as he could. The arrows went into the ground and if that boy's arrow came as close as the length of his little finger, then he won. We measured our little fingers with a piece of wood. Sometimes we would shoot arrows to see who could shoot the highest or the longest distance. We used to bet maybe a kid. They don't use bow and arrows around here any more. Some of the Christian Indians told the Agent the boys were gambling with bows and arrows, and he said we mustn't play with them any more. We also had buckskin slingshots. We used to kill rabbits and prairie dogs. [Birds?] Yes, but not the bluebird and some others, only a little brown bird. Our slingshots were about a foot and a half long. If they are longer, they twist. [Did you play any other games when you were a boy?] Three or four of us would get together and have races or wrestle. One or two of us might ride on another boy's back and he would try to buck us off.

Trips to the trading store or to town are among the principal amusements and rewards, as are opportunities to attend ceremonials, especially the "squaw dance," Night Way, and Mountain Top Way chants. Occasionally preadolescent girls dance in the "squaw dance" (see *The Navaho*, Chapter 7) but boys seldom participate until they are in middle or late teens. They start to join in the singing earlier, as they do at the curing chants and Blessing Way. In most areas girls do not sing publicly, but in the privacy of the hogan, or when out herding sheep, youngsters of both sexes sing a good deal. The family takes pride in teaching them to sing and also to do simple dances. It is not at all uncommon to hear a little girl or boy of three or under singing a quite difficult song from one of the chants. At that age they do so without embarrassment, even in the presence of outsiders. Later, however, their singing takes place mostly when they are off alone herding or riding horseback by themselves. The gradual participation of the boys in public singing begins very shyly.

Most Navaho games have a ritual context. In fact Navahos say that playing the old games at the proper time will help to bring rain and good crops. Of the old games proper for children one virtually never sees shinny played any more (though note the reference to this game in the immediately preceding quotation), and a Navaho equivalent of "prisoner's base" is passing out of use. Organized games are seldom seen except near schools or in those areas where white influence is great. However, the age-old amusement of imitating the activities of elders continues. The following description from *Son of Old Man Hat* refers to two generations ago but could be of yesterday.

One summer, just as the corn was getting ripe, a woman and her daughter came to our place to help us. She was a relative of my mother's. A lot of crows were getting after our corn, and I used to go to the cornfield and watch and scare the crows away. The girl's mother said, "Go with the boy, so that he won't hurry home. You can stay with him until you get hungry, and then you can both come back." The girl and I were the same size. She was half Navajo and half Mexican.

So we stayed where the crows always went, way in the end of the cornfield. We made a little brush hogan, and she made a knife out of a tin can and got some corn and cut it up and started grinding it. But we had no fire with us, so she ground the corn for nothing. She said she was going to make corn bread, but we didn't have a fire, we weren't allowed to carry fire around. When she sat in this little brush hogan I'd be lying right close beside her, "because," I thought, "she's my wife, and I'm her husband." I remembered what my mother had said when I asked her about men and women. She'd said, "The man who goes around with a woman is husband to the woman, and she's wife to the man." So I thought, "I'm a husband to this girl, and she's a wife to me." [4]

CHILD TRAINING: WHITE STYLE

GOING TO SCHOOL

As it has been intimated, by no means all Navaho children go to school, even in these days. But most families where there are a number of children see to it that at least one attends school. Definite policies of selectivity are followed. In some families those who have better memories and are quicker to learn are chosen. But in at least the poorer families the prevailing tendency has been to send the more delicate or crippled children who are less useful in the home economy. A tenth-grader in one of the boarding schools wrote of her selection thus:

[4] For source, see p. 267.

One time the principal from Leupp came to our home. He asked my mother to put my older brother to school. But he was the only one that had to take care of the sheep and other things. So she put me to school in place of him.

In the early 1900's, persuasion often took the form of literally kidnaping scholars for the boarding schools. In addition, Indians who had been to school were sometimes sent around the Reservation to hold out promises of good food, free clothes, and comfortable buildings to lure reluctant pupils. Parents retaliated by hiding their children when the school people came in view. Prior to 1930, government schools for the Indians were most often characterized by bleak barracks-like buildings and a lock-step life. Homesick children were intimidated from running away by stern measures.

I was at school and I ran away and it took me all night to walk home and in the morning my father said, "What did you run away for?" and I said, "The disciplinarian was going to strap me and the bandmaster struck my finger. That hurt a lot." Then a policeman came and took me back. The Agency superintendent said, "Why did you run away?" and I told him and he said, "I know how to stop you, you will have a strapping." And another time I ran away and when they took me back they put handcuffs on my ankles with a long chain between and at night they would put one handcuff around the bed. I wouldn't go to the dining room and for four days I didn't eat and then the Superintendent came and he tried to make me eat but I wouldn't. He took the handcuffs off and then I went to the dining room and I ate and it made me sick. So for a little while I just took some milk and bread.

Going to the modern day school does not involve any such abrupt transition for the child. In many places the children go to and from school every day by bus; in others they live in simple dormitories at the school through the week and return home for Saturdays and Sundays. Naturally less is accomplished academically by this means than where the children live continuously away from their homes, but the gains in contentment and in making the process of change less drastic are of great importance. Moreover, it gives the parents a chance to take some part in the educational process.

Entering a boarding school even today, when former militaristic, coercive methods have been abandoned, is a severe break with familiar ways and people. Although both parents and children see the desirability of this sort of education increasingly, the adjustments

CLEANLINESS — SOAP AND WATER AT A DAY SCHOOL

CLEANLINESS — YUCCA ROOT SUDS AT HOME

necessary are far greater than for a white child entering boarding school. A girl in the eleventh grade wrote of her experience:

In 1933 (when I was 11) my daddy decided to sent us to school. My mother made me a new skirt and a new blouse. My daddy bought me a new pair of shoes. He also bought a whole suit clothes for my brother Bill. In the fall when school started we sure got excited. We sure wanted to come to school. The next day a man came in a car, we got in a car with my daddy. My mother stayed at home with my little brother and sister.

Finally we came to Shiprock. We went to the office. Dick was the boys' adviser that time. He is the one that interpreted for my daddy. My daddy said, "I brought my children to school." The principal said, "You are late in bringing your children to school. The dormitory are all full and there isn't any vacant seats in the dining room. At the same time you don't need them to come to school, because the way I see it, they sure are dressed fine and I know you have plenty of food for them at home."

My daddy said, "I know I can take care of them myself. But I didn't just bring them here just to sleep on nice beds and eat at the table. At home they didn't sleep on beds or eat at tables. They can sleep on the floor or in the corner, and eat without sitting at the table. The main thing I brought them here for is to learn English."

Finally the principal said, "All right you can leave them here."

We went into the office and he named us Ruth and Bill. The boys adviser took Bill to the boys' building and the girls' matron took me to the girls' building. The matron gave me some clothes and she took me down to the basement and there was a girl with a scissor and a comb. She cut my hair and I felt so funny with my hair short. I took my bath and put on all the clothes that she gave me. Just then my daddy came to take my squaw clothes. When he saw me with my hair short, he laughed and I felt so shy.

The first thing I got so interested in was going up and down the steps. The next morning I went to school with the first graders.

This fifth-grader tells us more of what happens in school.

When I come to school I was just a little girl. There were many other little girls. One of them was Mae Belle. I did not know anybody in this school I came with my father and mother. They told me to come to school so I could learn something, so I could help my family when I grow up to be a big girl.

So they just left me here in the morning when the children were coming to school. One of the girls took me up to the school office, and they put me in the first grade. When they put me in there I did not know what to do. When my teacher spoke to me I did not know what she was saying. And my friend Mae Belle did not know anything when she came to school. When I got to know Mae Belle we started to work together. We all first learn to write and spell. We learn to spell cat and cow, pig, bag, and boy, girl, things like that. In the afternoon we all go to sleep in the schoolroom. Then we get up and play for a little while, and we have to eat our milk and bread in the schoolroom.

When we get through eating we go out of school and go back to the building. And we get in line and start going to the dining room. We eat in the dining room. Sometimes we stay in there until we through eating. Then we go out of the dining room. Then we play all in the evening. When the girls tell us to go inside that means it is time for us to go to bed. When we go to bed we say a prayer. Then get in our bed, all go to sleep, and not talk to someone who is next to you. If we talk we all get punished. Even if just one is talking to someone we all get the punishment for it.

When we get up in the morning we all brush our teeth. If we won't brush them, we will have some dirty teeth. Then we go to the dining room to eat. When we come back from the dining room, we are all getting ready for school, and then go to school. We go in the school room and sit down and wait for the teacher to tell us what to do.

I find out it was better to go to school than to stay at home. So I tell mother and father that I like to stay in school for ever. From that time I stay in school. When I was in the third grade I learn to talk in English; from that time on I can speak in English. I have found that you do not forget once you learn English. You can always remember it when you are at home or outside. When my father wants to talk to an English man, he always wants us to talk for him, and then tell him what the white man says. Or when the white man comes to our home, we talk for my father and mother.

Sometimes the experience was more unpleasant.

I enter school when I was six years old, my sister and I came to school at the same time. When I first came to school I sure was scared and pretty near cry all day. . . .

When it is almost time for us to go to school some of the Big Girls had to be over at the little girls' building to help wash the little girls and comb their hair for them and scrub them. They used to scrub us with the scrubbing brush. Sometimes we cry when they were scrubbing us.

And when there was a fire drill at night the same girls that scrub us have to carry us out at night. If we don't wake up when they tell us, they just hit us and slap us before they take us outside.

A fifth-grade boy has a philosophical recollection of his early school days.

When I was a Beginner we just eat and sleep in the afternoon. We sleep in the afternoon and we eat in the morning.

I was too much of a roughneck when I was in the small boys' building. That time the boys' adviser used to whip me when I was bad. And Billy was my friend, he always whip me too; every time when I do bad things, he always whip me.

However school life is not all work and sorrow nor even seriousness, as this account, by a boy whose family lived near the boarding school testifies.

Last year I went to school too at Tuba City. That time I was in the fifth grade. We go any place we want to last year. We were good and bad. Sometimes we go to our homes in the wash. We always go from here to the Kerley Trading post. We play on a rock. We roll the rock down the hill. We rolled a big rock down. There were some boys down near it. They saw the rock coming, so they know what to do. They ran under a pointed rock so the rock jumped over them. The rock broke all to pieces. We laughed about the rock, how it broke up. When the rock fell it made a big hole.

Then we came to the trading post. We bought some candy and some apples for each of us. We ran a race to the tree. The first boy that got to the tree got all the apples. I won, so they gave me all the apples, and I gave them back to them again.

Then we ate the apples and ate some candy too. We ate Baby Ruth and O'Henry. It was good. Then we licked out our tongues.

We go on to our hogans. We eat again. We eat fried bread, and coffee and sugar before the war started. Then we start back to our building.

We came on the other side of the store and up a big hill. Then we start playing again. We play in the reeds. We play Tarzan. We yell and howl; we swing on trees and roll rocks. We saw a donkey sleeping in the grass. We have some rope, so we rope the donkey. One donkey was little, so we did not bother him because he was too little. We start bumpety on the donkey. I sit on the donkey first. He bump me into the bushes. Then Frank sit on it. He start bump and bump him in the sage bushes. We start back to the building.

We came back to the building and saw the boys marching to the dining room. We came in the building, wash, ran out and ran to the dining room. We start to eat. We came out of the dining room. All five of us almost got punished, but we are all right now. We laughed about what we did.

The psychological conflicts and stresses which are perhaps the most momentous for the personality formation of Navaho children taught by white teachers in any school do not appear overtly in these autobiographical excerpts. These arise from two features of white culture: (1) the great stress upon competition between individuals; (2) the lack of definite status for the child at each age level. The Navaho is completely unaccustomed to an explicitly stated hierarchical ranking of persons such as is carried out in the grading system in white schools. At first, at least, being singled out from one's fellows for superior performance is embarrassing or actively disturbing rather than rewarding. It is likewise a strain to have quasi-adult demands put upon one. Navaho practice is to expect only so much from children at each age level. The white tendency is to project adult standards down into all except the earliest childhood. It is frequently observed that Navaho children who leave the hogans calm and well-poised return at the end of the first school year nervous and tense. This is less true of children attending the present Indian Service day and semi-boarding schools.

COMING HOME

The greatest advantage of the day school is that the continuity of home life is preserved. Most younger children come home from boarding schools for the summer, to be sure, but many of the older ones get summer jobs at or near the school and spend only a week or two or no time at all at home. When finally the school course is completed and there is a permanent return to the family, the adjustment is often painful on both sides. The boy or girl has become accustomed to white food, white clothing, white standards of cleanliness. He is torn between his abiding affection for his family and his drive to live up to what he has been taught are higher standards. Very few of the children who wrote autobiographies spoke of returning to their homes after school. Most of them said they would "get a job" or "make some money" or "work for the government." One cannot say, of course, whether this represented genuine desire for such a future or was just the natural goal to mention in the school setting.

Their impulsion, conditioned in early childhood, to participate reverently in the native ceremonials conflicts with what they hear in school about "ignorant superstitions." Generally the "ignorant superstitions" win out in the end, but only after a deal of discomfort. The discomfort causes the home-coming student to make remarks which annoy or hurt his unschooled relatives, and a vicious circle is set up. The matter is further complicated by the real ignorance, on the part of the school child, of Navaho myths and religious procedure. One of the older boys wrote:

I do not know any sings because I am in school studying things. I never seen yeibichai yet.

The type of conflict and confusion which arises is well brought out in the following interview with a young English-speaking woman.

That lady, she told me the world would come to an end. I didn't believe that. Everything is changing. The world isn't the same. We haven't got lots of things like animals that we used to have. I think the world will end soon. That lady said when the world ended Jesus would come. He would talk to everyone and He would find out if he was a Christian. If he was, He would take him up to Heaven, but everyone else He would leave here and they will burn up. [Does it help you to be baptized?] Yes, that means you are a Christian and that you tried to live a life like Christians. . . . Some of the people at home, they laughed at us. They said you can't use pollen any more. But that isn't true. You can use pollen if you are a Christian. One old man, he hates the Christians. He said it was wrong to believe there was a Heaven and that Jesus was coming. I talked right up to him one day. I said you'd better not say those things. When you get old you will have bad things happen to you. But he thinks when you die that that is the end of you — then you are gone, you don't live any more. [Do many Navaho believe that?] Yes, lots of them. [Don't they think they will live in another world like this one?] Well, they just think they come to an end.

Stresses of this type, though most severe in the English-speaking generation, also have their impact upon those who have not come so much under white influence. It is a commonplace to hear old Singers complain that they lack their accustomed acolytes or, if they do have apprentices, that these young men want to learn only the bare essentials while the details of myths and the fine points of practice are forgotten. Plaints of this sort are constantly heard:

Children are too lazy these days. They teach them in the schools that they don't need to mind their mothers and fathers. They are supposed to

go the white man's way and we don't know that. So we can't even wake
them up in the morning. We try to teach them to go out and roll in the
snow the way we did when we were their age, but they won't do that.
They even cuss their parents out.

Well, it's no wonder it doesn't rain any more like it used to. The
reason that isn't a grass meadow any more but just a bunch of washes
isn't because we have too many sheep like the white people say. It's because these young boys aren't learning what they should and aren't doing
what they should. They even sing Night Way songs in the summer and
do those dances. We were taught that this would pack the ground so
hard that the grass would stop growing.

The following excerpts taken from the autobiography of a middle-
aged Navaho, who returned from school in 1906 at the age of about
twelve, indicate some of the difficulties schooling raised at that time.
This boy didn't know how to get home, and was staying with some
school friends twenty to thirty miles from where his family lived.
While some of the details would be different today, many would be
unchanged.

One day after that another man come. When he first came inside the
hogan, we was sitting there. He asked the people, "Who came back here
from school?" One of the men says, "These three here." "Which one is
living down at Marking-on-Rock?" I says, "Me." "Well," he says, "get
ready. I am after you." I had a suit case with me; I says that's all the load
I got, nothing else. He says, "Your father is just this side of Gallup this
morning. He sent me over here to get you." . . . When we come there
where my father was, there's three mens there and one woman. After I
shake hands with these people there, one of them was my father but I
didn't remember him.

. . . My father is living way back over here with my brother. We
stayed down there three days and then we start coming down this way to
Marking-on-Rock. Ride double again with my father. . . . Got to Marking-on-Rock just about sundown.

When I got home I seen my two sisters and my brother. I remember
my brother but my two sisters I forgot all about them.

My father has cornfield all fenced up with wooden fence. I seen some
very nice corn there. Next day I start to hoe, hoed some corn with my
father. I learned some songs in the school from the other boys. When I
got right in the middle of the cornfield, start hoeing, start singing that
song there. That was my great mistake, to sing that song right in the
middle of the cornfield. Father says, "Whup, whup, don't you sing that

song in the middle of the corn. That's a *yeibichai* song," he says. I started
to ask about it. "No," he says, "we won't talk about it, mustn't talk about
it in the middle of the corn. Wait till after fall and everything is dry and
then it's time for to sing that song." . . . After that he told me mustn't
sing that song but we can sing Corn Song in the corn field whenever
they working there — or Cornbeetle Song. That's all he says.

We heard that a man is coming from Ramah that night — he's going
to sing Blessing Way. I been riding some down there at the store, ride a
horse down there. . . . Told the storekeeper they going to have Sing up
there at my place. This wasn't the storekeeper that was trading there the
time I left [for school]; this was another one. I told him that I start
from here at that store. He asked me how I like the school. I says all
right; told him I was going back. He says tomorrow when they going
to have the Sing, tomorrow night he'll come down and see how they
going to do. I stayed there pretty near all day and come back home. The
Singer had come.

There was just a few people there that first night. Long after nine
o'clock Singer says he going to do some singing. The patient was there.
Old man ask him what was the matter with him; what was his trouble.
Patient says he had bad dreams pretty often, and I don't know what "bad
dreams" mean. After I came back from school I not trying to believe
Navaho way, I believe American way. I don't know any more Navaho
way than before I went to school. The patient start to telling story about
his dreams. . . .

We had that white man over there the last night for part of the time.
He sit by me and I sit with him. When the Sing starts he says, "Aren't
they foolish?" he says. That's the first time I learned about that Way,
Blessing Way Sing.

[One day his sister wanted him to ride with her to Ramah.] This is
to my other sister, where she is living, we going. We got there late in
the afternoon. That's where that little canyon is this side of Ramah.

When we got there my sister started to talk about the Sing. They
want to put a Sing over there, that is Blessing Way. The reason they
want to do that, I was away in school. They say they should put that
Sing, I mean they said they should have done it for me just after I came
back from school. They ask me did I want it. Told them I don't want it.
They keep asking me till I say, "Yeah."

But I got no moccasins. They got to make moccasins for me first. First
they just start to talk about it. After I say all right, then there's some
people what's living round there, they come there and they put up new
hogan. Told the other people down there they was going to had a Sing.
My father come down over there and make moccasin for me. My sister

had a little buckskin, just fit my feet. Get that hogan finish and moccasin finish, sent man over here for the medicine man. I think they gave him $12.00 money, good saddle blanket, two sheep. He come over. He come over the same day man went for him.

When the sun is down, after dark, Singer ask me a lot of questions about school. First thing he ask me how I went out there, on a horse or in a wagon? I start to tell him how I first start over here — in a buggy and four horses. Told him how we went through there and pick up one Mexican boy. We stayed up there at the Mexican place one night. Told him I was going to try to run away from there; I got afraid about wolves and coyotes and wild cows and so I didn't start to run off. Next day we start from there to Grants. We got down there about afternoon, took a train from there to Albuquerque, same night we got to school. Gave him the whole story till I started from and he ask me what kind of place that was. Told him it was good place to stay. He asked me did I was lonesome when I was down there. "Yeah," I tell him, "Yeah, for a little while." When I got used to it, then all same as home. We used to have good place to sleep night. Go to school in the morning and work the other half the day. And good place to eat — lota eat down there. Lota boys and girls, different tribes. Told him I wasn't coming home, only one of the boys start telling me to go home with him. This boy was from Fort Defiance. I and him go to the superintendent and we ask him about it. He let me go, so I come.

Singer said he seen me when I was a little boy over there at Ramah and ever since when I was herding down here with my brother, he know me. He didn't do much that night, he only do some praying. He start off with a pray. He let me hold two pieces of medicine while he pray for me. When he start off with the prayer, he told me to keep up good, say the words plain. Then when he started talking it was pretty hard for me to follow. Some places he have to say it two times for me. He didn't supposed to go back, he says. He did go back two, three times. Then, so's he wouldn't have to go back, he put another man next to him and whenever I didn't say the prayer this other man says it for me . . .

After they sung over me there, they tell me lota things what not to do. They told me I shouldn't cuss the sheep or boys or children. Mustn't play with dog or sheep, and told me I should do just like what they told me. I hear some old story when the Singer came there that first night. This Singer says we got to go a long way. I talk to two of the boys, two of my sister's boys. One of them went to school over here at the mission. We talk English together. They told us we couldn't talk English together while they having the Sing. So I kinda start to believe what they says, and that's the first time when they sing over me, when I come back from school.

On questioning, this man said he didn't want the Sing at first because he didn't want to undress before all those people. His sister and father were the principal urgers. His brother didn't come to the Sing; he was busy. His father and sisters talked about the old ways, and he started to believe them. Then at the start of the Sing, the first night, the medicine man talked to him and told him that he had been to school, learned a lot of things, white man's ways. "But you're not a white man. What are you going to do when you have learned white men's ways? That won't make you white; you'll still be Navaho. Now, white man's way is one way and Navaho way is another, and you better learn the Navaho way."

When I bring in the sheep that night, I asked my sister why did they had a Sing for me. She told me ask my father. My father was still there and I ask him about it. He says, "We didn't put you in school; your brother did," he says, "And we was all so glad you got back over here without anything wrong with you. And Navaho, all the Navaho, they all do the same thing — whenever they send the children to school, they do the same thing; they put up the Blessing Way. They all have to put up the Blessing Sing for children." He says, "That's the way we Navaho work it with our children when our children goes to school." He told me, "That's about all I can tell you. There's some more reason for it but that's too hard for you to understand." He told me some of the people says that school is very good for the children and he thinks it's good, too, himself.

On another occasion this man spoke with real regret of his not having gone further in school. He said the storekeeper talked to him about it a good deal, and he surely wanted to go back, but his father and sisters said no. He said that if he had gone to school longer, he didn't believe he would have come back home to stay at all, except maybe for a visit now and then. He didn't know where he would have gone, but he thought he would have got a good job somewhere.

Thus the conflict between the older and the younger generation, which seems to be a part of many cultures, is here greatly intensified by the introduction of foreign ideas and ways among the young folks and the interference with the methods developed by countless generations of Navahos for teaching children the customs and beliefs of the tribe. Friction often arises over matters which are trivial in themselves but which have gained symbolic importance. For example, if the returned schoolchild insists on aping white etiquette, this can prove most irritating to his elders. Navahos do not customarily say "good-by" when leaving an individual or a group; they simply walk off, even when departing for an absence of some duration. When they shake hands they do not exert pressure but keep the hand relatively limp — it is more a hand-clasp than a hand-shake. The act of hand-shaking is a more formal gesture than with white people. Usually, one offers the hand only to persons whom one has not seen for some time and when shaking hands with a number of persons a fairly definite order of precedence is observed. Young Navahos who depart from these and other points of "good manners" shock and disturb many of their elders. Conversely, the young people sometimes feel called upon to be apologetic to their white friends about the behavior of their parents. An unhappily frequent remark of the young "agency Navahos" is "These Navahos are kinda funny."

It is only in the case of school children that there is any marked conflict between home standards and age-group standards. In white society every little clique-like group of children is apt to have its own sub-culture and each child is torn between the demands and expectations of his parents and the pressures for conformity put upon him by his age-fellows. In Navaho society, except under the full impact of white ways, such problems are minor. Among the children themselves age lines are much more fluid — partly because there are no school "grades" to give a symbolic value to the separation of children of various ages. Moreover, in the old Navaho way, children and adults do not belong to two separate worlds. The same set of standards prevails in most things for all ages, from the child (as soon as he can talk) to the very old people. Generalizations were really "general" and easy to apply in the old Navaho world, and the child was taught a way of thinking suitable to such a world.

The fact that even today these generalizations are usually so unverbalized and are taken so much as a matter of course makes it particularly difficult for the child who has lived for some time in a boarding school to see where he is going wrong, from the family's point of view. The whole system is so non-contractual, so automatic, that the older members of the group find it hard to explain in words what it is that the school boy is failing to do or is doing wrong.

This, indeed, is probably one of the reasons why the graduates of boarding schools have thus far failed to provide leadership that is more than superficial and temporary. They are often articulate — at least in English. They can write letters to the newspapers and in other ways attract the attention of that part of the white population that has an interest in Navahos. With increasing frequency they are elected as "Chapter officers" and even as delegates to the tribal council. But this is because the actual leaders have discovered the usefulness of intermediaries who can handle English. However, real leadership inevitably rests upon the leader's intimate understanding of the native social organization, an understanding which comes only from full participation, from being a cog which meshes perfectly with other cogs. Such participation is seldom possible for the man or woman who has spent six to ten years almost completely away from the world of the hogans, because conscious training and verbal instruction are no adequate substitutes for continuous apprenticeship.

Navaho personality as formed in the pre-school years and the conditions of life as it still goes on in adult years in the hogans are not as yet geared to the demands of white men and the psychological atmosphere in schools taught and directed by white men. Until The People have gradually worked out adjustive techniques for reconciling their child training and their life ways with the inexorable realities created by white pressures, one must expect many disoriented and unhappy persons. In the social sphere one must expect disorganization and the increase in recourse to witchcraft and "good" supernatural practices.

3.

ADULT LIFE

AMONG The People — except for youth in boarding school — there is no period of several years when the individual is neither a child nor an adult, such as the adolescent in white American society today. The Navaho's physical maturity and social maturity are more nearly coincidental.

In the old days the Navaho girl was ready for adult life after her first menstruation. "A girl's first bleeding is an order from the Holy People to marry," The People still say, and womanhood is announced with a dramatic rite. While there is no analogous rite for boys, the lad who has reached physical maturity is also nearly ready for marriage.

THE GIRL'S PUBERTY RITE

WHEN a Navaho girl first menstruates, a four-night ceremonial is held for her, with an all-night singing on the final night. This is an extremely important social and religious occasion for girls. Those who are at boarding school frequently go home when their menses commence so that the ceremony can be held properly, although sometimes it is postponed until a vacation brings them home in the normal course of events. This illustrates an important point of difference in the whole Navaho attitude toward sex as contrasted to that of white people. With Navahos, to become a woman is something to be proud of and to announce to the whole community, not something to hide and be ashamed of.

The first night's ceremony consists in tying the girl's hair with a special thong. She must stay by herself when not actually participating in the ceremonial and must eat only certain foods. Each day at dawn and usually at noon she races to the east. Others may run with her for all or part of the way but they may not pass her, lest they grow old before she does. Each day there is also a "molding" ceremony. The girl lies on a blanket in front of the hogan door between a line of women to the south and a line of men to the north.

An older woman who has been chosen as a kind of model kneads the girl's body and straightens her hair. This is to make her shapely and beautiful, like Changing Woman.

During the first three days a quantity of corn is ground by the girl and her relatives. On the evening of the fourth day this ground corn is mixed into a batter and placed in a corn-husk-lined pit oven. Then the personal property of the girl (clothes, jewelry, blankets, horse trappings), and also that of her family and of such friends and relatives as wish it, are brought into the hogan where the ceremonial is being carried on. This pile of personal belongings is blessed during the all-night singing, which usually begins a little before midnight with the consecration of the hogan by rubbing pollen on the roof beams. The ceremonial practitioner leads the singing of a number of groups of songs, and then in turn other persons will sing songs they know. Shortly before dawn there is a ceremonial washing of the girl's hair. Then follows the race. Next the girl cuts the cake which has been baking all night. She returns to the ceremonial hogan to have her hair brushed with a special brush to the accompaniment of a song and to have her cheeks painted with lines of white. (Such spectators as desire it are also painted.) Then comes the final molding. The ceremonial ends when the girl distributes large pieces of the cake to the ceremonial practitioner and to those who have sung their songs the previous night, and smaller ones to all the relatives and friends who are assembled. At the time of second menstruation the whole four-day rite should be repeated, but many individuals have this ceremony only once.

The girl who has had the puberty rite is considered ready for marriage. She can dance in the "squaw dance" which is roughly equivalent to a debutante ball. The chances are that shortly thereafter a marriage may be arranged for her.

THE BOY BECOMES AN ADULT

A boy's sexual maturity is, of course, less clear-cut than a girl's. Since Navaho customs with regard to modesty prevent noticing pubic hair, change of voice is the principal criterion. Only after this change has occurred will a boy normally take a sweatbath alone, although he might earlier join older relatives in one. Also, in the old days, and in conservative areas today, at puberty he would begin to be careful in the wearing of the breechcloth. A breechcloth is worn occasionally from the age of four or five, but a young boy will usually wear one only when he participates in a rite which requires stripping to the breechcloth.

One boy's father spoke to him in this way when his voice began to change:

This comes in place for us men like a girl's first bleed. The time has now come when you will want women pretty bad. From now on you mustn't hand anything to your sisters or play with them any more. You must get ready to be married. Watch and see how these young people living together, see what a boy should do for a woman. You must watch that all the time from now on so you could do that too. You must stay away from your sisters and from your female cross cousins. Pretty soon we are going to marry you to one of the girls.

GETTING MARRIED

MARRIAGE is regarded by The People as the natural, indeed the inevitable, thing. This conviction is indicated by the fact that auto-biographies obtained from Navahos frequently make no mention of marriage at all, even though the informant may have been married several times. The scant attention given to this topic may come partly from reticence in discussing personal affairs, but it can also be traced to the feeling that only failure to marry is worth mention-ing. Spinsters are virtually unknown among The People, and bach-elors are rare. In the old days a few men (some of them probably hermaphrodites or homosexuals) donned women's clothing and took up women's occupations. Some such persons are still known, but all of them are middle-aged or older. It may be that the bach-elors in their thirties who live in various communities today are individuals of these two types who fear the ridicule of white persons and so do not change clothing.

The old custom was for girls to marry within a year or so after first menstruation and for boys to be married by the time they were seventeen or eighteen. Among non-school children today many mar-riages occur in the early teens, but school and economic pressures now tend to bring about delays. Furthermore, the Navaho Council has passed a regulation forbidding marriage for girls under eighteen and boys under twenty-one. Such a ruling is virtually impossible to enforce rigidly, partly because of the prevailing uncertainty about ages, but in any case these days some girls do not marry until their late teens, and boys who finish high school wait until their early or even middle twenties. If any young man or woman seems to be putting off marriage too long, he or she will be formally requested by relatives to marry.

MARRIAGE ARRANGEMENTS

Though the Navahos have been introduced to the white concept of romantic love in schools, it is still not widely held, and almost no emphasis is placed on psychological compatibility as a prerequisite for marriage. The Navaho theory is that one woman will do as well as another, so long as she is healthy, industrious, and competent. Girls who are known as good weavers are more in demand. Some value is placed on youth and virginity. Girls who are considered extremely ugly are harder for their families to marry off. Otherwise there are few physical or psychological qualifications for marriage, and the majority of marriages are still arranged by the parents or other adult relatives.

The primary considerations are economic factors, the clans of the young people, and previous alliances between the two families. If a young man has made a successful marriage, it is considered highly suitable that his younger brother [1] should marry the wife's younger sister or that her younger brother should marry the husband's sister. There are a very great number of such reciprocal exchanges where both families have been satisfied with a previous arrangement. When a husband or a wife dies an obligation is felt to replace the dead mate (especially a wife) from the same family or clan.

The boy's family normally takes the initiative in arranging a marriage. His maternal uncle (today more often his father) or his mother will sound out the girl's mother or mother's brother or her father. If the reaction is favorable, a definite proposal will be made. This involves naming a date and settling the marriage gift to be made by the boy's family to the girl's family.

The general theory of this bridal gift seems to rest upon residence with the girl's people. That is, they provide most of the livestock, utensils, and equipment with which the young couple set up housekeeping. The bridal gift is the contribution of the groom's family.

It must not be supposed that Navaho girls ordinarily resent these

---

[1] This means, of course, not only a full biological brother but also "brothers" in the extended family (cousins on the mother's side).

arrangements. On the contrary, from the Navaho point of view, it is precisely the exchange of property which regularizes the marriage, assuring respect for the wife and security (economic and otherwise) for the children.

It is common for white men to refer to this gift as the "bride price," but this phrase is very misleading because it implies to most people that the bride is "bought," that she becomes a chattel of the husband. Nothing could be farther from the truth. Her family will always interfere if the husband mistreats her. If mistreatment goes too far and too long, her relatives will send the husband packing, and native opinion dictates that in this case the bridal gift is not returnable. This means that the boy's family have an interest in seeing that he behaves properly so that the marriage is not disrupted and their original investment lost. On the other hand, the girl's family are constrained to see that she keeps her part of the bargain, for if the marriage is dissolved through her fault they must return the livestock or other property that constituted the bridal gift.

While the girl most definitely does not become a chattel of the husband, there is one sense in which the arrangement is that of purchase. Among The People, sexual rights are property rights. There is no doubt that Navahos feel that sexual access is bought and paid for and that denial of such access demands return of the bridal gift. The Navaho view is clearly set forth in the following remarks of an older man who returned after an absence of some months to the young wife to whom he had been married for a year, to find that she didn't want to have anything more to do with him. "I paid for it all right. If she don't want to stay with me, they ought to give those sheep back because I didn't punish her or anything."

The size of the gift depends, naturally, upon the economic standing of the two families involved. For a family of average income, twenty sheep is the usual gift. Ten horses used to be the conventional offer for a wealthy girl. Today "twenty-five dollars and some sheep and horses" is often stated to be the consideration involved between well-to-do families.

The gift will vary also with the desirability of the girl, as previously described. If a girl who is alleged to be a virgin turns out not to be, all or part of the bridal gift must be returned. A wealthy older man will make a very high offer for a fourteen-year-old girl. The reverse also holds, however. A widow or divorcee in her middle

DAY-SCHOOL CHILDREN WATCHING A "DISAPPEARING PENNY"

EARNING BY DOING — PLAYING "STORE"

USEFUL SKILLS FOR OLDER SCHOOLBOYS

thirties will go to an attractive or promising young man fifteen years younger without a gift. If she is well-off, the husband thus has a chance for prosperity without hard work. This situation appeals to poorer families with many sons. Hence the number of marriages where the groom is considerably younger than the bride is quite high.

Before a girl is definitely promised, her family almost always consults with her. Some young girls are perfectly willing to marry old men who have blankets, sheep, and jewelry. Strenuous objections on the girl's part are usually respected unless it is felt that she is being needlessly willful or stubborn. Occasionally, however, the girl will not state her objection but will disappear into the woods the day the marriage is to take place. Once in a while the bride has never seen the groom until the actual ceremony and takes a violent dislike to him. In this event she may weep wildly after the marriage and refuse point blank to go off alone with the man. In other instances young girls appear to have real terror of the sex act and will run off or refuse to cohabit. In all such cases Navahos take the situation philosophically and do not insist that the marriage be consummated. The girl will usually later marry another man and accept the sexual side of marriage.

THE WEDDING

The marriage ceremony takes place at the home of the bride's parents. The groom enters the hogan and walks sunwise around the fire to a seat on the northwest side. The girl is led by her father to a place next to the groom. The father takes a new basket filled with corn mush and points the opening in the design to the east. He makes a cross and a circle in corn pollen upon the surface of the basket and turns the design opening toward the young people. The two then wash each other's hands in water. The man takes a pinch of mush from where the pollen touches the circle to the east, then bits from the south, west, and north sides. The girl follows him in each of these acts. In some localities the couple is expected to consume all the mush. Usually, however, after prayers and sometimes songs the assembled relatives and friends eat the rest of the mush. The two fathers (or distinguished older men who happen to be present) deliver little sermons on the reciprocal duties of husband and wife, how they should get along together, and the like. If the mush has been finished by the guests, the person eating the last portion is said to have won the basket; but in most areas he is expected to present the basket either to the mother of the bride or the mother of the groom. The gathering does not break up until Blessing Way songs have been sung at dawn.

MARRIED LIFE

IN the majority of instances the new family does not live alone, at least during the first years of marriage. This means that either the husband or the wife must adjust to a new group of people with somewhat different habits. When the marriage involves movement many miles from home, the adjustment must be to a whole community of strangers and to a different landscape. To a Navaho, who has very strong ties with his family and his native place, such an adjustment must indeed be difficult. One of the authors took a man in his fifties about forty miles over the mountain to his old home. As he looked at the high red mesas, he observed wistfully,

I used to live in this country all right. I moved all around and up over those hills. It's a pretty good country and I used to get very homesick for it. But I left it when I was young [to get married] and went over to Ramah and never came back. Now I got old over there.

In most cases husbands and wives continue to consider themselves as members of the groups to which they belonged before marriage rather than as parts of a new and independent unit. Thus their economic and other interests are not always identical and are often in conflict.

The man is unquestionably the official head of the family. In most families there are pretty well distinguished "spheres of influence." The husband's decisions are generally final in all matters pertaining to farming, horses, and cattle, and sometimes to sheep and goats. But often the wife or the group of women claim — and exercise — the right to use their own judgment as far as the sheep and goats are concerned. They are more likely to be influenced by the opinions of their brothers or uncles than by those of husbands or fathers. The husband ordinarily conducts negotiations with the trader in disposing of wool and lambs, but the wife is likely to have set a minimum price in advance and woe to her man if he lets her expectations down!

Within the hogan and in the area immediately surrounding it, woman's supremacy is seldom challenged. In some families a strong-willed and sharp-tongued woman makes by far the greater number of ultimate decisions in most realms. It is very common when one is hiring an interpreter or a guide for a trip to have the man say, "I'll have to ask my wife first." In other families the wife's authority is less evident, and yet there is cumulative indication that the power behind the scene in an extended family or "outfit" is wielded by the women in many instances.

In terms of the traditional conceptions of men and of women, The People are promoting the economic security of the society when they place a large share of the property and its control in the hands of women. Women are thought of as more stable. They do not go around gambling and wasting money in drink and other ways to as large an extent as the men. Their interests are centered on family and children so that they can be expected to use the resources placed in their hands to promote the stability of the family and the welfare of their children. There is a compensation for men in that they maintain control of the horses, which provides them with independence from a too constraining family life.

Only about one woman out of three and one man out of four reaches old age with the same spouse, and men who have had six or seven different wives in succession are frequently encountered. Some of these changes are the result of deaths, but the majority are consequent upon desertion. "Divorce" is simple, consisting ordinarily in the return of one partner or the other to his or her own people. Sometimes desertion is not altogether voluntary. A man who is lazy or too quarrelsome may be made so uncomfortable by his wife and her people that he is practically forced out. Occasionally, indeed, the wife's father or uncles may tell the husband in no uncertain terms to get out.

Marriages which last a few years have a good chance of continuing indefinitely. Out of 500 broken marriages in the Ramah area about half the breaks occurred during the first year and another third before the end of the second year. In short, less than one separation in five took place after the couple had lived together three years. This seems to be partly because children are a strong integrating force and become some guarantee of the stability of a marriage. Mutual affection for the children is important, but it is also through the children that the economic resources of husband and wife eventually fuse in a manner that is not at all true of the initial period. Finally, there is the factor of the time required for the adjustment of two persons who were usually virtual strangers before the marriage.

Relatives on both sides see in a marriage that fails a threat not only to original investment but to future good feeling and coöperation of all types between the two families. Hence the husband and wife are usually made to feel that a breakup is a defeat and implies some deficiency on the part of one or both of them. When a dissolution of one marriage is not only an economic inconvenience but also imperils other marriages between two family groups, the elders and all the brothers and sisters involved do their best to reconcile the estranged pair, and each side admonishes its representative to mend his or her ways. If the whole security, economic and otherwise, of the individual depends upon the full affection and support of his immediate and clan relatives, such sanctions are exceedingly powerful. Today, in the regions where white influence has been strongest, all the family and clan pressures whereby individuals were to some extent kept in line are beginning to lose their power. A returned boarding-school boy who has had the experience of living apart from his relatives, who speaks English, and can get along in the white world may take a job in a white town off the Reservation until the storm over his desertion of wife and children has blown over.

For other reasons, too, divorce is probably a bit more frequent at present than it was a generation or two ago. Navahos are generally under more severe pressures. Because they are uneasy and worried, they are irritable and more touchy in all human relations. The conflict between the old Navaho pattern of marriage and the white conception of romantic love and individual choice which the young people are learning in school probably adds another strain.

Remarriage may follow rather quickly after "divorce." In the event of death, the survivor is expected to wait a decent interval (two years according to old custom but often a shorter time now) and is threatened with visitations of the ghost of the deceased if this waiting period is not observed. The new mate is commonly a sister or brother (full, or from the extended family or clan) of the dead one. This is the preferred pattern and offers economic and other advantages to both extended families. It may be followed even in the case of divorce, unless enough bad feeling has grown up between the two groups to block such a procedure. Normally there is no bridal gift when a woman marries for a second or third time.

The emotional life even in stable marriages is typically rather labile, at least into late middle life when, as such persons will often say, "My wife and I are so used to each other now that we never fight any more." In early and middle adulthood intermittent quarrels and temporary separations are frequent. Reconciliation is effected in most cases by relatives of one or both partners and sometimes, as a last resort, by the headman.

The following account of a successful attempt to reconcile a husband and wife, which occurred near Crownpoint in 1933, illustrates not only Navaho attitudes and practice with regard to marriage but also their attitudes toward sex and leadership in operation. The husband, his father, mother, brother, and sister, and the wife, with her father, maternal uncle, maternal grandfather, and sister were present. There were also three older men not immediately related to either family, one of whom acted as an informal "chairman." Tension was marked; everyone perspired heavily and opened his mouth to get started as if his throat were too tight to speak through the teeth in the normal Navaho way.

The chairman began by asking questions of the boy. "How long have you been married?" "Four years." "Where did you meet?" "At a 'squaw dance.'" "Where did you go?" "To my mother's hogan." His parents interposed, saying that he had been with them and not with the girl. The girl stood unmoving, with her eyes fixed on the boy. At times she looked as if she were about to cry; at others she hid a smile behind her blanket. The boy maintained that they had never had sex relations on this first occasion.

Then the girl was asked to stand before the old men. She said that she and her husband had never had intercourse before the marriage ceremony. One of the old men got angry at this point and said that he knew the girl at this period, that he had told her several times to stop her doings with men. She stayed silent during and after this outburst.

The chairman asked the pair if they mutually enjoyed their sexual relations at present. Both said that they did, that the trouble came from the fact that they had no property of their own and that the family of each interfered too much.

After extended recriminations by members of both families, the chairman made a long talk in which he said that the girl had made mistakes before marriage, that she had a bad reputation, that she had "caught" the boy at a "squaw dance" and had not entered into marriage with him after customary and proper negotiations between the two families, that for this reason they had got off to a bad start, but that she had apparently settled down and was trying to live decently. He suggested that their families build them a hogan several miles from where they now lived, where they would be alone, and that each family contribute some sheep and goats to the young couple. He asked the husband and wife if they were agreeable to this. They were.

Then everyone shook hands all round, the members of the two families with each other and with the peacemakers. The tension was broken by friendly laughter and joking.

When such an attempt at reconciliation fails and one partner still is reluctant to break up the marriage, he or she is likely to make a somewhat formalized speech in the presence of relatives from one or both families. The speech will run along these lines:

It's no use. My wife (husband) has got the best of everything. You other people have tried the best you could for me. But my wife (husband) wants to quit anyway. She (he) has done all these things: [reiterates list of grievances]. It's all through, all over with. There is nothing more to say about it.

SEX LIFE

It may be doubted whether sex is at first a strong bond in Navaho marriages that are arranged. The man can obtain extramarital sexual satisfaction with a minimum of inconvenience. Evidence indicates that girls who are virgins do not find much pleasure in intercourse for some time. Probably some of this difficulty is due to the practice of many mothers, who tell their daughters that first intercourse will be painful.

After the couple has become sexually adjusted, the element of sexual attraction may become very powerful. Despite the rarity of romantic love, Navahos are often the victims of strong sexual jealousy, and even between well-adjusted pairs jealous quarrels are frequent. Partly, no doubt, this is because sexual rights are property rights, and it is an insult to the pride of possession to know or suspect that one is sharing with an outsider. There is a strong probability

that conservative whites — notably missionaries — encourage sexual
jealousy in order to break up the old Navaho pattern of polygamy.

The attitude of the Navaho toward sex is — like that of many
other peoples — complex. On the one hand, from early childhood,
sexuality is accepted as a natural and normal part of life, and this may
be an explanation of the fact that impotence in men and frigidity
in women appear to be excessively rare. In some ways Navahos view
sex with much less prudery and it gives rise to fewer conflicts among
them than it does among most Christian peoples. The acceptance
of masturbation as a normal part of the young child's life has already
been mentioned. Physical maturity in girls is straightforwardly
made the basis of a public ceremony rather than as in white society
being implicit but unmentioned as in debutante balls and religious
confirmation in some churches. Most sexual matters are discussed
in a more open and matter-of-fact fashion than among white people.
The observer gets a sense that the attitude is less often prurient, more
often healthy. The notion that women are, or ought to be, too
"pure" to be interested in sex, that they merely submit to intercourse
as part of their marital duties and in order to have children, is definitely not current among Navahos. Indeed many women have a
local reputation for being desirous, active, or initiatory in sex matters. If a woman ceases to participate in sexual relations because of
ill health, it is accepted as right and proper that her husband will
either leave her and remarry or take a second wife.

On the other hand, many data indicate fear and distrust of sex
and of things associated with sex. Though menstruation is not regarded as in any sense shameful, there is a morbid fear of menstrual
blood. Humpbacks are thought to result from eating food prepared
by a menstruant woman with blood on her hands, and exaggerated
precautions are taken to protect ceremonies from contamination by
menstruant women.

Men and women are excessively modest about exposing the genitals to the view of members of the opposite or even the same sex.
Adult members of the same sex will go a little distance apart and
turn their backs upon each other when they urinate. Although
there is no hesitancy about referring to the natural functions even
in mixed company, and in an automobile filled with men and women
one woman will ask without embarrassment to have the car stopped
so that she can urinate, the act itself is carefully concealed. Men

never take sweatbaths in mixed company, and they cover their genitals with their hands until they are safely within the darkness of
the sweathouse. A mother continues to wear her dress during childbirth, even though only women are present. Intercourse seldom
takes place except under cover of darkness and with very little dis-
robing. Indeed it is widely believed that a man who looks upon the
sex organs of a woman will be struck by lightning.

Perhaps the most general Navaho concept of sex may be expressed
as power-danger. This is the reason for the emphasis upon contin-
ence during war and hunting activities and in connection with
other ceremonials. The old taboo upon intercourse for the first four
nights of marriage was probably based on the feelings that sex is so
powerful and so dangerous that one must show self-control for a
while before venturing the risks. The parallel to ceremonial power
is very close. Navahos want and value both powers, but they must
be prepared for and guarded against with many precautions and
restrictions. Like other strong things, in the Navaho way of thinking, sex is a two-edged sword.

This concept of sex is imparted to children very early in life. As
we saw in the preceding chapter, children who are approaching the
age when they might indulge in heterosexual activities are frequently
and strongly warned against them.

We tell even little children that boys and girls must not touch each
other. They can play together but they must not touch each other. We
say to the girl that a boy may bite her ear off, or the boy may get mad
and break her head with a stone.

Small boys are sometimes told that the girl's vagina will bite off or
injure the penis, and it is significant that one of the best-known
Navaho myths is that of the *vagina dentata*. All such warnings,
which might be motivated only by the practical consideration of
protecting immature children from too much sexual experimenta-
tion and preventing pregnancy in adolescent girls, stress the danger
of sex and are couched in terms that might implant a lasting uneasiness about the sex act.

Sex is the subject of patterned jokes between certain classes of
relatives, and words and topics which would be beyond the pale in
mixed white society abound, but sexual activity is not a subject for
idle boasting among Navahos. Except when under white influence,

young men seem almost never to brag of conquests and even those who are close friends seldom talk about girls except in a very general way or in the framework of a joke that is so standardized as to be impersonal. If a boy's family or his intimates refer to an affair of which they suspect him, he becomes tongue-tied and shamefaced. This is partly the result of the fact that Navaho society is too closely knit to make such boasting appropriate — not altogether because of attitudes toward sex as such.

The strength of the sex drive varies greatly as between individuals, but the number and variety of cautions and sanctions against sexual excess suggest that among The People lust requires curbing. In the old days there were severe and even brutal punishments for adulterous women; these were doubtless regarded partly as violations of the required fidelity to a husband, but probably they were also intended as a check on undue sexual activity. It is believed that too frequent intercourse, even between married people, will lead to madness, to bleeding in the genitals, or to being struck by lightning. It is sometimes said that a couple who really desire children should not cohabit oftener than every four or five nights. One word for madness is used both of women who are sexually hyperactive and of prostitutes. However, the taboos on unlimited sexuality are not always observed today. Woman are heard to make such remarks as "It's pretty hard to make a man stay away from you, even the few days that you're menstruating."

Indeed, there is much material which suggests that in these days sex, like alcohol, is a measure of escape for some men and women. Especially for those who are caught between two ways of life — who are held by neither the old native restraints nor the white standards which they do not fully comprehend — indiscriminate sexuality takes its place with drunkenness as expression of the felt futility of existence.

THE OLD AGE TRAIL

LATE maturity and early old age usually bring prestige and authority. But when physical vigor markedly diminishes and when there are mental signs of senility, the picture alters rapidly.

Declining years are a period of dependence, loss of authority, and ill health. The People have no illusions about them. At best, old age is a bad time in the Navaho way of thinking, nor do they disguise this fact with sentimentality. The following passage echoes representative sentiments.

Mr. Mustache was talking to the bunch before the Sing started. He said getting old was like a hill. "A man's life up to 40 is like going up a hill. It seems a pretty long time, your life up to 40, then right after that you start getting old; it's like you were going down hill. Every day something new happens to you, some new wrinkle comes on you or your hair gets white. It seems like you are going down hill, and you hurry more. When you are young, if you get a new hat, new clothes, it looks pretty good, people like to look at you, but when you are old, the new things don't look any good on you, just look funny. The young people, they watch you, the way you do things, and they laughing at you. When you are young you like all your food, all the different kinds of meat, the way they taste. When you are old you can't taste nothing hardly, it all taste the same, and you haven't any teeth to bite it with anyway.

"The way I look at it," says Mr. Mustache, "here you are over here, and over there are the People that make old age and put it on you. They look at you and they talk about you. One says, 'He has a pretty good tooth there, let's pull it out. Let's put the deaf in his ears, make his eyes so he can't see. He's got a lot of hair, let's pull it out. You work on one knee there, and make it bad for him, and I'll work on the other.' An old man is like a baby, needs some one to look after him, but he is worse than a baby, the baby has it better. The mother will care for and wash the baby, but nobody will do that for the old man. No one wants to come near him. At night when he tries to sleep his body itches all over, and he scratches all the time, tears his clothes off and don't sleep good. His skin and body have no sickness, just need scratching."

Someone else went on. "It is truth. Old age is something we all got to go through. All the young ones, boys, girls, even babies and the womens, they all got to go, and white people and Navaho and Mexicans, and all different tribes, it don't make no difference. There is no way around, all got to go through old age."

A Navaho leader in his late forties expressed himself as follows:

The best period in a man's life lies between the ages of 25 and 60. At 25 you begin to know things. You know what is right and what is wrong. You begin to learn a lot of stories about the old days, and you begin to learn more all the time. After 60 they begin to slip away from you and you forget things.

The treatment of the aged varies greatly. A Singer who retains his memory can continue to be an important person even when

physically very weak, and in some families all the aged are treated
with great respect and consideration. But sometimes the very old
are neglected, and there is often a strong element of fear in the attitude of younger people toward the aged. One Navaho said:

Some people aged like Ned or this old man here [about 70 years],
Navahos are kind of afraid of people about that age, they say they might
be witch, and if you don't feed them they will go off and they will work
against you some way. One of your children will get it, or woman will
get it. So that is more why we feed always in our way.

DEATH

THE People believe that, as life begins when wind enters the body
through its orifices (particularly the ears), so death occurs when
wind leaves the body through the fingers. They say you can see the
trail of the first death in the whorls of the fingertips.

Death is the end of all good things to The People. No Navaho
looks forward to life in the hereafter as a reward for good deeds on
earth. At best, existence in the afterworld is uninviting. To the
living, the dead are objects of horror who must be buried with elab-
orate precautions. Only thus, Navahos believe, can they prevent the
malevolent ghost from returning to plague The People.

DEATH RITES

There are a number of major local variations in the customs of
disposing of the corpse, but a general pattern may be sketched as
follows:

So long as there were captive slaves, they were made to risk the
contamination of burying the dead. Today the task of burial is sur-
rendered to white men whenever possible. All day schools are supplied with coffins, or lumber for them, and staff members take over
responsibility for many burials.

Otherwise, since ghosts are believed to be especially malevolent
toward their own relatives, Navahos who are no kindred of the deceased are hired by the family to dispose of the body. If the relatives
must themselves carry out the work and if the deceased was not an
infant or one who died of old age, four (or two) mourners are
selected. One of these is a near relative or clansman of the deceased;
another is commonly taken from the clan of the father, the wife, or
the husband of the dead person. One of the number is chosen as a
sort of "master of ceremonies."

The mourners unfasten their hair and strip to the breechcloth. Then they bathe the corpse and dress it in fine garments, placing the left moccasin on the right foot and the right moccasin on the left foot, in the manner prescribed by the origin myth. Often the dying person has been moved outside the dwelling or to a brush shelter; but if death has occurred within a hogan, the body is removed through a hole made in the north side and carried in minutely prescribed fashion to its burial place. If the body is transported on a horse it is put on from the wrong (i.e. right) side. The mourners preserve complete silence, communicating with each other when absolutely necessary by signs. The route they take is called the death line, and no one dares cross it until the four days of mourning are past. If another Navaho accidentally draws near the funeral party he is vigorously warned away by the chief mourner.

With the body are deposited valuable possessions: jewelry, saddles, blankets. Dishes (formerly pots) are broken. The saddle may also be partially destroyed before disposition. One or more horses or sheep may be killed. The body and grave offerings are often placed in a rock niche in an out-of-the-way place, and the opening is sealed with rocks against the intrusion of coyotes and other animals. Where such niches are not available (and sometimes by preference) a grave is dug in a secluded spot where the ground is soft and sandy. In recent times the number of inhumations in Christian cemeteries has markedly increased. By no means all of those so interred were practicing Christians. A Christian burial was — from the family's point of view — an expedient for getting white men to dispose of the corpse and to avoid its being tampered with.

When the burial is not in a cemetery the burial party returns from the grave by hopping and skipping steps over another route which completes a circle. They often burn the hogan in which death occurred. They purify themselves in the smoke of a sage fire. For four days they must remain apart, observing many restrictions on eating and on behavior. Members of the immediate family sit and weep silently in another hogan. They may not eat until the burial party has returned and for four days their behavior is also subject to restrictions.

When death occurs in the dead of winter and the ground is frozen so hard as to make burial impossible, the procedure is often simplified by leaving the corpse in the hogan and tearing the structure down to cover it. The family moves and observes the four days of restrictions wherever it settles down temporarily. A person who has been killed by lightning will ordinarily be left completely untouched. No burial of any sort takes place.

4.

THE "PSYCHOLOGY"

of THE PEOPLE

QUOTATION marks are used in the title and many subheadings of this chapter to remind the reader that the words so enclosed are rough and ready labels tending to have different meanings for different people. The meanings intended here should be derived from the examples given rather than from the sense the reader may be accustomed to give to the term.

The purpose of this chapter is to describe certain ways of feeling and reacting that are typically Navaho, neglecting those which are broadly human. Not all of the statements made here will hold true for every Navaho, and their relative importance and emphasis will vary greatly even among those to whom they do apply. The conditions of life in different portions of the Navaho country are so different, the range of white influence varies on such a wide scale, the chance happenings which influence Navahos' lives — as they do the lives of all human beings — are so numerous that the best that can be done is to point out certain tendencies that have considerable value as statistical generalizations.

What individuals learn from their training in a particular society is never symmetrical and coherent, and rarely is it fully integrated. All healthy personalities are somewhat elastic and can, without being shattered, behave in different situations according to the most apparently incongruous and discrepant patterns. Some of these discrepancies are doubtless a consequence of variations in the biologically inherited constitution. Others result from accidents of the life experience. Although child training in Navaho society is, or has been, fairly well standardized, the individuality of parents certainly influences their children's personalities as much as or more than convention and cultural tradition. Domestic influences differ enough from family to family to produce quite a variety of personality structures.

But while any individual's personality is the resultant of a unique combination of hereditary, domestic, and cultural influences, it is a fact of ordinary experience that some types of personality are much more common in one social group than in another. In any stable society the system of child training tends to tone down variation due to biological inheritance, to restrain spontaneity and creative activity, to make most persons more or less like the majority, the average. Socialization tends to give each maturing individual the habits and thought ways of the reputable members of the community. Just as the members of any group tend to behave alike, so also their conflicts and maladjustments tend to be similar and characteristic of their society — as long as most individuals are subjected to about the same childhood pressures and are forced as adults to adjust to about the same situations.

On the basis of experience it can be said that the chances are good that any given Navaho will respond to some circumstances in a manner that is characteristically distinct from what might be expected from white men or from Indians of other tribes. This is not to say either that the item under discussion is true of every Navaho or that it is not manifested by some white men and other Indians. When, for example, it is said that the feelings between a boy and his maternal uncle are likely to be mixed, it should not be inferred that no nephews have a single-hearted devotion to their uncles; what is meant is that the betting odds favor a two-sided emotional quality in the relationship. Nevertheless, such statements help in understanding and predicting the behavior of The People, for they are applicable to the greater number of instances.

BENEATH THE SURFACE OF HUMAN RELATIONS

RELATIVES, as has been said, are the focal points of the Navaho's human world, and experiences with them constitute models for all personal relationships. If we look beneath the official codes which pattern dealings with relatives, what emotional tones most often color the interaction between various pairs?

If one visits the several hogans occupied by an extended family, the outward aspect of things will be calm in ninety-nine cases out of a hundred. People seem to be behaving toward each other very much as would be expected in terms of age, sex, and kinship position. Everything moves smoothly without many explicit directions except to the younger children. As a matter of fact, the members of stable extended families develop such habitual ways of working together that the performance, on superficial inspection, often seems to resemble that within an ant hill.

But the apparently effortless functioning which prevails a good deal of the time is not achieved without friction which erupts now and then in open quarrels. Out of a total of 859 references to "threats" found in an extensive body of interviews with Navahos, 219 were "threats" from social relationships. Of these, 20 per cent referred to quarrels within the family.[1]

Outbreaks of physical violence occur only during drinking or when tension has reached the breaking point. However, a deal of quiet seething beneath the outwardly calm surface may be said to be the rule. Some of this seething becomes transformed into fear of witches and into using "witches" as scapegoats to provide psychological relief. Some hostility is also drained off by the broad and sometimes boisterous jokes which various classes of relatives are permitted to carry out against each other. Which individuals are in a state of suppressed antagonism or what the factional line-up in a family group may be at a given time depends, of course, upon the "temperaments" of persons who are expected to get along with each other and upon chance events. Nevertheless, the social structure and cultural demands tend to give common features to the strains existing between kinfolk.

In spite of the tender attachments which unquestionably exist between Navaho family members, in spite of the cultural pattern of diffuse, unspecialized devotion to all relatives, there is an uneasy, sometimes a seamy, side to the relationships between kinsmen. A strong case could be made out for the view that many of the ceremonials are, at bottom, cures for anti-social tendencies against close kin, and that their varying symbolism reflects various forms of the mild or serious neuroses produced by family life.

PARENTS AND CHILD

Among the reasons for tension between husband and wife, discord over the rearing of children is conspicuously absent. Clashes about authority over the children occur mainly when white influence

---

[1] For source of these data, see the article by Leighton and Leighton listed in the references on p. 267.

is strong, for the Navaho point of view is that children belong first and foremost to the mother and her family. In cases of separation, immature children almost invariably stay with the mother. Only when the mother dies and her sisters or mother are unable or unwilling to assume responsibility for her children are they reared by the father and his family.

Sometimes a Navaho shows resentment when he and his mother have been abandoned by the father. More commonly, children do not take sides in any way in quarrels between the parents. When "divorce" results, the child's affectional ties to the father usually remain unbroken. If the child was an infant and hardly knew his father when the divorce occurred, or if the child does not see the father again for a long time, indifference — rather than hostility — is the usual attitude.

Scrupulous fairness toward the various children in a family is the rule. Occasionally a half-witted or otherwise ill-favored child is neglected, though such misfortune is just as often compensated for by extra tenderness. If there is a son or daughter toward whom a mother or father feels extraordinarily drawn, the parent may symbolize his oneness with the youngster by inhaling the breath of the child four times in the same way that the dawn air is breathed in four times at the end of a chant or that an especially treasured gift (particularly of ceremonial property) is drawn toward the lips and the breath taken in sharply four times "to become one with it — making it yours."

On the whole, the feelings of a child for his parents are much less likely to be seriously mixed than is the case among white people. It is significant that although Navaho chant legends tend to have a standard plot that centers on disobedient or unhappy children, the denouement of the myth never provides for the child's vengeance on the parents.

The child's feeling for his mother throughout his life is in some ways the most positively toned relationship in Navaho society. In childhood youngsters are being constantly admonished by grandparents and other adult relatives, "Always speak nicely to your mother. Always be kind to her." Neglect of a mother on the part of an adult is harshly censured by the community. A son who has married into a group that lives some distance off is criticized if he does not visit his mother regularly. Although mothers and daughters have more in common and so might be expected to feel closer to each other, the tie between mothers and adult sons appears to be equally strong. Only in heavily disguised fashion (in dreams, in stories about ghosts and witches) do we get any evidence of mixed feelings about the mother. Psychoanalysts claim that in white society fantasies of destruction of women by eating them are evidence of deep aggression against the mother. Such themes are prominent in Navaho witchcraft tales. However, instances of open aggression against the mother even in stories and dreams are exceedingly rare. But the total data suggest a component of resentment which is so deeply suppressed that even the oblique traces in dreams and folk tales are thickly veiled.

The relationship of children and fathers is also dominantly a warm one. The stereotype of the harsh, tyrannical father is lacking in Navaho culture. The child's affection for his father may be less profound than that for the mother, but there is less apt to be a hint of suppressed resentment toward the father. At most there is a generalized attitude that he is less dependable than the mother because he is so often away from home or might possibly go away for good. But this seems to be accepted as one of the basic facts of life.

The ties between son and father through close occupational association are often heightened after the son's marriage by the favorable light in which the father's gentleness is placed by the demands and orders of the father-in-law. Sometimes a married daughter will resent her father's attitude toward her husband, but a wife is more likely to side with her father and mother in family quarrels than with her husband. The affection her father lavishes upon her children is usually more than compensation for any slights he may put upon her husband.

SISTER AND SISTER

The relationship of sisters is usually one of solidarity. Occasionally there is rivalry between adult sisters, and where matrilocal residence prevails this usually arises from jealousy over a common husband. Even this is very much less frequent than might be expected. Otherwise the interests of adult sisters tend to be merged, except where one or more have gone off to live in separate locations. Generally speaking, one sister is equivalent to another among The People; it is "one for all and all for one." This means that they help each other out in any crisis. It also means (and this sometimes makes for tension) that any woman feels some personal responsibility for the debts or for the misdeeds of her sisters. The important thing is that this relationship ordinarily remains close and intimate throughout life — which is no longer the normal expectation in white society.

BROTHER AND BROTHER

Brothers feel toward each other much as sisters do, except that brothers are more likely to be divided in residence and thus in economic allegiance. Nevertheless a great deal of reciprocity goes on even between adult brothers who live with the families of their wives. In some regions brothers make a point of assisting each other with plowing and harvesting, even when they have married into quite distinct family groups. Sometimes they feel the need to stick together as absentee owners who are being defrauded by their sisters' families and others resident at the old homestead. Adult brothers not only give each other mutual aid of various sorts; they often travel in company, take sweatbaths together, and consult each other over the marriages of their children and other problems. Their manner with one another is free and easy, and they indulge in patterned jests whenever they meet.

Sometimes, of course, there are economic rivalries or bitterness over the way an estate has been divided. Another source of tension is a struggle for power between two or more brothers who have married sisters. As the father-in-law grows older, one of the sons-in-law gradually assumes the male direction of the extended family. In many cases this post falls to the son-in-law who is recognized as the most energetic, the most experienced, or the most intelligent. Sometimes, however, there is frank or hidden competition, in which the wives may also participate.

BROTHER AND SISTER

The relationship between brothers and sisters is perhaps the most curious and interesting of all the pairs. Feelings are undoubtedly polarized in two directions. At one pole there is much attraction, much genuine warmth and affection; at the other, periodic friction is the rule. The latter stems from Navaho social organization, which gives each the duty of interfering in the life of the other and causes each to be caught in an emotional cross-fire. The sister is commonly responsible to the brother for the sheep and other property which he has left at his maternal home, yet she is concerned to see that as much of it as possible stays there or is used for family ceremonials and that eventually her children should inherit the bulk of it. The brother usually wants to please his sister and his own clanfolk generally, but he is also under opposing pressures from his wife and children. On the other hand, the brother has certain responsibilities for the upbringing and the marriage of his sister's children, especially the girls. His recommendations may not always accord with those of the sister's husband (the father of the children), in which case the sister must choose between her brother and her husband. The wife's brother is also expected to see to it that her husband does not too flagrantly or publicly transgress the codes governing extra-marital sexuality.

We have been speaking as if but a single brother and a single sister were involved. No neat formula can be given for determining which brother will consult with which sister. Some precedence is given to age, but factors such as residence, intelligence, and personal compatibility all enter in. This is another example of the preëminence of personal considerations over behavior by formal rule, so common in Navaho culture.

Here is one fifty-year-old man's description of how he deals with this problem:

I always tell my oldest sister first when I am going to have a ceremony or any other doings. She can tell the next one. I don't pay so much attention to my younger sisters.

Whenever I don't do right, my oldest sister scolds me. If I dance with somebody I shouldn't at the "squaw dance" she gets mad at me, real bad. Or if I don't take her advice about something, if she don't get her own way, she sure scolds. Or if I do something without telling her about it first.

I must always tell her what's going to happen. I tell my oldest sister my oldest girl is ready to get married. I ask her: "What shall I do about it?" She says, "All right. Let's tell our other sisters. We'll fix this up just the way me and her want to do it." And then I have to say, "Yes, let's keep it that way."

A woman of about the same age who had seven living brothers gave this account of her choice.

I always ask the one of my brothers who has the best head. I thought about which one of my brothers will be the best. For I knew already which one knew more than the others. Some of my younger brothers, they drink a lot and do a lot of wrong things. If I picked out one of those boys for talking things over with, people would laugh about them and about me. So I picked out the best one, the one I can depend on. I think everything which he tells me will turn out all right.

The strength of the taboos on physical contact between mature brothers and sisters and the gossip about incest suggest that, in the isolated conditions under which most Navaho children grow up, the incipient sexual attraction between brother and sister is strong and temptation must be sharply curtailed. It may be that the popular form of mating where a brother and sister from one family marry a sister and brother from another is an unconscious substitution for incestuous desires. Certainly the training in avoidance of physical contact begins early and is carried to what are, from the white point of view, extremes. One Navaho man in his thirties described the attitude and practice of his people as follows.

When girls are very small, we teach them to keep their skirts down. We say, "If anyone sees up your legs they will go blind." When we all grow up so we think about these things, we are told not to touch our sister. After she or her brother is married, if she asks for a shoe or a plate he can't hand it to her. He puts it on the ground first. Then she takes it. If she wants to change her skirt she has to go outside or wait till her brother is gone. They say a brother must never see her knees or her breasts. [If she has a baby does she nurse it if her brother is in the hogan?] Yes, but she covers it up.

UNCLE OR AUNT AND NIECE OR NEPHEW

The mother's brother was, and to an appreciable degree still is, a severe disciplinarian. On the other hand, his sister's children can look forward to assistance, profitable instruction, and inheritance from him. Yet the uncle is torn between the claims of his sister's children and those of his own sons and daughters. Since his sister's son ordinarily becomes a member of still a third extended family group, whereas her daughter continues to live where the uncle grew up and with his own mother and sisters, friction between a young man and his mother's brothers is more frequent than between a young woman and her maternal uncles. The brother-sister and the mother's brother-sororal nephew relationships are the most bipolarized in Navaho society. The strongly institutionalized joking patterns between the latter pair are useful safety-valves, but the incidence of dramatic quarrels proves that hate, though outweighed by love most of the time, is very powerful.

As has been previously indicated, the sisters of the mother are secondary and substitute mothers throughout childhood, and this relationship prevails throughout life.

Uncles and aunts on the father's side usually play a much less important role in the individual's life. The brothers of the father, though not called by the same kinship term as the father, are to some extent identified with him. However, although dealings with the paternal uncles and aunts are ordinarily pleasant, a child's contacts with them are usually less frequent and intense than with those on the mother's side.

GRANDPARENTS AND GRANDCHILD

The child usually sees his father's parents much less frequently than his mother's but both sets of grandparents tend to behave toward their grandchildren much as do white grandparents. That is, they are dominantly solicitous and indulgent. Navaho children likewise respond with warm affection.

The principal differences from white relationships arise from the greater degree of mutual responsibilities among Navaho grandparents and grandchildren. The mother's parents, in particular, take much more responsibility for the training and discipline of their grandchildren. (Indeed their behavior would be resented as interference by most white parents.) In turn, Navaho children are often obligated to cut wood, haul water, and otherwise look after a feeble or incapacitated grandparent. Sometimes a child of nine or ten is assigned to live in the grandparental hogan, which may partially prevent his normal play with other children.

This is probably one of a number of experiences that leads to the mixed feelings which Navahos later in life exhibit toward their elders. A number of autobiographies suggest that adult Navahos have conscious or semiconscious resentments at having been exploited as children by older relatives. Perhaps this experience contributes to the suspiciousness with which many of The People regard all figures of authority.

NAVAHO "PSYCHOLOGICAL" TRAITS

HAVING seen something of the feelings which individuals have for each other in the familial world of The People, let us look now at a few traits which seem common to most Navahos. Again it should be remembered that the quotation marks warn the reader against accepting the term at face value.

"CURIOSITY"

A feature that strikes anyone who has contact with The People is their intense interest in one's past history, family situation, purposes in traveling through their country. "Where are you going?" "What for?" "Where do you live?" "Is that your wife with you?" "How long have you been married?" "How many children do you have?" "How does it happen you don't have more than that?" "How much did your car cost?" "Where did you buy it?" An interminable barrage of these and similar questions is directed by the most casual acquaintances at the traveler who speaks even a little Navaho. English-speaking Navahos may be more inhibited in a chance encounter because they have been rebuffed or taught in school that it isn't "polite" to be so inquisitive. It is the writers' experience, however, that when one has established a friendly relationship with a schooled Navaho, he or she is equally prone to make numerous, detailed, and personal inquiries.

During the course of the war the writers have been much impressed by the differing attitudes of certain Pueblo and Navaho Indians. Before the United States entered the struggle it was most exceptional to have these Pueblo Indians ask a single question about the war in Europe. To them it was apparently remote, uninteresting, unimportant. But Navaho friends who lived many miles from the railroad and, knowing no English, never read newspapers, would almost invariably ask: "What is happening in the war?" "What is he-who-smells-his-own moustache [Hitler] doing now?" "Who is winning, the Germans or the English?" The People had made up widely current designations for other nationalities. The English were "islanders"; the French "those of queer speech"; the Russians "lawless ones"; the Germans "metal hats." Navahos followed the varying fortunes of these nations with the keenest curiosity. Information gleaned by one Indian from a white trader or traveler and passed on and on in the community (often acquiring distortions or embellishments) would supply endless hours of conversation. After the American declaration of war, the Pueblo friends began to ask some questions. But these never sprang from disinterested curiosity;

they always had a bearing on when a given individual might expect to be drafted, when the war would be over so that certain relatives would get home again, and the like.

This contrast may be generalized beyond the war. To the Pueblo Indians, their village is enough. They are supremely uncurious about the outside world. The Navaho is not so "ethnocentric." He continually demands information about great cities, ocean boats, other ways of life. His imagination roves beyond the bounds of the immediate destiny of The People. For example, thoughtful older men these days are full of theories about how to win the peace. They are apt to say, "We hope that *this* time you white people will be wiser than you were last time. Don't you see that unless you kill every German — man, woman, and child — you'll have to fight this war all over again in another twenty years?" Such matters are long discussed over hogan and camp fires.

"SHYNESS–SHAME"

By white standards, adult Navahos are hypersensitive to shame or ridicule. This may be illustrated by incidents from quite varied spheres of life. One of the reasons that The People are often unwilling to be photographed or are indignant when they are snapped without their permission is that they are sensitive about being seen by others in "old clothes." A very common experience is to have an individual or a group say that they would like to have their pictures taken but that they must "get ready" first. When they have put on their best clothes and their finest jewelry, they are quite willing to be photographed. The same attitude is exemplified in the unwillingness to attend a festive gathering unless new garments are available.

Once a Navaho family in the Ramah region was converted to Mormonism. For a month they faithfully gave up the use of coffee. Their mentor had supplied them with quantities of Postum as a gift, and they appeared to be quite content with this beverage. But when the rumor began to go around that they no longer drank coffee because they were too poor to buy it, this they could not stand. Mormonism and abstinence from coffee both went by the board.

In the presence of strangers (especially white strangers) adults commonly manifest embarrassment. They stand with heads hung down and are notably inarticulate. They hide their faces with a blanket while eating. Sometimes when a relative brings a simple message or a single query from a distance he will hang about for hours rather than deliver it while white visitors remain. Women express shyness by a particular, patterned gesture. (See illustration, "Woman Showing Shyness," by Paul J. Woolf.)

Several sources of irritation to white men result from Navaho attitudes toward "shaming." A Navaho who speaks some English will indicate assent or comprehension when he has not understood at all — lest he be "shamed."

Many differences in Navaho etiquette which whites are apt to interpret as rudeness are easily understood in terms of the "shyness" concept. When a visitor arrives, white people think it proper to show welcome immediately with expressions of greeting and pleasure. But Navaho politeness is to ignore the visitor at first, lest he be embarrassed. There is a point at which "shyness" grades into resentment. Sometimes when an unwelcome government official or white missionary arrives at a hogan he sees a circle of persons all sitting with heads bowed down. This may mean that his visit or his questions are a source of annoyance. But the same behavior may also mean that the family is grieved, embarrassed, or perplexed.

The line between "shyness" and "respect" is also not the line with which white people are familiar. When they press for an explanation as to why some Navaho has or has not done something, they are often told, "Well, he got ashamed," or "He is too shy." But the Navaho word which English-speakers usually render as "shamed" or "shy" is actually a composite of these two notions with that of respect, and in discussing relationships of respect-avoidance such as that between son-in-law and mother-in-law the same word-root is constantly used. The hesitancy in speaking in front of unknown white persons is thus, in part, the type of embarrassment which whites themselves also often feel before a much more prominent or powerful person than themselves. Where the white person tends to overcompensate for his feeling of inadequacy by braggadocio or overweening behavior, the Navaho stands speechless, with his head down, turning from side to side, twisting his hands. The Navahos are always talking about "shaming," "being ashamed," or "acting ashamed" (to use the translation that they usually choose).

Control of the individual is achieved in Navaho society primarily by "lateral sanctions" rather than by sanctions from above. That is, the Navaho from childhood on is brought into line more by the reactions of all the people around him rather than by orders and threats of punishment from someone who stands above him in a hierarchy. "Shame" is the agony of being found wanting and exposed to the disapproval of others, as opposed to the fear that some single superior person will use his power to deprive one of rewards and privileges if specified tasks are not carried out according to instructions.

Navaho sensitivity to "shame" likewise largely takes the place that remorse and self-punishment have in preventing antisocial conduct in white society. Navahos do not lie awake nights worrying about the undiscovered "bad" things they have done. Because they have not internalized the standards of their parents and other elders but, rather, accept these standards as part of the external environment to which an adjustment must be made, "divine discontent" is an emotion foreign to the normal Navaho. It is believed by some that "progress" occurs in societies of the Christian tradition largely because each socialized individual is trying to avoid the self-reproach that would be incurred by failing to live up to the ideals inculcated in childhood. Navaho society is (or would be if not under continual pressure from white society) much more static, since "shame" ("I would feel very uncomfortable if anyone saw me deviating from accepted norms") plays the psychological role which "conscience" or "guilt" ("I am unworthy for I am not living up to the high standards represented by my parents") has in the Christian tradition.

"Conscience" is related to the belief in an omnipotent God who knows all. "Shame" naturally develops as a major sanction in societies where almost identical fears are shared and in which there is so little privacy and such constant face-to-face relationships among the people who really count in each other's lives that small peccadilloes cannot be hidden. In white society the child doesn't see the parent in many life situations. The small boy has only his father's own account of his importance in the office. But a small Navaho boy cannot be fooled as to the respect which other adults have (or lack) for his father. In the circumstances of Navaho life a pose of omnipotence or omniscience on the part of parents would be speedily and almost daily exposed.

"PERSONAL WITHDRAWAL"

White Americans give great praise to the "go-getter," to the person
of initiative who not only accepts but seeks personal responsibility.
From the white point of view Navahos often seem irresponsible.
At best, they will — when working for white people — do what
they are told and no more. Even if the situation changes, they continue mechanically to carry out instructions as given. It is hard to
get them to take authority over others. Claims of competence are
seldom made; a "medicine man" who has Reservation-wide fame
will say, "I don't know much. I know a little." It is hard to pin
them down as to which member of a group made — or should make
— decisions. When questioned by white men on almost any topic,
their characteristic tactic appears to be that of outright evasion. Even
a freely volunteered utterance is replete with "it seems," "maybe,"
"it looks like," *they say,* *that one says,* and the like.

But "passivity" or "personal withdrawal" describes the Navaho
attitude better than "irresponsibility." The same individual who carries out great responsibilities in a ceremonial seems unable to do so
when working for a white man. This paradox is to be understood
in terms of another: the Navaho, though decidedly an individualist
in some ways, is essentially group-minded. His whole training and
experience predispose him to work best as a member of a familiar
group where authority is diffuse, informal, and shared, and where
adequate performance is enforced by the subtle sanctions of "shaming." [2] To accept authority over his fellows or to take initiative in any
obvious fashion has for the Navaho the psychological meaning of
separating him from the social group to which he looks for both
support and regulation. Evasion of direct personal decision and displacement of individual authority are essential to the localizing of
authority in the group where, to the Navaho way of thinking, it
belongs. But a sense of responsibility is none the less real for being
divided and shared, for being — to the white person — vague and
unfixed.

Behavior results from forces that have direction. Therefore, all
behavior depends to a large degree on the "mental picture" an individual has of the situation in which he is acting. When the

[2] "Shaming" cultures are mainly homogeneous, group-minded cultures. Cf. the
Japanese.

Navaho operates in a context where he knows what is expected of him and of others, he feels secure. His behavior may be unobtrusive, but it is not precisely passive or withdrawn. In an uncharted or new situation such as one he enters when he works for or with white people, the Navaho feels insecure because the psychological directions are not defined: the Navaho does not know what action will lead to what result.

Just as the Navaho child in a strange situation will sit tight (making no effort to get out of a car, or refusing to get dressed in a doctor's office even though these routines had long since been learned), so the adult Navaho faces white exploitation with passive resistance; he masks fear of the unknown by quiet unmovingness, by the appearance of stolidity. Perhaps in some instances Navahos' "passivity" is a way of getting others to act for them. Perhaps sometimes the psychological meaning is that of being passive so as not to let others see your torture or anxiety in the hope that this will stop the motivation for tormenting you. Perhaps "personal withdrawal" is a more and more frequent Navaho response because The People have found from recent experiences that it doesn't do them any good to be other than passive, that action leads them only into more trouble.

"SPACE–TIME VAGUENESS"

Navaho conceptions of space and time are hopelessly fluid from the white point of view. The "Navaho mile" is notorious among the white men of the Navaho country, for they know all too well that when a Navaho says a place is a mile off it may be five hundred yards or ten miles away.

White employers of Navahos are wont to complain, "Those Indians have no idea of the meaning of time. 'Right now' may be in fifteen minutes or six hours." Part of what these white people refer to depends undoubtedly upon that greater leisureliness, that unhurriedness which tends to be a hallmark of most rural peoples. Most white men, however — whether country- or city-bred — have been trained to be clock-watchers since they were infants fed on a schedule. The experience of the Navahos has been quite different. To be sure, they distinguish about eight positions of the sun during the day and about four points of time at night (using the moon and stars), but these bear a varying relationship to an absolute time system in accord with the seasons of the year. Navahos have discovered the importance of the clock in getting along in white society, and many who cannot read or write nevertheless have learned to tell time and have even bought watches or clocks. If a job with white people is important to a Navaho who has to depend upon "sun time," he will often arrive at work an hour or two early in order to take no chances with a system which, from his point of view, is arbitrary because it is not geared to observable natural phenomena.

While much of what seems to white men to be indifference to time is very similar to that found in other societies which are not adjusted to western industrialism, it must not be assumed that this is equally true of all "simple" societies which lack written languages. Navahos remember seasons of the year and sequences of events rather accurately — in fact, the correctness of their memories over many years in these respects often astonishes white people. It is on absolute dates that they err. A Navaho mother always knows which of her children is older or younger than another. She can tell whether a child was born at lambing time or during the corn harvest. She will also remember that her younger sister was born during the great influenza epidemic of 1918-19 and that her brother was born at the time her uncle went off as a soldier during World War I. But she is as likely as not to insist that this sister is "forty years old" and the brother "fifty-five." It is an actual experience that one mother gave her daughter's age as five in July, as six and a half during October of the same year, and as five during June of the following year, and there is every reason to believe that she was trying her best to be truthful on each occasion. The writers have many records where the same individual has, within the span of a few years, given with equal positiveness absolutely irreconcilable ages for himself or members of his family. In contrast, an Eskimo group is very good at remembering actual dates but untrustworthy as to sequences.

"EMOTIONAL VOLATILITY"

To the superficial observer, The People seem stolid. A man has his finger cut off and never once cries out. Observers who were trying to test the inherited sensitivity to certain chemicals almost gave up the attempt because Navahos would chew bitter papers without comment or manifestation of annoyance. An occasional white man, noticing reactions of this kind and victimized by the fixed notion that the American Indian is impassive, will say, "These Indians haven't got any feelings — really." Another superficial but more sentimental observer will state just as positively, "They're just happy children."

The truth is more complicated. Navahos are renowned, among the outsiders who know them, for their wit and humor and for their capacity to have a good time. Geniality and capacity to associate with others without rancor or a desire to dominate characterize the ceremonials and festive occasions. Their affectional life is as warm as it is mobile. In spite of the theoretically fixed patterns of behavior between relatives, reactions are on an emotional basis and depend on individual motivations at the time. Navahos laugh and joke a great deal and, to the white man who sees them only on pleasurable occasions, their nature seems to be lighthearted to the point of irresponsibility.

However, those who know them more intimately realize fully that there is a more somber side to the Navaho character. Almost all Navahos will, on occasion, become tense, fearful, and suspicious when what is going on hardly warrants such attitudes — from the standpoint of a detached and "objective" observer. This is a partial explanation of their curiosity: they ask personal questions, even of strangers, because anything unusual is potentially a threat. Also many Navahos appear to experience periods of depression, of morbid preoccupation with their health, and of withdrawal into themselves. And so while it would be very incorrect to place a one-sided emphasis upon the uneasiness in Navaho psychology, still we must recognize the presence of such trends.

Another reflection of their general uneasiness is found in the fact that, while some Navahos do have a great drive to get rich (and one must ask how much of this is due to white influence), the majority seem to be interested only in safety. This, to many white teachers, makes them seem "utterly without ambition." They themselves will sometimes say, "All we want is enough to eat for ourselves and our families." What is not said but is often implied, by context or in other ways, is that life is so dangerous and such terrible things can happen to people that anyone is foolish to ask for more than security. Hence the predominant drive is for moderate material well-being.

Perhaps some readers who are familiar with modern psychological theories are asking: how can the anxiety level be so high among a people where infants are nursed whenever they want to be, where childhood disciplines are so permissive, where there is so much affection for children? It is true that, if the writings of certain psychoanalysts and other child psychiatrists and psychologists were literally true (and were the whole truth), adult Navahos would inevitably have calm and beautifully adjusted personalities. However, this is certainly not the case. In spite of the fact that Navaho infants receive a maximum of protection and gratification, when they grow to be adults they are very moody and worry a great deal. The explanation is probably not that the theorists are utterly wrong but that they claim too much for the earliest years and do not pay enough attention to later events and to the total situation in which the mature person finds himself. Infantile indulgence probably does constitute the firmest foundation upon which, if later circumstances are reasonably favorable, a secure and confident adult personality can be developed. But it affords only a possible basis; it does not, in and of itself, promise fulfillment. The high degree of tension observed among adult Navahos may be traced partly to the exceedingly grave pressures to which Navaho society is at present subject, and also to the conflicts caused by weaning, other experiences of later childhood, and beliefs about supernatural forces. These days most Navaho groups are "worked up" about something most of the time.

The main point is the changeability of Navaho emotions. Navahos are moody. Their feelings run the gamut from bubbling jocularity to despair, from inert apathy to destructive violence, within quite a brief space of time. The distance from laughter to tears is often a short one. They are impulsive rather than spontaneous. Few Navahos indeed are capable of sustained personal autonomy; they are too responsive to the pressure of public opinion. Their outer and inner lives are too seldom firmly integrated. They have often achieved a measure of self-control under many conditions which will deceive the casual white observer, who would be astonished to see these apparently well-disciplined adults burst easily into tears of homesickness or give vent to violent rages on slight provocation.

The sexual jealousy of Navahos has been mentioned. Some of it is undoubtedly conventional, but undoubtedly it is often very deeply and personally felt. Occasionally a rejected spouse will deliberately overstrain himself by carrying a huge rock — "he hurt himself because he wanted to die." Marital quarrels and jealousy are indeed frequently ascribed as causes for suicide, exceeded only in number by the desire to escape going to prison or to evade other consequences of past acts. Third most frequent is grief over the death of a relative; fourth, brooding over incurable illness. It is interesting to note that, of known suicides (which are not very frequent), males outnumber females more than ten to one. Shooting is the most common method, hanging next in frequency. Jumping off a cliff was most usual in the past.

"REALISM—UNREALISM"

In certain respects The People are about as matter-of-fact, practical, hard-headed citizens as can be found. Like white Americans, they tend insistently to ask the question, "What good is it?" They are interested in learning skills that will help them to make a living. Their talk is of crops and weather and health. They will argue about government policies and other practical measures. They will even discuss with considerable zest the classification of a clan or a ceremonial. But you can never whip up a heated dispute among them over abstract goals and final philosophical issues. Their feet are firmly on the earth.

Yet their talk is also of ghosts and prowling were-animals. To many white people the fact that The People can believe "such superstitious nonsense" is proof positive that "they don't think like we do." Missionaries and physicians sometimes speak as if the reports of ghosts and witch activities on the part of Navahos were strictly comparable to the hallucinations and delusional experiences of the mentally unbalanced. Such a conclusion overlooks the part played by cultural tradition (as opposed to the individual's "mentality") in interpreting the evidence of the senses.

As A. I. Hallowell has written, "psychologically, the actual order of reality in which human beings live is constituted in large measure by the traditional concepts and beliefs that are held. . . . Indians are able to point out plenty of tangible empirical evidence that supports the interpretation of the realities that their culture imposes upon their minds." [3] If you are skeptical about the tales of the Hero Twins slaying the monsters, for example, your Navaho friend

[3] "Fear and Anxiety as Cultural and Individual Variables in a Primitive Society," *Journal of Social Psychology*, 1938, 9, 25–47, p. 38.

is likely to ask how *you* explain the fossil bones of great animals which admittedly may be seen in Navaho country. The night is huge and dark; in every direction there is silence; and strange forms and shadows sometimes give a start even to those who have not been brought up to believe in ghosts. But if you *have* been brought up to believe in ghosts and witches, then you have a ready-made scheme for interpreting, for elaborating from a simple, actual sensory experience. Suppose a person is alone in a hogan at night and a bit of dirt falls in from the roof. If he is a white man, he is likely to attribute it to wind, or perhaps to a mouse on the roof; but if he is a Navaho, this is a signal which has symbolic significance — it is a sure sign that a were-animal is on top of the hogan. All subsequent sights and sounds fall into line in accord with the central premise activated by the falling of the dirt, and the Navaho is likely to tremble with apprehension a good part of the night. The next morning there is a search for tracks. There are always animal tracks around Navaho hogans, and if a set of dog tracks are discovered which are (or seem to be) a bit bigger than average, this proves that it was a "witch-bear" for sure. And so it goes. But the important thing to remember is that such fears are not *all* "in their minds"; that they are documented, in part at least, by sound and concrete evidence of the senses, white as well as Navaho. The white man is justified only in quarreling with the Navaho interpretation of this evidence. Almost all people believe what they find others believing — those others with whom they identify themselves. A Navaho believes that the lava flows are the congealed blood of monsters slain by the Hero Twins because everybody who is anybody in his world says so. White men also believe many things on authority, not because they themselves have seen the evidence and worked out the theory from first principles themselves.

"IMAGINATION"

Another Navaho quality which is essential to the continuation of The People's "unrealistic" experiences is their extreme imaginativeness. This is one feature of their "psychology" about which there can hardly be a quarrel. Lively imagination stands out in their adaptations of borrowed arts (weaving, silversmithing, drypainting), in their ceremonials, in their myths and other phases of their phantasy life. Possibly this almost hyperactive imagination is, in part, a product of the tension between the outward control which is preserved most of the time and unresolved pressures from impulses. Imagination may provide a main outlet for the disharmony between inner and outer life.

In any case, their interest in the human worlds beyond their own, their flexibility and adaptability, certainly bear a relationship to this development of the imaginative faculties. And The People turn only part of their energies to the outer, practical world; the rest is resolutely reserved for the inner life. Perhaps this is why, for all their hard-headed practicality, they have made so few strictly mechanical inventions. They have seen the possibilities offered by the gadgets of others (imagination) and have utilized them, but they themselves have devised almost no new "things." Perhaps this quality is best summed up by the comparison which a physician once made between the Navaho and the eminently practical Eskimo, "The Eskimo has the mind of a surgeon, the Navaho that of a psychiatrist." The People are concerned with human relations and are sensitive to mystic imponderables as contrasted with the more mechanical and utilitarian minds of Eskimos.

PART II

TESTING THE PEOPLE'S CHILDREN

5.

WHERE AND HOW
the TESTING WAS DONE

Up to this point this book has summarized knowledge of individual development and of Navaho "psychology" as learned from the writers' field studies and from published materials. The remainder of the book will be devoted to reporting upon and discussing the investigations carried on in 1942 by the Indian Education Research project. New data were gathered, principally through the efforts of nine persons.[1] The project represented an attempt to evaluate previous impressions of anthropologists and other people who knew the Navaho as to the working of the "minds" and "emotions" of The People, by applying more objective, and particularly more standardized methods. The reason for making such an attempt was the wish to know as much as possible about Navaho attitudes, sentiments, and ways of reacting in order to plan intelligently for future administration and development of the tribe.

For a number of reasons it was decided to test children of school age rather than individuals of all ages. For one, the children of today are the adults of tomorrow, to whom plans for the future of The People must be geared. A practical consideration was the fact that school children were relatively available for testing, an important point in this sparsely settled country where travel is difficult. Moreover, many of the tests that seemed suitable had been standardized only for children. There can be no doubt that the material is incomplete because it lacks data on adults or on preschool children, and perhaps some day the study will be continued to complete it in these directions, with alterations in the tests to fit the ages of the individuals studied.

The 211 children examined in the present project ranged from those who passed their sixth birthday during the calendar year 1942 to those who were eighteen during the same year. These children

[1] See Acknowledgments in the Preface.

were tested in three Navaho communities — Shiprock, Ramah, and Navaho Mountain — which will be described later in this chapter.

METHODS OF TESTING THE CHILDREN

THE procedures used can be divided roughly as follows: interviews with adults who knew the children and their families; medical examinations; intelligence tests; a battery of tests to sample attitudes, sentiments, and emotional reactions; and projective tests.

INTERVIEWS

Interviews were conducted by the supervising teachers at Shiprock and Navaho Mountain and by the single investigator at Ramah, in each case with the assistance of interpreters. Nearly all the families of the children studied were visited and the parents were questioned about the child's place in the family, his early training, his skills, health, and relationships with his playmates and elders. While asking questions there was an opportunity to observe the behavior of various people in the home, the degree of comfort or poverty, and the extent to which articles of white manufacture were present. Interview material also includes school records, data regarding the family secured from neighbors or relatives or various government offices, and teachers' estimates of the child's ability and personality.

EXAMINATIONS AND TESTS

Physical Examinations were made of about three quarters of the sample of children, the rest not being available in the time allotted. All examinations were made by one of the writers of this volume (Dr. Leighton).

Intelligence Tests included the Arthur Point Performance Scale and the Goodenough Draw-A-Man Test. Neither required the use of English, writing, arithmetic, or other skills learned only in school. However, both had to be explained through an interpreter to children not well acquainted with English. The Arthur was given by two people familiar with intelligence testing, the Goodenough by the person who collected the other drawings.[2] In general, the Arthur Test does not give satisfactory results beyond the age of fifteen, and the Goodenough is limited to children under twelve.

[2] See *Projective Tests* below.

The Psychological Battery was the name given to the collection of tests used to sample the children's attitudes, sentiments, and emotional reactions. It was a matter of question and answer, and could be given by the teachers with the aid of interpreters. Since language played so large a part in this, and also in one of the projective tests described below (Thematic Apperception), a small experiment was made to see if the results, when an interpreter was used, were very different from those obtained by a tester who could speak and understand Navaho himself. In a few instances where it was tried, it appeared that without an interpreter replies were usually fuller but were similar qualitatively to those intermediated by translation. Readers who wish more details on this Battery will find in Appendix I samples of the tests used and replies obtained.

The *Projective Tests* included Free Drawings, a modification of Murray's Thematic Apperception Test, and the Rorschach Psychodiagnostic Test. The idea of these tests is to present to the child standardized material, but material so vague and unpatterned that he will "project" his own personal situation and character into it in carrying out the instructions. For example, for the Free Drawings he is given certain limited varieties of paper, paints, and pencils and told to draw anything he likes. While he may borrow ideas from his neighbors if other children are also drawing, he will shape his pictures in accordance with his own interests and will choose colors that he himself likes. In the Thematic Apperception Test he is shown a number of pictures and asked to tell a story about each one. Without recognizing that he is doing so, he will take his stories from his own experience and thereby tell things about himself that he may not realize consciously and could not tell if asked directly. The Rorschach is the most standardized of the three tests, and the most indefinite. The child is shown a succession of ink blots and asked to say what they look like to him. From studying his method of interpreting these blots, one can infer his characteristic ways of dealing with the world of his experience. References to literature on these tests and samples of Navaho results with some of them will be found in Appendixes and Bibliography.

While these various tests differ in important respects, it is worth noting that they also overlap each other to a considerable extent. For example, one can estimate "intelligence" from the projective tests as well as from the intelligence tests; one learns a good deal about the child's family and personal relations from the Thematic Appercep-tion Test as well as from interviewing those who know him; both the Rorschach and Thematic Apperception Tests supply information about the pattern of the child's reaction to life situations. Thus, in addition to testing a number of different aspects of the child's per-sonality by the use of so many procedures, it was also possible to check one procedure against another and to see which test gave the most reliable and useful information for the time and effort it re-quired. It is not possible to discuss all these aspects of the program here, but critiques of the various tests will be published as listed in the Bibliography.

NUMBER OF CHILDREN STUDIED

The number of children tested in each of the three localities is shown in Table 1.

Not all the children were given every test. Sometimes they were ill when the tester was available; some families moved out of reach;

TABLE 1

Number of Navaho Children Studied, by Community, Sex, and Schooling

	Shiprock	Ramah	Navaho Mt.	All Communities
Total Number	99	49	63	211
Boys	47	25	36	108
Girls	52	24	27	103
Schooled [a]	99 (100%)	6 (12%)	26 (41%)	132 (62%)

[a] A distinction is made between "schooling" and "education" because even the chil-dren who do not attend school receive a definite, though nonacademic, education from other Navahos.

in other cases there was not enough time to test each child and a selection had to be made. The number who took each test is shown in Table 2.

SELECTING COMMUNITIES FOR STUDY

With such a large number of individuals and such a wide geo-graphic spread, all generalizations about The People as a tribe are hazardous. Details of local variations are for specialists, but two general tendencies are worth noting.

The first of these is that, while intra-tribal linguistic differences are for all practical purposes trifling, there are two subdialectic divi-

sions, roughly "eastern" and "western." They are distinguished by
certain preferences in phrasing and idiom and by a very few variations in words. For example, at Navaho Mountain they say *zas* for
"snow," whereas at Shiprock and Ramah they say *yas*. The western
groups and the eastern groups are sometimes known as the "*zas*
people" and the "*yas* people" respectively.

TABLE 2

NUMBER OF NAVAHO CHILDREN WHO TOOK VARIOUS TESTS,
BY COMMUNITY

	Shiprock		Ramah		Navaho Mt.		All Communities	
	Number	Per Cent	Number	Per Cent	Number	Per Cent	Number	Per Cent
Number of Children	99	100	49	100	63	100	211	100
Physical Exam. . .	72	72	37	75	42	66	151	71
Free Drawings . .	82	82	34	70	32	51	148	70
Goodenough . . .	47	47	. . .	. . .	. . .	. . .	47	22
Arthur	92	92	33	67	33	52	158	75
Battery	94	94	34	69	53	84	181	85
Thematic	42	42	30	61	37	59	109	51
Rorschach	43	43	28	55	39	62	110	52

For the second general difference one can say that in physical type
westerners and northerners (Navaho Mountain and Shiprock) tend
in general to be taller and heavier than easterners and southerners
(Ramah). This difference is very likely because of the fact that
northern and western Navahos have had some intermixture with the
larger-framed Plains Indians, while eastern and southern Navahos
were more influenced by the smaller Pueblo peoples.

In spite of the hazards, for purposes of planning it is necessary to
be able to deal with The People as a single group with certain general
characteristics rather than as a number of different groups varying
from each other in details. Thus it became an aim of the Project to
find what was the range of variation within the tribe both in respect
to Navaho culture and to white influences. In order to do this, it was
decided to select children for testing from three localities which
differ from each other but at the same time have features common
to large areas. Naturally such factors as availability of personnel,
schools, and facts known about the region also played a part.

Finally, the three communities of Shiprock, Ramah, and Navaho

Mountain were settled upon. Shiprock stands for that part of the
eastern Reservation which is most densely settled and most prosperous; also it has had the greatest amount of contact with white
men. Ramah represents the regions beyond the limits of the Reservation where The People are in direct competition with white men and
have much less governmental protection and regulation than within
Reservation boundaries. Navaho Mountain furnishes an example of
a remote area where population is scanty, white contacts are few, and
life goes on according to ancient Navaho ways. There follows a
somewhat detailed description of these three areas and the methods
of working in each.

THE PEOPLE OF SHIPROCK:
SOPHISTICATION AND HOSTILITY BY THE RIVER

THE Shiprock area is located in northern New Mexico, not far from
the Colorado and Arizona borders, on the San Juan River. Except
for the irrigated portions near the river, the country is dry, gravelly,
and fairly flat. The region is about 4,000 feet above sea level, with
extremes of heat and cold; the highest recorded temperature is 106
degrees Fahrenheit in the shade, and the lowest 14 degrees below
zero. At such an altitude and with limited rainfall (average annual
precipitation 15.7 inches), the vegetation is chiefly desert in type, with
very few trees. Where the land slopes up toward the distant mountains, pinyons, cedars, and sage appear.

The western horizon is filled with the Lukachukai range and the
Carriso mountains, which contain vanadium deposits that are now
being mined commercially. Northward the land rises toward Mesa
Verde and Sleeping Ute Mountain. The San Juan snakes its way
northwestward between Carriso and the Sleeping Ute. To the east
the sharp sandstone ridge known as the Hogback separates Navaho
farmers on the north side of the San Juan from Mormon and other
white ranchers whose irrigated lands reach eastward and then north
into Colorado along the river. (See Map I.) On the south bank the
Reservation extends for some miles beyond the Hogback. This ridge
and similar smaller formations hold superficial veins of coal which
are dug by both Navaho and white owners. A number of oil deposits were located in the Shiprock area in 1923 only one of which is
being worked at present. Recently helium also has been discovered.

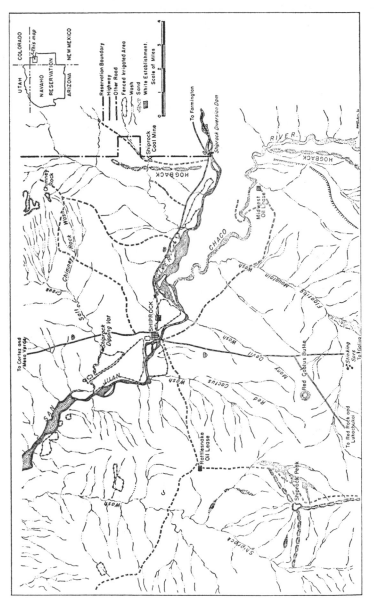

I. SHIPROCK REGION

The flat country is dominated by the great volcanic rock which gives its name to the area. Early white visitors to the region saw the rock as a ship with sails billowing. To the Navahos, however, it looked like a great bird, and their name for it is Winged Rock. To them it is a place of tragedy and terror, where no "good Navaho" will go. Very few indeed — and these of the most acculturated group — have ever climbed upon it, although many have herded their flocks near its base.

The legend that best accounts for this avoidance concerns a time when the tribe was hard pressed by its enemies. The "medicine men" prayed for help. The holy ones heard their cry, and the earth rose, lifting the Navahos with it, and carried them as on a wave to the east, settling where Shiprock now stands. Thus they were saved from their enemies, and they continued to live on the rock, coming down from it only to get water or to till their fields. One day while the men were at work on the farms a terrible storm arose. Lightning struck the rock and split off the trail. The men could not climb up, nor could the women, children, and old people come down. All on the rock perished, and their bodies remain on its top. Thus the rock is a sort of grave which no Navaho but a witch would approach. The People do not like white men to climb on it either, lest they stir up the spirits of the dead.

About five miles northeast of the rock, near the point where the main highway north from Gallup crosses the river, is located the government establishment — a boarding school, a hospital, various other official buildings, employees' quarters — and missions and trading posts. The government plant is old and outmoded, damaged by occasional floods, and subject to so much alkali seepage that the ground is poor for agricultural purposes. Nevertheless, until new buildings are put up in a better location, it remains the headquarters for a large population and one of the most prosperous on the Reservation.

There are no figures specifically for Shiprock, and indeed it is difficult to set the limits for any such "community." Estimates for District 12 in which it lies, an area of about 2,000 square miles, indicate that between 3,000 and 6,000 Navahos live here, a maximum population density of 2.7 per square mile. This would not be possible except for the irrigated farm lands and the mountains which provide valuable summer pasturage.

The 1940 per capita income was $82.52, of which 21 per cent was derived from agriculture, 46 per cent from livestock, and 20 per cent from wage work. (These sources accounted for 14 per cent, 44 per cent, and 30 per cent respectively of the tribal income in the same year.) Shiprock had the next-to-highest amount of wage income of all the districts, the highest non-wage commercial income, and also the highest non-commercial income. Its total income was the second largest of any District on the Reservation. There were 1,505 individual farm tracts which produced crops valued at $93,099. District 12 contains about 20 per cent of all the farm acreage of the Reservation, and 9,849 acres were irrigated in 1940.

White influence has been considerable for many years, partly from government representatives, partly from the white ranchers and traders in the eastern valley. White pressure has also come from the missionaries. Various religious groups have worked in Shiprock at different times; at the time of the study Roman Catholics, Christian Reformed, Navaho Christian Fellowship (conducted by a Navaho), and a nondenominational mission were located there. The boarding school was built between 1900 and 1905; the 40-bed hospital somewhat later. The school founder remained for many years as superintendent of what was then the Northern Navaho Reservation. He was a man of strong character and great determination, who bent his energies to replacing Navaho ways with white ways as rapidly as possible and by any means he could think of. He induced the men to cut their hair, for example, by refusing to issue wagons to those with long hair. No group on the Reservation has been exposed to so many years of high-pressure administration; it seems likely that this is partly responsible for the fact that Shiprock is the center of anti-white feeling and resistance to government programs for the Navahos.

The peyote and certain other religious cults flourish here and have strong anti-white associations. Witchcraft talk is common. In short, all the available facts suggest that this is an area of marked uneasiness, probably the result of the kind of cultural change to which it has been subjected, which finds outlets in emotional religious cults, in opposition to the government, and in the expression of aggression against other Navahos through witchcraft and numerous quarrels. The farmers' organization in District 12 has a long record of internal conflict and disputes over leadership.

On the positive side, white contacts are doubtless partly responsible for the high income at Shiprock, for the gradual improvement of farming practices, and for the facts that many adults speak some English and a considerable number speak it really well. There are more Navahos in this region than elsewhere who live like white people, with homes practically the same as those of neighboring white ranchers. With all this, of course, people here are more at the mercy of the fluctuations of the market for agricultural products than are their less "progressive" brethren who use most of their goods at home.

The single biological family is the principal working unit, with less emphasis on "extended families" and much less on "outfits" than is common in other areas.[3] More than one wife in a family is extremely rare. This may reflect the influence of the former superintendent and the missionaries, but it is also similar to what one finds in the social organization around Chinle, where irrigated fields and orchards are also common, but white influence has been comparatively slight.

TESTING SHIPROCK CHILDREN

The children tested came from families living within bus-range of Shiprock where they came daily to school. In the year of the study (1942–43) there were 304 boarding pupils and 108 day pupils on the roll, many of the boarding pupils coming from distant parts of the Reservation. Although nearly all of the day pupils were included in the testing, it is clearly apparent that they may not represent adequately the estimated 1,800–2,700 children of the Shiprock population. No attempt was made to get a properly assorted sample, as there was little basis for knowing what such a sample should include. There were necessarily many more children from families living near the school than from those scattered through District 12.

The testing program was carried out under the direction of Miss Rachel Jordan, one of the high-school teachers, who was relieved of her teaching responsibilities during the year of the Project. She was assisted principally by Miss Josephine Howard who was lent by the United Pueblos Agency to give the Arthur Test; by Miss Lillian Lincheze, a Navaho apprentice teacher, who administered the Psychological Battery and collected Goodenough drawings and Free

[3] See *The Navaho*, Chapter 3, for discussion of these groupings.

Drawings; by Miss Alice Leonard, also a Navaho and a recent Ship-rock graduate, who acted as interpreter and did a large amount of secretarial work; and by Dr. Leighton, who came for a month to give physical examinations and Rorschach and Thematic Appercep-tion tests.

All the testing was carried out at the school since all of the subjects were pupils. Miss Howard gave the Arthur Tests very soon after school started in the fall. She worked in a room in the employees' club to which children were brought from their classrooms one at a time. Except for the recess period when teachers often came to observe, there were few distractions. For many of the children in-structions could be given in English, but with a certain number, especially the smallest ones and the older ones coming to school for the first time, Miss Leonard had to interpret Miss Howard's direc-tions. Most of the children worked well and appeared interested in the different parts of the Arthur Test.

Miss Lincheze administered the Battery during the fall months and gathered the drawings in December and January. Since she was herself Navaho, no interpreter was required. As far as possible the Battery was given in English; when necessary a standard translation into Navaho, prepared by Mr. Robert Young, was used. The test was done individually and in a private room. The drawings, on the other hand, were made in groups of ten to twelve. As many of the children as could be provided with equipment at one time were called in from their classrooms to a special room and were brought back repeatedly for one- to two-hour periods until each had drawn the Goodenough man and eight free drawings. In many cases, absence from school would extend the length of time it took to collect a given child's drawings over many weeks.

The Rorschach and Thematic Apperception Tests and physical examinations were given by Dr. Leighton in January. The physicals came first, as it seemed advisable to make some sort of contact with the children before starting on the projective tests. All the boys or all the girls on the list from each schoolroom were brought in at one time and examined in turn. Miss Leonard assisted by giving direc-tions and doing some of the clerical work. Because of Navaho mod-esty requirements it did not seem wise to ask the children to strip below the waist, especially as the physicals were being used in part as a means of establishing rapport between them and the examiner.

Height and weight of each child were obtained from schoolroom records.

After completing the physical examinations, first the Rorschach and then the Thematic Apperception Test were administered to half the children on the list. Had time allowed, it would have been preferable to give these two tests to every child. Children were brought singly to a room in the employees' club and given both tests at one sitting. The Rorschach was always given first because it does not require story-telling, and it was thought that if it followed the Thematic, where stories are requested, the children would try to make up a story for the blots also. A few children were too shy to utter a word; a few others failed to grasp the instructions; but on the whole there did not seem to be any particular difficulty in connection with these tests. Most of the children below the fourth or fifth grade preferred to speak Navaho and have Miss Leonard interpret, though there were a few who insisted on speaking English brokenly. All of the older children gave their responses in English. In many cases limitations of their command of English and difficulty of putting their ideas into a foreign idiom stood in the way of obtaining the full and refined data one expects from children of their age and intelligence. Yet, in spite of this, the basic patterns of their individual personalities were clearly revealed.

Meanwhile Miss Jordan was making the acquaintance of the families of the children, interviewing them, and gathering information about them from school and other government records. This was the part of the Shiprock program about which there was the most doubt and uneasiness in the minds of the Research Committee. Shiprock has such a reputation for being unfriendly to white people that it has not often been a field of investigation for anthropologists, and no one knew how the families would react to being visited and questioned. Miss Jordan started out very cautiously by simply going to see the families and finding out if they expected to send their children to school. Many of the parents expressed astonishment that someone from the school should come to see them and said it was the first time they could remember such an occurrence. When, in the course of repeated visits, they discovered that Miss Jordan was not going to take anything away from them or impose some new government regulation but was really interested in their children and in them, they warmed up considerably and did not show any unusual reluctance to talk about the youngsters selected for testing. There were a few families who refused to tell anything that was asked, but the more common experience was for them to answer questions willingly and soon to begin coming to see Miss Jordan when they had business at the school or the trading posts. Many of the parents spoke no English or too little for Miss Jordan's purposes, in which case Miss Leonard or one of the English-speaking Navaho women in the vicinity of the school acted as interpreter.

At Shiprock more than elsewhere, visits had to be repeated several times in order to obtain the desired information. This was largely because both the Navahos and Miss Jordan felt the need of establishing an acquaintanceship before feeling able either to ask or answer the questions the research required. The Indians were prepared, on the basis of their previous experience with white men, to meet with disapproval when they told of their methods of training their children, or even when they let a white person into their homes. It is greatly to Miss Jordan's credit that she was able to dispel their suspicions and to gain their confidence to the point that some of them invited her to attend ceremonials in their homes.

THE PEOPLE OF RAMAH: UNEASINESS AND CONFLICT IN "THE CHECKERBOARD"

THE Ramah Navahos take their name from a little Mormon settlement outside the Reservation in western New Mexico, 44 miles southeast of Gallup. (See Map II.) The Indians live in and beyond "The Checkerboard"[4] in a belt of varying width which extends for 30 miles southward from Ramah. The total area includes 505 square miles, but only 230 are Navaho-owned or leased by or for The People. Figures for Ramah are taken from records of one of the writers (Dr. Kluckhohn) or from information obtained at the United Pueblos Agency. Although they are not strictly comparable with those for Navaho Mountain and Shiprock, in that many of them can be given in greater detail (social statistics, livestock ownership, etc.), while income data were estimated differently, they are the best data available.

Prevalent elevations are around 7,000 feet, which gives the region a steppe climate. Broad rolling valleys covered with grass or sage are bordered with wooded ridges which in some spots are replaced by

---

[4] So called because alternate square miles to a depth of 40 miles on either side of the tracks were given to the Santa Fe railroad when it was built.

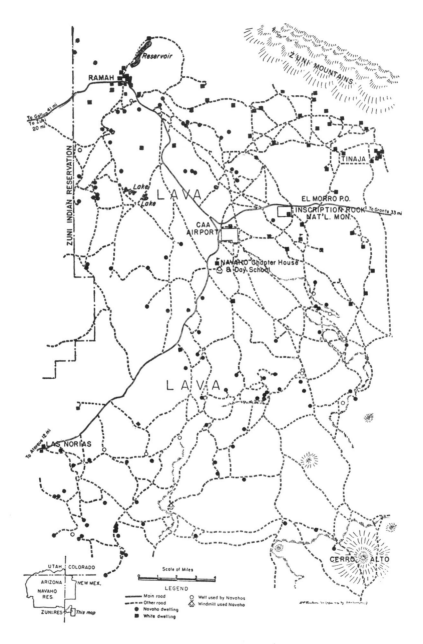

Reservoir

RAMAH

To Gallup 41 mi
To Zuni
20 mi

ZUNI MOUNTAINS

ZUNI INDIAN RESERVATION

Lake
Lake

LAVA

TINAJA

EL MORRO P.O.
INSCRIPTION ROCK
NAT'L. MON.

To Grants 33 mi

CAA
AIRPORT

NAVAHO Chapter House
& Day School

LAVA

To Atarque 12 mi
LAS NORIAS

CERRO ALTO

UTAH | COLORADO

ARIZONA | NEW MEX.

NAVAHO
RES.

ZUNI RES. | This map

Scale of Miles

LEGEND

——— Main road
-·-·- Other road
● Navaho dwelling
■ White dwelling

○ Well used by Navahos
⊗ Windmill used Navaho

II. RAMAH REGION

red or striped sandstone cliffs. One of these is famed as El Morro or Inscription Rock, named from the notations scratched on it by early Spanish explorers. Because the Ramah area is so high above sea level, killing frosts often occur late in the spring and early in the autumn. Annual precipitation averages 14.9 inches, but over a ten-year period it has varied from 6.7 to 23 inches. Drought conditions have occurred in three years out of the ten, and the whole rainfall for a summer month has been known to fall within a single 24-hour period. The deepest snowfall (30 inches) was recorded on November 22, 1931; it killed much of the livestock, brought long hunger to many humans, and starvation and death by freezing to a few. Monthly average temperatures vary from 25 degrees Fahrenheit during January to 66.2 in July. Winter temperatures sometimes go to 30 degrees below zero and July temperatures to 95 above. Nights are invariably cool, even in summer.

There are many trees, with pinyon and juniper characteristic, but with yellow pine and oak frequent at higher elevations. There are two principal natural vegetation combinations: coniferous trees with underlying short grasses on the tablelands; short grasses and short to waist-high shrubs in the drainage ways and on the extensive flats. Generally speaking, the soils contain too little organic matter and are too alkaline. The best lands, both for farming and for grazing, are in the northeastern portion of the area along the base of the Zuni Mountains and are mostly occupied by white ranchers. The worst lands are in and along the lava beds which mark the central and southeastern parts of the area.

The history of Navaho occupancy is that of being gradually pushed more and more into the less desirable lands. Before Fort Sumner The People hunted in the Ramah country and apparently cultivated a few fields. After release from captivity, a few related families drifted into this region instead of settling on the Reservation. They chose the well-watered valley, now covered mostly by the Ramah reservoir, which was known to Navahos then as "Grass-onion place" because of wild onions that flourished there. In 1882 a Mormon colony arrived, and the Indians were "persuaded" to relinquish the choicest areas. At about the same time Spanish-speaking ranchers began to come across the mountains from Cubero, San Rafael, and other settlements. As white population increased, the Navahos were pushed little by little into the lava country. Meanwhile, their own numbers had grown and had been augmented by other families driven south through the expansion of white population into the lands nearer Gallup. In the 1920's homesteaders from Texas and Oklahoma began to take up acreages which The People had been using without legal claims. Today there is no land unclaimed; fencing has increased enormously within the last decade.

A recent count in the Ramah region showed 109 dwellings occupied by The People and 86 occupied by white men (outside the village of Ramah). The 502 Navahos made up 88 biological families, with 14 isolated individuals. Seventy-one of the biological families were combined into 28 extended families, and 59 of the biological families formed 8 "outfits." Sixteen clans were represented, but 419 of the population were members of the Meadow, Bitter-Water, Sour-Water, Chiricahua-Apache, and Close-to-the-Rock clans.

The People farmed 158 different pieces of land, amounting to 3,000 acres. They owned 18,940 sheep and goats, 108 cattle, 310 horses, but these were very unequally distributed. There were only 53 herds of sheep and goats, which ranged in size from 16 to 3,247 head. The average yield of wool was 6 pounds per head. Lambs sold in October weighed from 25 to 70 pounds. In general, poor families were dependent upon agriculture and wage work, well-off groups upon livestock.

Although figures for 1940 are lacking it seems probable that the per capita income for Ramah was between those of Shiprock and Navaho Mountain, in the neighborhood of $72. By 1943 official figures placed it at $104.47, the rise almost surely due to the great increase in wage work available as a result of the war and the not inconsiderable amount of money being paid to families of Navaho men serving in the armed forces. Similar increases would probably be found in other areas.

The land situation is the keynote to Navaho-white relations in the Ramah area. The People feel themselves crowded. They feel they have been exploited by domineering whites who knew how to manipulate the white man's laws. Otherwise the effect of contact has been much less important than might be supposed. While since 1880 the Ramah Navahos have been in continuous touch with English- and Spanish-speaking white people, the culture of these whites has been so simple and the linguistic barrier so great that white influence has been slight except in the realms of technology and economy. However, there are more adult Navahos at Ramah who speak a little Spanish than there are persons who speak any English at all.

The Navahos here have been much less exposed to white agencies, such as schools and missions, which deliberately set about to change their way of life than have The People of the Reservation. Although for a time in the 1920's local Mormons were appointed to supervise the Ramah Navahos and did see to it that some youngsters were sent off to school, the Indian Service has paid only sporadic attention to this group until very recently. The first school was not opened until 1943. Missionaries have never been stationed closer than thirty miles away, and their visits have been few and infrequent. A few years ago the center of Indian Service control over the Ramah Navaho shifted from the Navajo Central Agency at Window Rock to the United Pueblos Agency at Albuquerque. This change made for confusion in the minds of the Navahos, as does the fact that their lands are under the jurisdiction of still another administrative agency, that of Federal Grazing District 7.

The outstanding features are the uneasiness in the face of white pressures, similar to that found at Shiprock but a little less intense, and the prevalence of old patterns of life. It may be that this greater preservation of familiar ways and values makes the anxiety less far-reaching here. The diversity of superficial contacts with other cultures and the isolation from the rest of the tribe should also be stressed. Besides the influences of Mormons, Texans, and Spanish-Americans, Zuni influences are of some importance, for much of the Ramah area borders on the Zuni Reservation, and some Navaho hogans are less than four miles from the Zuni farming village of Pescado. Both Zunis and Navahos trade in Ramah village. Although the Ramah Navahos are cut off by the Zuni Reservation and by white settlements from direct geographical contact with other Navaho groups, visits and exchanges of ceremonial practitioners are almost weekly occurrences. In certain respects the cultural position of Ramah is intermediate between that of Navaho Mountain and Shiprock, but the common factors of peripherality and isolation make the psychological flavor of Ramah much like that of Navaho Mountain.

TESTING RAMAH CHILDREN

The Ramah area had been known to both writers of this volume for some time. Dr. Kluckhohn had visited it for many years and studied the Navahos there; Dr. Leighton had made another investigation over a four-month period in 1940. Because of this previous acquaintance, it was possible to list families in the region who exemplified the range of social and economic conditions and the degree of white influence in the community. Children of the desired ages were selected from those families for testing. Had the time been unlimited, it would have been best to take only one child from each family and thereby spread out the sampling, but for convenience and speed it was decided to test all children between six and eighteen in each of the chosen families.

A further deciding factor for this method of selection was the lack of a school or any other central place to which the children came. This made it necessary for Dr. Leighton to visit each family and do the testing at the child's home. Such a procedure had the very great advantage of giving her an opportunity to see the family in action and to observe the outward evidences of interpersonal relationships within the groups. At the same time there were a number of real disadvantages, as will be seen in the account of the testing below. Since all these factors played a part in interviewing families in all three areas, though not in the testing at Shiprock or Navaho Mountain, a description of an actual trip at Ramah will serve to give the reader an understanding of the problems encountered in gathering the Navaho data.

Dr. Leighton was boarding at the small country hotel in the Mormon village. The Indian Office supplied a half-ton truck which served to transport testing materials and camping equipment as well as tester and interpreter. The interpreter, Mrs. Bertha Lorenzo, was a most essential part of the entourage as few Navahos spoke English and Dr. Leighton spoke no Navaho. Mrs. Lorenzo lived with her family a short distance from Ramah and was employed by the month for this project. Although family complications occasionally interfered with plans, for the most part she was on call at any time and was willing to stay away from home for several days at a time when the work demanded it.

The usual procedure was to start out early one morning with supplies for a three- or four-day trip and go to camp with one or more families in the same general neighborhood, observing, interviewing, and testing until the family was "finished." A frequent variation was to visit several families on a days' trip and make appointments for a time when we might return and find the children at home. In either case it was usually necessary to explain what we wanted to do and why.[5] We would tell them that a good many Navahos, and also white people who were interested in the Navahos, were not satisfied with the kind of education the children were getting in the schools and wanted to improve it so that the children would be able to get along better and make a better living when they grew up. It had been decided that the best way to make such improvements was to first find out what the children were like and how they lived. We also wanted to see how healthy they were. We then explained that we would like to give the children some little tests that were not very hard and were really mostly like games, and then we would like to ask the older people about the children and how they raised them. Besides that we would give each child a physical examination just the way the doctors did for the boys who were drafted, and if we found any sickness we had a few medicines to help them out. We added that because we could see that the children were working, except for the little ones, we would be willing to pay them for the time they worked with us and couldn't do their usual jobs.

There follows a somewhat edited account of a trip, excerpted from Dr. Leighton's field notes.

October 7. Bertha and I finally got off with our equipment about 10 o'clock and reached our destination 30 miles away about 2 o'clock. This was the home of Gordo whose two children were on our list. The older, a girl of 10, had been tested previously, but the 5-year-old boy had been bashful, and there had been too many adults around to make a good testing situation. Moreover his mother had been too busy helping get in the harvest to answer our questions about the children at that time. We found Mrs. Gordo and the two children sitting outside their house picking over pinto beans. She told us she was all out of groceries and was getting these beans ready to take to the store to trade.

Since part of our mission was to win the confidence of the little boy, we sat down with the rest and helped with the beans. When they were finished we got out our groceries and they cooked supper for all of us. Meanwhile the boy was playing around us and seemed very friendly. He was especially pleased with presents of candy and cigarettes. His mother told us one reason he was scared of us before was that his father used to try to make him behave by warning him that, if he didn't, some white women would catch him and put him under their skirts and smother him. The mother kept sending him away from where we were shelling beans. Bertha thought this was because his

---

[5] "We" is used advisedly, for conversation always involved both Dr. Leighton and Mrs. Lorenzo and it must have been somewhat modified in translation.

clothes were very ragged, but it seemed equally probable to me that it was because he got in the way of the work. Mrs. Gordo did not think there was much chance that he would work with us, but she was willing to have us try it.

After supper the girl went to water the horses and the boy to take the little flock back to some older members of the family who lived in a hogan a quarter of a mile away. When they returned we had nearly finished questioning the mother, and after a cigarette all around, the children drew some pictures for us. They had made a few on our first visit, but they did it much more spontaneously this time. The little boy kept appealing to his sister or mother to look at his drawings, but they paid little attention. After they were finished he always declined to say what they represented.

Mrs. Gordo was chatting with us while the children painted. She said she would have to get up early, finish a corral fence around some corn, and then thrash and winnow some more beans. I asked when we could test the boy. At first she detailed all the difficulties, then said she would wait to begin her labors until we had finished "those games." She doubted we could do anything requiring language, as "he is poor at that and bashful besides."

Our hostess said we were welcome to sleep wherever we liked, inside or out. We chose to stay inside as it was chilly. Since they live in a Mexican-style house without the central Navaho smokehole, it was both warm and stuffy when they closed the door for the night. Every time I woke from a restless sleep I heard loud scratchings from the children or their mother. By morning I discovered for myself what made them scratch! The boy said *shimá* [mother] twice; but, when his mother did not respond, he subsided.

October 8. Before sunup Mrs. Gordo was stirring. Soon her daughter and I followed her, and later Bertha and the little boy. While we had breakfast the mother warned the boy that if he acted scared of me I would not give him any more candy. After eating, the daughter went to look for the horses, and we began to give the boy the Arthur Test. He was not scared, but he tended to give up rather easily. Some parts of it he said he liked. We attempted the Battery, starting by asking him if he had ever been happy. He said yes, but seemed unable or unwilling to describe an instance. Mrs. Gordo tried to discourage us from further "questioning," and it appeared to be pretty useless. So we ended with a physical examination to which he submitted willingly.

While we packed up our things to go, Mrs. Gordo dressed in her best to have a picture taken. She declined to have the boy photographed, presumably because he had no good clothes to put on. Meanwhile word had been sent that we should stop at the hogan near by to prescribe for some sore ears. It turned out to be mumps in a younger sister of Mrs. Gordo. All the family had had it in succession. We gave the patient some aspirin, asked directions for reaching the next family we wanted to test, and started off.

These people were living at a sheep camp in the lava beds, "where the roads go this way and that way" as the Navahos would tell us. After several wrong turns we finally located them. The children we wanted were two daughters

of a man named Harry and a third girl who lived with the family and herded
their sheep. Harry had gone to work building the day school, and his family
had moved over to join that of his wife's mother, Mrs. Mucho. We found them
living in two brush enclosures, with a red truck in the distance and a good
wagon and water barrel near the shelters. Mrs. Mucho was sitting with a
little girl in one shelter, another woman in the other, and Mrs. Harry with her
youngest baby was under a tree near by. Two other little girls were playing
around the truck. This was our first encounter with this family.

We shook hands with Mrs. Mucho and offered her a cigarette which she
refused. We sat in silence for some minutes until she inquired what we wanted.
We had hardly finished explaining when she began to say she didn't want us
to test these children because she knew it was just to line them up for the day
school. We told her this was not so, but it had no effect. She went on to say
that the two we wanted to work with stuttered so they could hardly speak,
they didn't talk much even to the family, and they weren't big enough to take
tests anyway. Moreover she wasn't going to have them go to the day school,
especially the one she was raising. During this tirade the girls' mother said
nothing. The little girls kept a safe distance but came to where their mother
was sitting to peek at us through the brush now and then. When the smallest
one started to cry, the grandmother pointed to us, and Bertha said she was
telling her that I would take her away if she cried. There was no shaking
Mrs. Mucho's belief, apparently, though we brought up every argument we
could think of.

After some time Mucho arrived, came into the shelter, and shook my hand
quite affably. We explained it all to him, and he said that the decision was up
to the women. Finally, Mrs. Harry spoke up from behind her tree. She said
she thought it was all right for us to test the children, but she was afraid her
mother had spoiled it for us by the talk she had been making, which the
children had heard. She called the younger of the ones we wanted over and
asked if she would do it, but the child said, "No." Mrs. Harry said she guessed
the child had taken her grandmother's advice. Mucho made some dark remarks about white people who go behind hills and take pictures of children
pretending they are making pictures of the view. Then he walked off.

We asked about the older girl, but Mrs. Mucho said she couldn't spare her
from the herding. She said the girl's family had let them have her when she
was little to take care of the crippled woman in the other shelter, and now she
was just the same as their child. She never came near when there was any
company, anyhow.

As an afterthought, Mrs. Mucho began to fuss about how we knew the children's names, and how Dr. Kluckhohn knew them when we said we got them
from him. She wanted to know why Dr. Kluckhohn never came to see them.
I told her it would be easy to find out their names, as from their father for
instance, without coming away out where it was so hard to locate them. Also
maybe she acted towards all white visitors the way she had towards us, so of
course they wouldn't come here much.

Finally I told her that I wasn't mad at her, but that I didn't know how to answer her except by telling the truth, and she didn't believe that, so there was no use in our staying. I said I hoped she would watch carefully to see what children went to the day school when it was finished, and if not all the ones I had tested went, then she would know that I had been telling her the truth. Mucho (who had returned) and Mrs. Harry laughed a little at this.

We departed, somewhat shattered by this first absolute refusal to coöperate, and headed for our good friend Carlos and his family, stopping for lunch on the way. Carlos, his daughters Bianca and Rosa, and a couple of his grandsons were working on beans, thrashing and winnowing them and sacking them in hundred-pound bags. They came over soon after we drove up and we gave them some pictures we had taken on a previous visit. Carlos told us he had more than 20 of the bags of beans. He had been expecting us to come with the doctor from Zuni for a monthly clinic in a few days and had thought he would miss us as he had to cart his beans to the store. One of Carlos' sons-in-law was sitting near by playing with his little girl. He disappeared as Mrs. Carlos, his mother-in-law, rode up with the flock of sheep.

Seventeen-year-old Bianca said jokingly that she guessed she would kill one of the sheep so we could take her to Ojo Caliente, the Zuni farming village, to trade the meat for melons. To this Carlos and his wife added their pleas, and Carlos said he thought I might do this for them since they permitted the government doctor to hold his clinic in their house. I demurred at first, but then gave in and agreed to take them after testing a little boy who lived only a mile or two away. It seemed like an excellent opportunity to see this family, three of whose children we had tested, in a way I never had before.

By this time it was late afternoon. The testing was to take place next morning and our trip in the afternoon. The rest of the day was spent in joyful preparation for the trading expedition. Before we slept three ancient sheep had been butchered. They said the Zunis didn't care how tough the meat was. A kid was killed and part of it cooked for our supper.

October 9. Everyone was up early today to get ready. Bertha and I drove to the family we were to test as soon as breakfast was finished. It turned out to be the most poorly kept home we had visited, with the buildings out of repair, the inside untidy, the bedding still lying on the floor, and even left-over food scattered around. Most of the members of the family were ill-dressed. Our subject, a boy of ten named David, was quite elegant by contrast, with new denim pants, a new bright yellow rayon shirt, and a new neckerchief. He is a half-orphan who lives with his paternal grandmother. His father had been working in a defense plant and had recently paid a visit home, bringing new clothes for his son. In addition to the boy and the grandmother there was his aunt and her husband, two children by a former husband, and a year-old baby by the present one. The baby was far from clean when we first saw it, and two days later it was still dirty in the same places.

They had had word we were coming to work with David, and the grandmother had insisted that he be excused from work until we arrived. The rest of the family were busy hauling ears of corn from their field with an ancient wagon. David was glad to work with us. He said through Bertha that he would rather do our kind of work than help haul corn. He is the only child at Ramah to express such feelings.

We took him and the testing materials a little way from the hogan outdoors. First we gave him the Arthur Test, then the Battery, Rorschach, and Thematic Apperception. He applied himself fairly well but was easily distracted by anything that happened in the neighborhood. While we were doing the Battery a truck containing the Navaho policeman, another Navaho, and a Laguna Indian who was working at the day school drove up. While the policeman delivered a message to the family, the Laguna came and watched what we were doing and asked us questions. David had nothing to say under these circumstances. When they left, the grandmother and an uncle, who had just returned from driving cows across country to the railroad for a white rancher, came to watch. Again David ceased to respond until the grandmother left and he told the uncle to take himself off. We finished with a physical examination and tried to persuade him to make some drawings. He said he didn't know how, and his grandmother agreed, saying that whenever his father gave him a pencil to practice with, the others in the family took it away from him, as they did with everything else he had. When we finished I asked him if he preferred only money, or a little money and a jackknife. He said he wanted money and he wanted it right away. He asserted that he was going to spend it on tobacco.

This description covers only three days, but what has been given will suffice to show the kind of experience one can expect to encounter. While the personalities and items would vary for Shiprock and Navaho Mountain, the general flavor would be much the same, with some people friendly, some hostile, some neutral; success here, failure there; Navaho ways modifying plans constantly; and numerous distractions from the main program.

THE PEOPLE OF NAVAHO MOUNTAIN: HARMONY IN THE BACKWOODS

THE majestic dome-shaped mass which is called Navaho Mountain rises so alone above the Rainbow Plateau that it serves as a landmark over thousands of square miles, a blue shadow straddling the Utah-Arizona line. Until a few generations ago The People thought of this as Piute Indian territory, and the ordinary Navaho name for the mountain translates literally as "Enemies' Hiding Place." There are still a few Piutes in this neighborhood, but they have intermarried with the Navahos and have largely adopted Navaho ways. To a certain extent the Piutes here have been pushed out of the way by the invading Navahos much as the Ramah Navahos are being elbowed aside by intruding whites. Even before Fort Sumner, but especially in the decades immediately following the captivity, Navaho families used to come into the Navaho Mountain country to hunt, collect pinyon nuts or graze their livestock for a while. But apparently no Navaho considered this "home" until about 1898, when a man we will call First Settler, with his three wives, children, and one son-in-law, began to move north from Shonto each winter to occupy lands south and east of the Mountain as winter range. About 1918 this extended family (which had meanwhile grown a good deal) commenced to make the region a year-round residence. When First Settler died, his sister's daughter and some of her children came to claim their inheritance and remained. Most of the present population are descended from First Settler or this niece.

Navaho Mountain figures prominently in the mythology of The People. The sacred name for it means "Pollen Mountain." Because the mountain is so holy it is fearsome, and no Navahos dwell upon it — indeed they are afraid to remain on it overnight. The People live mainly on the sagebrush flats of Rainbow Plateau to the south and east of the Mountain and in the deep canyons (Piute Canyon, Navaho Canyon, and their branches). (See Map III.)

The research group includes those families who trade (partially at least) at Navaho Mountain Trading Post and who send their children to the Navaho Mountain Day School. Because of seasonal moves and families whose local group-association is variable, it is impossible to specify exactly the size of this group, but it numbers about 200. Thanks to a study made by Malcolm Carr Collier, we have some useful facts on the 140 persons living closest to the trading post in 1938.

Of these 140 Navahos, 117 were descended from either First Settler or his niece; 38, in fact, could trace their descent to both. Only one man in the whole community could not claim a blood relationship with someone else who lived there. The 140 people belonged to 9 different clans, but 111 were members of the Salt or Bitter-Water clans. They lived, in 1938, in nine separate groups of hogans. The largest of these extended families included 34 persons, the smallest seven. Figure 1, a much abbreviated "family tree" of the six Navaho Mountain children described in Chapter 9, serves to show the high degree of common heredity and the limitation of clans.

There is no very complete information on the economic life of the people in the immediate vicinity of Navaho Mountain, but as at Ship-

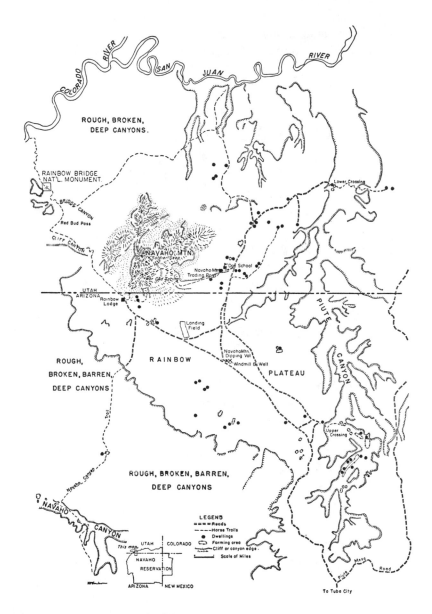

ROUGH, BROKEN,
DEEP CANYONS.

RAINBOW BRIDGE
NAT'L. MONUMENT.

BRIDGE CANYON

Red Bud Pass

CLIFF CANYON

NAVAHO MTN.

Soldier Seep

Navaho Mtn.
Trading Post

Gas Springs

Day School

UTAH
ARIZONA
Rainbow
Lodge

Landing
Field

Navaho Mtn.
Dipping Vat

Windmill & Well

ROUGH,
BROKEN, BARREN,
DEEP CANYONS

R A I N B O W

P L A T E A U

P I U T E   C A N Y O N

Upper
Crossing

Lower Crossing

Trail

Navaho Canyon

ROUGH, BROKEN, BARREN,
DEEP CANYONS

NAVAHO

CANYON

This map

UTAH   COLORADO

NAVAHO
RESERVATION

ARIZONA   NEW MEXICO

LEGEND

Roads
Horse Trails
Dwellings
Farming area
Cliff or canyon edge
Scale of Miles

Piute   Mesa   Road

To Tuba City

COLORADO   RIVER

SAN   JUAN   RIVER

III. NAVAHO MOUNTAIN REGION

rock something can be gleaned from the official figures for the district (District 2:1,711 square miles) in which it lies.

The density of population is the smallest on the Reservation — 0.7 persons per square mile — while the average for the Reservation is about 2 per square mile, and one district has as many as four.

The per capita income for 1940 was $62.81. The percentage of this income which is commercial is the smallest for any district (58 per

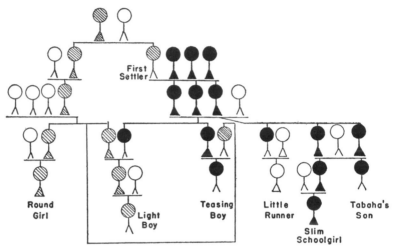

Fig. 1. Lines and solid blocking of heads and skirts indicate membership in the Bitter-Water or Salt clans respectively. Blank figures belong to a variety of clans. Lines directly beneath figures indicate husband and wife.

cent). Wage income for 1940 was only $5.09 per capita (10 per cent), while the Navaho average was $24.30 (30 per cent). Sixty per cent of the total income came from livestock and 20 per cent from agriculture, whereas the tribal averages were 44 per cent and 14 per cent respectively.

A harvest was taken from 1,077 acres, 253 of which (in Navaho and Piute Canyons) were irrigated. Individual farm tracts numbered 280 and produced crops (corn, squash, watermelons, potatoes, peaches, alfalfa, and a few beans) valued at $15,370.

The government has developed water resources in District 2 through two drilled wells with windmills, two dug wells, seven springs with troughs, and three earth reservoirs for impounding run-off water. One windmill and one reservoir are on Rainbow Plateau.

The outstanding features of the Navaho Mountain group are their internal harmony and the small amount of white influence. The two facts are of course interrelated, but part of the peacefulness of the Navaho Mountain Navaho is also due to everybody's being related to everybody else, which, among The People, reduces overt hostility and increases a tendency toward coöperation. Moreover, they are isolated by deep canyons and other geographical barriers from most other Navahos.

The small degree of white contact results from the isolated location. It is 175 miles from the nearest town on the railroad, and a part of the last 65 miles of "automobile road" is simply a trail marked with white paint across the rocks. This circumstance has been partially counterbalanced in recent years by the fact that travelers are attracted to the area to see Rainbow Bridge in the canyons north of Navaho Mountain. However, until 1925 there was not even a wagon road to the base of the Mountain. Before that the closest trading store was 60 miles away by a trail so narrow at one point that wagons had to be taken apart, carried piece by piece up a steep defile, and reassembled.

No trading post was established in the immediate vicinity until 1928; no permanent post until 1932. Three traders and their families have done business at the Mountain at different times, and since the day school was built in 1936 there have been three teachers in succession. Other white contacts occur with the people who run the outfitting post for parties to Rainbow Bridge, and with occasional governmental and other visitors.

While the number of white people is small, the Navahos have a much more intimate relationship with them here than at either Shiprock or Ramah. One bit of evidence of this is the fact that Navaho Mountain women have learned to make yeast bread to bake in their three-legged iron Dutch ovens; this has never happened at Ramah, so far as is known, and is probably very rare at Shiprock. The fact that the white wife of the trader at Navaho Mountain at the time of the study had grown up among Navahos and spoke their language fluently was partly responsible for the intimacy of Navahos and white people at the Mountain.

Given the isolation, the peripheral location, and the unusually high degree of blood interrelationship, it is not surprising that this research group is characterized by conservatism and a "back-woodsy" flavor.

TESTING THE CHILDREN AT NAVAHO MOUNTAIN

The group of children studied included 63 between six and eighteen years of age. Of these, 26 were currently, or had been, in school, while the remaining 37 lacked this experience. This situation afforded an opportunity to observe the difference made by schooling in children of the same family, for in no case were all the children of a family "educated."

The testing program here was under the charge of Mrs. Lisbeth Eubank, who had been the day-school teacher for two years. During part of the time a second teacher was supplied to take part of the school work while Mrs. Eubank devoted more time to the study. Since the school is a community center frequently visited by the families when they come to the trading post, a number of the interviews could be held there, and the rest were collected on trips to the children's homes. School children were tested at school. Their brothers and sisters were brought in by the school bus for most of the testing, though the Psychological Battery was sometimes administered at their homes. Mrs. Eubank spoke a little Navaho but relied on the interpretation of Mr. and Mrs. Robert Tallsalt, the day-school assistants, for the tests and much of the interviewing. Dr. Leighton arrived in the last month of school to collect drawings, do physical examinations, and administer the Arthur, Rorschach, and Thematic Apperception Tests. Because it was late in the spring and the children's assistance was needed at home in some cases, fewer children were available than if other obligations had permitted Dr. Leighton to be at the Mountain earlier in the year.

The People at Navaho Mountain were, on the whole, extremely coöperative. This was due in part to their general good will towards white people, in part to interest in the school and anything calculated to improve conditions for their children, in part to the friendly attitude of the traders toward the study, but mostly to Mrs. Eubank's excellent relationships with the Indians. They trusted her, were grateful to her, and were willing to go to considerable inconvenience to do what she requested. Dr. Leighton's advent marked the first extended visit by a physician to the community. The Navahos utilized this to have their aches and pains investigated and even to have a physical examination "just to see what it was like." This was a surprise, for the air of conservatism and the high confidence in Navaho ceremonials to cure illness had led white men to think that white medicine would be of little interest to the Navaho Mountain community. What happened is evidence of Navaho curiosity and of their essentially practical way of accepting anything they think may benefit them. Had there been any taboo such as, "You must never go to another ceremonial if you have the doctor examine you," no patients would have appeared, and probably the children would have been warned not to submit to examination. As it was, they not only made use of Dr. Leighton's presence, but when the Tuba City doctor appeared on a flying visit one day with materials for inoculations, a large number of both adults and children were eager to be vaccinated.

6.

MENTAL
and PHYSICAL FITNESS

A POPULAR conception of many white Americans who have never dealt with Indians is that "Indians are Indians," different from white people, inferior to them — interesting, perhaps, as historical phenomena, as impediments to the westward sweep of European civilization, or as attractions in the circus. They are supposed to stand about with poker faces and say "Ugh" occasionally. Those who see them casually often think "Indians are dirty." The possible relationship of scant water supply to cleanliness customs, the fact that something may be going on behind the poker face, or even that this Indian is not exactly like that one, rarely comes to mind. The reverse of this view, that "Indians are just the same as white people," is also held by some whites and is equally inaccurate.

Indians, too, think in stereotypes. Those who have not had much experience with white men think that "all white men are alike," all are noisy, ill-mannered, waiting to do the Indian out of his property unless the Indian pretends he hasn't any or outsmarts him in some other way. The way to deal with white men is to "play dumb" and see what they do first. Perhaps, if Indians have had white friends, they swing to the other extreme and think that "white people are just as good as Indians."

This fixed way of thinking about each other imposes a serious barrier to useful mutual understanding. If one believes that another group of people are all alike and that they "got that way" by some mysterious and incomprehensible means, there is, naturally, no point to studying the individuals in the group. Further examples can be found in common opinions about non-Indians — "You can't trust a Jap," "All Russians are radicals," "Capitalists care for nothing but their profits," and as many more as there are different groups of people with different customs and habits. The trouble is that, once one subscribes to one of these "universals," he closes his mind and forgets the only real universal: "People are people."

While any sizable group of people will contain individuals of many types, different cultures tend to foster one or more particular "personality configurations" that suit the conditions of the society better than do other configurations. White American society, for example, encourages its members to develop those qualities demanded for competition. The prizes go to the ones who do better than their fellows and who can speak up for themselves, rather than to persons noted for their modesty or their kindness to others. Another society, on the other hand, will have rewards for coöperation in group endeavors rather than for individual achievement, and an aggressive, competitive person would find himself ostracized. In the chapters that follow, watch must be kept both for the range of variation among the children of The People that were tested and for the way in which different personality types get along in Navaho society.

When one tries to define "personality," he immediately discovers that it is not an easy thing to do. He can mention words sometimes used synonymously, like "character"; but if he then tries to define "character," he is just where he started. Moreover the term "personality" is used to express quite different concepts. In the everyday sense, it often means "charm." Kardiner defines it as "the point of contact between individual and environment."[1] Still others may mean personal idiosyncrasies.

In the present book "personality" is used to indicate the total integrate of facts about the individual, including his biological inheritance, his life experience, and the way in which he affects other people. Some of the qualities which make up "personality" are: degree of intelligence; capacity for love, anger, fear, or other feelings; aggressiveness or passivity; and the balance between interest in self and interest in others, to name a few. Many others might be listed. Thus, while it is impossible to study "personality" as a unit, one can find out something about it by investigating some of its parts. This could be compared to the process the doctor goes through in determining the health of a person — he does not examine the body as a unit, but he studies carefully each organic system and, from the conditions he finds therein, deduces the state of the patient as a whole. To be sure, many of the qualities included in "personality" are far from being units or simple affairs themselves. However, they are

[1] Abram Kardiner, *The Individual and His Society* (New York: Columbia University Press, 1939), p. xxi.

easier to study than "personality" as a whole, and some aspects of them can be tested with varying degrees of success. Two of these somewhat obvious "elements" of personality which have been tested in white culture to a large extent are intelligence and health. These will be discussed first.

HOW BRIGHT ARE NAVAHO CHILDREN?

ONE tends to think of intelligence as a well-defined entity, partly because there are so many intelligence tests and the estimation of a person's IQ is such a common event. Like "personality," however, "intelligence" is so difficult to define that even the experts do not attempt it. The tests to measure intelligence vary from those which depend largely on what a person has learned and remembers, to those which contain new tasks for everyone and are intended to evaluate what the person can do in a situation for which he is unprepared. Most of the tests have been designed for white children or adults and presuppose the sort of educational and cultural experience that the average white person receives. Naturally one would not expect an Indian child who had had no schooling and little contact with white culture to do well on such a test, and so the Research Committee endeavored to select some measure of intelligence that would not handicap the Indian children unduly in this way. Table 3 shows the degree of success of the Navaho children. Results of the same test among white children are used for comparison because this base will be familiar to most readers and because this test was devised for studying white children.

If one graphs these data shown in Table 3 according to level of intelligence, the distributions appear as in Figures 2 and 3.

Table 3 and Figure 2 show that the average for the tribe is somewhat lower than that for white children, with a larger percentage of children in the two lowest levels. There is, moreover, great difference in the proportions for Shiprock, Ramah, and Navaho Mountain as can be seen in Figure 3. The percentages for Shiprock are much the same as for the tribe and for white children, with a higher percentage of children in the "average" range than in even the white group. The Navaho Mountain bar shows a larger proportion of children in the lowest grade of intelligence. Ramah has its peak of incidence in the next-to-the-lowest grade.

The question must now be asked, how can this distribution be

TABLE 3

PERCENTAGES OF CHILDREN SHOWING VARIOUS IQ'S, NUMBER OF CHILDREN TESTED, AND MEDIAN AND AVERAGE IQ'S

Grade and IQ	Grace Arthur Point Performance Scale					Goodenough Draw-A-Man
	Shiprock [a] (per cent)	Ramah [a] (per cent)	Navaho Mountain [a] (per cent)	Tribal Average [a] (per cent)	Whites [b] (per cent)	Shiprock [c] (per cent)
Very superior . .	7	3	9	6	8	29
135–139	2	...	6	2.6	0.8	4
130–134	1	...	...	0.3	1.7	6
125–129	2	3	...	1.6	1.5	6
120–124	2	...	3	1.6	3.4	13
Superior	6	3	9	6	11	26
115–119	2	...	3	1.6	4.0	15
110–114	4	3	6	4.3	6.8	11
Average	54	23	38	38	45	33
105–109	9	10	3	7.3	9.5	9
100–104	11	10	23	14.0	10.0	9
95–99	17	...	6	7.3	10.0	11
90–94	17	3	6	8.6	15.0	4
Dull normal . . .	17	23	26	22	24	6
85–89	11	13	3	8.6	13.0	2
80–84	6	10	23	12.6	11.0	4
Borderline . . .	12	29	6	16	10	6
75–79	6	10	...	5.3	6.0	4
70–74	6	19	6	10.6	3.4	2
Mental deficiency	4	19	12	12	2.0	0
65–69	2	3	6	4.0	1.0	...
60–64	...	10	3	4.3	1.0	...
55–59	1	3	3	2.3	...	...
50–54	1	3	...	1.3	...	...
Number of children . . .	92	33	33	158	409	47
Median IQ . . .	94.7	81.7	95.0	—	—	—
Average IQ . . .	95.9	84.3	94.1	91.4	102.5 [d]	109.7

[a] Data for Navaho children are for those 6–15 years of age.

[b] Values are for white children 5–15 years of age. Source: Mary Grace Arthur, *A Point Scale of Performance Tests* (New York: Commonwealth Fund, 1933), Vol. II.

[c] Goodenough Tests were given only at Shiprock. Data are for children 6–12 years old.

[d] This is the average IQ earned by the standardization group. Dr. Arthur states that probably a much larger sample drawn from all over the United States would have averaged 100 or less.

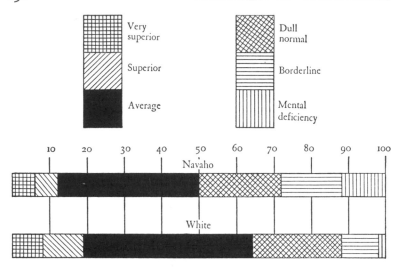

FIG. 2. Distribution of grades of intelligence, Arthur Test, white and Navaho children.

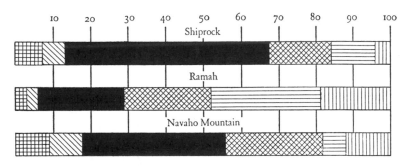

FIG. 3. Distribution of grades of intelligence, Arthur Test, children of three Navaho communities.

understood? How does it happen that Shiprock has more children of "average intelligence" than the white group? Why does Navaho Mountain have more children in the lowest level than the next-to-the-lowest? Are the Ramah children so much less intelligent than their tribal brothers and sisters? To start with, it must be pointed out that, with such small numbers of children, a regular distribution should not be expected, and it may even be that if 200 children had been tested at Shiprock instead of 100 the proportion in the "average" group would have been less. Another possibility is that the children sent to school from the Shiprock area are the ones best suited to

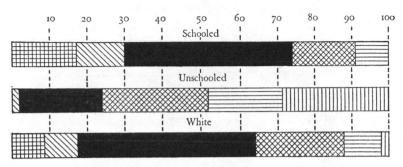

Fig. 4. Distribution of grades of intelligence, Arthur Test, schooled and un-schooled Navaho children and white schoolchildren.

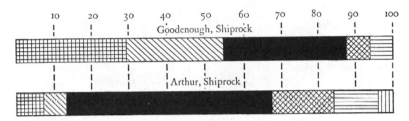

Fig. 5. Distribution of grades of intelligence, Arthur and Goodenough tests, Navaho children at Shiprock.

academic work and that children who do not succeed in school drop out.

In regard to the other two communities, it must be recalled that both at Ramah and Navaho Mountain some of the children tested had been to school and some had not. If the cases for the two areas are combined and then divided into school or non-school children, Table 4 and Figure 4 result.

It is evident that the factor of school education is extremely important in making a good showing on the Arthur Test unless one supposes that only the brighter children go to school. Of the Navaho children who have been to school, there is almost as high a percentage with average IQ's as among the white children, and there is a considerably higher percentage of high-level scores among the Navahos. Of the children who have had no schooling, only 24 per cent make an average or better rating, while 29 per cent appear to be mentally deficient. Although undoubtedly there are some children who are truly below average in intelligence, it is unlikely that there could be such a large percentage because of evidence from observa-

TABLE 4

Percentage Distribution of IQ's Earned on the Grace Arthur Point Performance Scale by Navaho Children (Ramah and Navaho Mountain Combined), Schooled and Unschooled, and by White Schoolchildren

Grade and IQ	Navaho Children [a] Schooled (per cent)	Navaho Children [a] Unschooled (per cent)	White Children [b] Schooled (per cent)
Very superior	17	0	8
135–139	9	...	0.8
130–134	...	...	1.7
125–129	4	...	1.5
120–124	4	...	3.4
Superior	13	2	11
115–119	4	...	4.0
110–114	9	2	6.8
Average	44	22	45
105–109	13	5	9.5
100–104	23	10	10.0
95–99	4	5	10.0
90–94	4	2	15.0
Dull normal	17	28	24
85–89	4	10	13.0
80–84	13	18	11.0
Borderline	9	19	10
75–79	...	7	6.0
70–74	9	12	3.4
Mental deficiency	0	29	2.0
65–69	...	12	1.0
60–64	...	10	1.0
55–59	...	5	...
50–54	...	2	...
Number of children	23	41	409
Median IQ	103.0	81.0	—
Average IQ	102.5	79.8	102.5

	Ramah Schooled	Ramah Unschooled	Navaho Mountain Schooled	Navaho Mountain Unschooled
Number of children	4	29	19	12
Median IQ	103.5	77.5	103	83.0
Average IQ	100	79.5	103	80.3

[a] Data are for children 6–15 years of age.
[b] Data are for children 5–15 years of age. Source: Mary Grace Arthur, *A Point Scale of Performance Tests* (New York: Commonwealth Fund, 1933), Vol. II.

tion and life-performance and estimates of intelligence from Rorschach and Thematic Apperception Tests. It is much more likely that the test fails to measure "native intelligence" and really requires a number of the experiences children meet with in school, even though it does not make use of English, arithmetic, or other subjects taught. Important among these experiences would be familiarity with being told by a strange white person to do an apparently senseless task. Probably also the handling of pencils and toys would give a schoolchild an advantage over one whose life had been mostly spent wandering through the sagebrush with a flock of sheep. It would be incorrect to claim that schooling makes the children more intelligent: rather it helps them to mobilize their own ability so that they can do well on the Arthur Test.

If school experience makes such a difference in IQ earned on this test, one might expect that the older children would tend to make a better showing than the younger ones. This was not the case, and irregularity of schooling may well be the reason. In white schools, a child of six is usually in his first year of training, and with each added year of age he has also another year of school. Navaho children, on the other hand, may begin school at any age from six on, and may drop out for varying periods at any age, so that a fifteen-year-old may be in his second year of school or a twelve-year-old in his sixth. Under these circumstances one could hardly expect a correlation of age with IQ.

There was little difference between boys and girls except at Navaho Mountain where the girls' average IQ was lower than that of the boys. This may well be due to the fact that fewer girls than boys tested had attended school.

The numbers of children are too small to prove beyond all doubt that this is a true picture of Navaho intelligence. However, the figures fit the situation, and it seems likely that, if a hundred times as many children had been tested, the results would still show the same trends and would still depend on the proportion of schooled children to unschooled for absolute values. It appears that, with a comparable amount of school experience, Navaho children would make at least as good a showing as white children. Of the sample tested, 73 per cent were schooled, or more than twice as large a proportion as the 25–30 per cent estimated for the whole Reservation.

From Table 3 and Figure 5 it is easily seen that the same Shiprock children get a considerably higher score on the Goodenough Draw-A-Man Test than on the Arthur Test. It is to be regretted that there are no Goodenough results for the other two areas to show whether children without school experience shared the advantage. The unsophisticated children of Ramah were amused at the instructions which, the interpreter said, sounded as if they were being told to make a husband for the tester, and they did not take the task seriously. In addition, several of them did not draw any pictures. At Navaho Mountain there was not time to do everything needed in the days between the tester's arrival and the closing of school.

In contrast to the Shiprock results, a group of white children from a small midwestern city who drew the Goodenough man and took an intelligence test similar to the Arthur, did less well where they had to picture a man than where the other type of performance was required. Success on the Goodenough requires drawing correct human proportions (within limits) and showing certain details of anatomy and clothing. As in most intelligence tests, the scoring is so arranged that the child of average intelligence should rate an IQ in the neighborhood of 100. On this basis, 73 per cent of the Shiprock children are "average" or better by Goodenough standards, whereas with the Arthur Test only 32 per cent fell in this category. Theoretically about 60 per cent of the white children should obtain "average" or better IQ's. The average IQ's in the two tests for Shiprock Navahos and midwest white children are shown in Table 5.

The Navaho language forces its speakers to pay attention to many details that go unspecified by speakers of English (see *The Navaho*, Chapter 8). While it is impossible to say with certainty that this sort

TABLE 5

Average IQ's for Shiprock Navahos and Midwest White Children, 6 through 11 Years of Age, on Two Intelligence Tests[a]

Test	Shiprock	Midwest
Arthur	94	113[b]
Goodenough	110	101

[a] Data from Robert J. Havighurst, Minna K. Gunther, and Inez Pratt, "Environment and the Draw-A-Man Test: The Performance of Indian Children," *Journal of Abnormal and Social Psychology* 41: 50–63 (1946), Table 1. Arthur average for Shiprock children differs from that shown in Table 3 because that table included older children.

[b] Score on the Cornell-Coxe Test, which is similar to the Arthur.

of language would train Navaho children to note details and proportions of men so that they would draw them more accurately when
asked to do so, still it seems likely that the habit of detailed observation thus engrained would give them an advantage which the more
generalized speech habits of white children fail to provide. It is not
that white children *cannot* observe just as accurately, but simply that
they are less in the habit of doing so from the requirements of their
speech than are Navaho children. Another cultural influence which
may give the Navaho an advantage is the traditional way of learning
new tasks: Navaho children watch and practice; they do not read the
method in a book nor acquire the needed information verbally. This,
too, would make it likely that they would have paid attention to
items which white children might disregard.

In conclusion, it appears that neither of the tests employed gives
a final and convincing evaluation of "intelligence" in all cases. In
the case of the Arthur Test, children who have not been to school
are penalized for their lack of experience, and in the case of the
Goodenough so many Navahos do average or better work that they
must have some advantage. In spite of these facts, and with these
imperfect methods, Navaho children still show as a group nearly the
same range and distribution of intelligence as was found in the group
of white children on whom the Arthur Test was standardized.

In this connection it is interesting to note that most of the five
groups of Indian children tested show consistently higher scores on
the Goodenough Test than on the Arthur. (See Table 6.) The table
also shows that Indian children who had regular school experience
were at no disadvantage on the Arthur Test, as compared with the
white children. Indeed, the Hopi averages were considerably above
those of the white children.

HOW HEALTHY ARE NAVAHO CHILDREN?

WHILE it is debatable whether health is an item in the usual concept
of "personality," few people would argue against the fact that health
plays an important part in the way a child develops. If he is strong
and well, his family will have certain expectations of him that they
will not entertain for a sickly child whom they will "baby" and give
more attention and indulgence than their other children. Moreover, a child who has frequent bouts of illness and suffers restrictions in activity because of them will have less self-confidence, for

TABLE 6

Average IQ's of Groups of Children, 6 through 11 Years of Age,
Tested with Grace Arthur Point Performance Scale
and Goodenough Draw-A-Man Test

Group	Arthur IQ[a]	Goodenough IQ[a]	Schooling Per cent attending school	Attend-ance[b]
Hopi				
Oraibi	112	111	100	R
First Mesa	111	117	100	R
Whites				
Arthur[c]	103	. . .	100	R
Midwest	. . .	101	100	R
Sioux				
Pine Ridge	101	102	100	R
Kyle	99	114	100	R
Zuni	100	112	100	R
Papago				
Topawa	100	109	100	F
Hickiwan	88	104	100	I
Navaho				
Shiprock	94	110	100	F
Navaho Mountain . . .	94[d]	. . .	61	I
Ramah	84[d]	. . .	12	I

[a] Data from Havighurst, Gunther, and Pratt, *loc. cit.*

[b] Symbols: R, regular (or presumably so); F, fairly regular; I, irregular.

[c] This is the Arthur standardization group, 5 through 15 years of age, reported in Arthur, *loc. cit.* Dr. Arthur states that probably a much larger sample drawn from all over the United States would have averaged 100 or less.

[d] These children were 6 through 15 years of age.

example, than one who is able to do whatever he wants. It has been pointed out many times also that state of health is an important determinant of what a child will do in school. In the South, children suffering with hookworm were very dull and apathetic until the infestation was removed. Then their alertness increased greatly. For all these reasons it seemed desirable to find out as much as possible about the health of the Navaho children being tested.

It has been stated before that all the Navaho physical examinations were made by a single physician, so that findings dependent upon

TABLE 7

PERCENTAGES OF NAVAHO CHILDREN SHOWING VARIOUS HEALTH CONDI-
TIONS, AND NUMBERS OF CHILDREN EXAMINED, BY COMMUNITY

Condition	Shiprock (per cent)	Ramah (per cent)	Navaho Mt. (per cent)	Tribal average (per cent)
Good health[a]	20	30	38	31
Undernourishment[b]	25	32	28	27
Decayed teeth[c]	47	54	27	44
Enlarged tonsils[d]	34	41	31	37
Removed tonsils	7	8	5	7
Colds[e]	44	43	31	40
Conjunctivitis[f]	1	5	7	4
Trachoma[g]	20	..	..	8
Tuberculosis suspected[h]	9	..	2	5
Acne[i]	4	9	7	6
Bone deformities[j]	4	3	7	5
Otitis media[k]	7	..	2	4
Miscellaneous[l]	7	14	13	8
Number of children	72	37	42	151

[a] Includes principally those with no physical defect, but also a few with slightly decayed teeth or mild acne.

[b] Largely a clinical judgment, substantiated in many cases by heights and weights. Some children seemed well-nourished at a given height and weight, while others of the same height and weight appeared scrawny, so that dependence upon figures alone would be unsatisfactory. Condition of the skin, amount of musculature, color, and activity, all play a part in "clinical judgment."

[c] Does not include filled teeth, only those uncared for. Except for Shiprock, very few children have any dental care, and even there it is intermittent.

[d] Covers all degrees of enlargement and infection.

[e] Vary in severity from a thick nasal discharge to crusts in the nose.

[f] Includes those cases of reddened eyes without trachoma.

[g] Active in only two cases; a matter of history in all the rest.

[h] Only those cases with X ray evidence of former infection (none active), and one boy who had been several years in a sanatorium and showed certain residua. All schoolchildren at Navaho Mountain had been X rayed a few months before the physical examinations took place because of the discovery of four active cases in the community. All the rest were said to be free of the disease.

[i] The only skin disease encountered, and it was not very severe.

[j] Includes two cases of probable old rickets, badly healed fractures, extra toes, and lost fingers.

[k] Active in only one instance. This figure may be low, as many eardrums were obscured by wax and could not be seen.

[l] Includes results of accidents, subjective visual difficulty, neurological changes in a leg, and scars.

clinical judgment are uniform to that extent. However, it is important to point out that, contrary to the usual lay opinion regarding the exactness of medical science, there are all too few absolute standards to determine health or disease. Two physicians will differ considerably as to what they call an "enlarged tonsil," or as to how thin a child must be before he is described as "undernourished." Such judgments can be refined if laboratory procedures and health histories are obtainable. No new laboratory work was done for this study, but in some cases previous records of X rays and other tests were present on the schoolroom health cards. In some cases also a good health history was available while in others this was entirely lacking.

Among the 151 children examined, the conditions noted in Table 7 were seen.

If the figures are combined for the three communities and arranged according to age-groups, they appear as shown in Table 8.

TABLE 8

PERCENTAGES OF NAVAHO CHILDREN SHOWING VARIOUS HEALTH CONDITIONS, AND NUMBERS OF CHILDREN EXAMINED, BY AGE-GROUPS

Condition [a]	5–7 yrs. (per cent)	8–10 yrs. (per cent)	11–13 yrs. (per cent)	14–18 yrs. (per cent)
Good health	3	13	37	65
Undernourishment	37	29	36	11
Decayed teeth	60	63	32	16
Enlarged tonsils	57	45	34	18
Colds	70	57	30	11
Conjunctivitis	10	5	2	. .
Trachoma	7	8	15	9
Tuberculosis	. .	9	7	4
Acne	. .	. .	3	22
Bone deformities	2	5	9	4
Otitis media	7	3	2	5
Miscellaneous	2	8	6	16
Number of children	30	38	46	37
Blood pressure	88/61	102/63	104/67	118/72
Average height (inches) . . .	45	51½	56½	62½
Average weight (pounds) . . .	46	62	81	116

[a] For definitions and qualifications, see notes to Table 7.

There are no very marked differences between boys and girls with respect to health.

Three rather striking facts emerge from these figures. One is that while Navaho children show a number of minor disease conditions, matters usually considered serious, such as trachoma and tuberculosis, are rare. Second, the older children show considerably fewer physical defects than the younger ones. Third, all things considered, Navaho Mountain children appear to be healthier than children from either Shiprock or Ramah.

As to point one, a number of things must be kept in mind. The largest group of children examined were in school, which means that no seriously ill children were seen. This would not apply at Ramah. Furthermore, there is a chance that, without laboratory tests, conditions present but not outspoken such as mild vitamin deficiencies or early tuberculosis were not detected. The large number of children who appear to be undernourished may be in a state where tuberculosis will develop even though they do not show evidence of it at present. Children who go to school, especially boarding school, regularly gain considerable weight in the first few weeks, sometimes as much as 10 or 15 pounds. Thus undernutrition should be less at Shiprock than elsewhere.

It may help in forming an opinion about Navaho health to see a few figures on the health of white public-school children examined by United States Public Health Service physicians over a five-year period twenty years before the present study. While these children were not comparable to Navaho children in many respects, and while the data are subject to all the qualifications applied to that for Navahos, still the figures are interesting. They are shown in Table 9, not to be taken as the final truth about white child health but to provide some basis for understanding the implications of the Navaho figures. In these few items, it can be seen that there is not much difference between these aspects of the health of white and Navaho children, except that Navahos seem to have better teeth and that their rate of tuberculosis is higher. It should be noted that the white tuberculosis rate is based on physical examination only, by which standard the Navaho figure would fall to 0.7 per cent.

That the figures do not give a full picture of health among Navaho children is evidenced by eye-witness accounts of the devastating epidemics of measles and other "childhood diseases," and by the com-

TABLE 9

PERCENTAGES OF WHITE AND NAVAHO CHILDREN SHOWING
VARIOUS HEALTH CONDITIONS

Condition	Whites[a] (per cent)	Navahos (per cent)
Good health	25	31
Decayed teeth	66	44
Enlarged tonsils	31	37
Removed tonsils	16	7
Tuberculosis or suspicion	0.3	5

[a] Data from Selwyn D. Collins, *Health of the School Child*, U. S. Public Health Service, Public Health Bulletin No. 200 (Washington: Government Printing Office, 1931).

parison, family after family, between the number of children who have been born and the number who survive. While vital statistics are still extremely unreliable among The People, talks with mothers give a strong impression that infant mortality is very high. Thus the children examined may be "naturally selected" for resistance to disease and general vigor as compared to the ones who never reached school age.

The second point raised for discussion is the difference in health between the younger and older children. One might conclude from the table that as the children grow older they also grow healthier. This is not necessarily the case, however, for the figures do not represent the same children at different ages, but different children of various ages. If survival of the fittest plays a part in the figures for the whole group, there is no reason to suppose that it ceases to operate when the child reaches six years. Thus, children between six and eighteen who become seriously ill have three alternatives: they recover, and may have acquired some immunity to their disease; they die; they remain invalids and are either kept at home or stay in a hospital. Except at Ramah, the examinations would have been limited to individuals in the first category.

Point three is that Navaho Mountain children appear to be healthier than the other two groups. This is particularly interesting in view of the fact that the average income is lowest there and that, by white standards, The People at Navaho Mountain are the most "backward." A number of factors may be responsible for this difference.

In the first place, since Navaho Mountain is primarily a herding

NAVAHOS LIKE THE COMICS TOO

WOMAN SHOWING SHYNESS

area, the diet may be more adequate because it contains more meat than that of the other localities. Moreover, all the meat comes from animals slaughtered at home (at Shiprock some may be bought), so that the blood and all the entrails add their contribution to nutrition and may play an important part in supplying needed vitamins and minerals. In addition, Navaho Mountain people probably use more hand-ground corn meal than milled flour; this too provides vitamins and minerals lacking in the more refined product. At both Shiprock and Ramah the higher incomes make it possible for The People to buy flour instead of grinding corn laboriously; although many families use their corn, they probably use more flour in proportion than at Navaho Mountain. Thus, while the Shiprock children may possibly have more to eat, particularly in number of calories, the Navaho Mountain children may have food that supplies their vitamin and mineral needs more adequately and so lays a better foundation for health. The relatively small amount of tooth decay at Navaho Mountain tends to substantiate this.

Another factor of importance is the sparse population, for germ-caused diseases will have less chance to spread where there is much space between families than where they are relatively close together. Related to this is the small number of white contacts. While white people need not necessarily be less healthy than Navahos, they may carry to the Navahos diseases to which they themselves are immune but to which the Navahos are highly susceptible.

It will be noted that Ramah seems to be the least healthy of the three communities. Here the income is lower than at Shiprock, but the sheep are probably fewer than at Navaho Mountain. The population density at Ramah is a little less than at Shiprock if only Navahos are counted, but, with the addition of the white people who live among the Navahos, the number of people per square mile exceeds that of Shiprock. Moreover, contacts with white men are frequent. Most important, perhaps, is that Ramah children were examined at home, so that family selection of school children on a health basis played no role.

As to the children's physical fitness, then, one could say that they do not seem to be seriously handicapped here any more than they are in regard to their intellectual endowment. However, it must not be forgotten that the basis for such an opinion is much less sound in the case of their health than in the case of their "intelligence."

7.

SOME ATTITUDES AND INTERESTS
of NAVAHO CHILDREN

MATERIAL for this chapter comes from the children's responses to the Psychological Battery mentioned in Chapter 5. Although this Battery had several different parts, only two are utilized here: Stewart's Emotional Response Test and Bavelas' Moral Ideology Test.

For the Emotional Response Test, the examiner begins by asking the child, "Have you ever been happy?" If he says, "Yes," as is usually the case, the examiner then says, "Tell me a time when you were happy." While some children will deny that they were ever happy when thus called upon for an instance, and others will say that they are happy all the time, or that they are happy "over every little thing that comes up," a good proportion will produce an adequate example of happy occasions. The examiner endeavors to secure three such examples, then continues the questioning with sadness, fear, anger, and shame. Finally he asks, "What is the best thing that could happen to you?" and "What is the worst thing that could happen to you?"

If the average number of responses made by Navaho children to the various questions are arranged in order beginning with the question most freely answered, this list results: Fear, 3.0 responses per child; Happiness, 2.5; Shame, 1.4; Sadness, 1.3; Anger, 1.1; Best Thing, 1.0 (only one was requested); Worst Thing, 0.8. Examples of the responses obtained from a few children are reproduced in Appendix I. The order for middle-western white children who took the same test was: Happiness, 2.9; Sadness, 2.3; Anger, 2.3; Fear, 2.2; Shame, 1.9; Best Thing, 1.1; Worst Thing, 0.8.[1]

The Moral Ideology Test consists in asking the child, "What is a good thing that a boy (or girl) your age could do so that people

---

[1] Comparative data for white and Indian children used in this chapter are from Robert J. Havighurst, "Comparison of American Indian Children and White Children by Means of the Emotional Response Test" and "The Comparison of Indian Children and White Children by Means of the Moral Ideology Test" (both ms., Indian Education Research Project, University of Chicago).

would praise him (her) or be pleased?" After the child responds, he is asked, "Who would praise him (her) or be pleased?" Three examples are requested. Then the same questions are repeated with "bad" and "blame" substituted for "good" and "praise." The average number of examples of "good" and "bad" acts given by each child was 5.8 (6 were requested), while the average number of "praisers" and "blamers" was 8.7 (6 were requested).

At the Universtity of Chicago the children's responses were studied and were grouped into different categories. One such category of the "Happiness" responses was Holidays (celebrating native feasts; tribal ceremonials; participating in tribal dances; celebrating Fourth of July or other white-culture holidays; birthdays; weddings). Eventually one could see certain themes emerging from the material. The persons involved in the responses, as praisers or blamers in the Moral Ideology Test and in association with the different "emotions" in the Emotional Response Test, were also studied.

It should be pointed out that both these tests required the child to give examples of behavior — some his own, some that of a hypothetical "child of his age." His choice would undoubtedly be conditioned by his willingness to appear in an unfavorable light (as in Shame), by his notion of what the examiner would approve or disapprove and his relationship to her, by cultural values regarding the "emotions" and "morals" under examination, and by whether he felt himself the subject of discussion or really was thinking of the abstract "child his age."

Under these circumstances it is impossible to list the examples given and suppose that this is the complete range of conditions under which Navaho children feel happy, angry, sad, and so on, or that this and this constitutes "good behavior" to Navahos while that and that is "bad behavior." It can be said with assurance that these are the items the Navaho children mentioned when questioned, but it must be borne in mind that there may be other equally or more important items which they either unconsciously or purposely suppressed or forgot to mention. For example, at Shiprock the small children frequently named the ch'įįdii, which is variously translated "ghost" or "evil spirit," as a thing that frightened them, while older children rarely spoke of it. At Navaho Mountain, on the other hand, children of all ages spoke of the ch'įįdii freely. This difference might be due to greater sophistication and a giving up of tribal ideology to some extent by older children at Shiprock, or it might represent a recognition based on bitter experience that white people don't believe in *ch'įįdii* and make fun of Navahos who do. Although the Battery was administered by a Navaho teacher at Shiprock, still the setting was white, and the teacher herself may have seemed more white than Navaho to the children.

The difference between Navaho and white children in the rank order of the average number of responses to the various "emotions" illustrates what is meant by the way in which cultural values will affect the test. The Navaho list is headed by instances of Fear, while this ranks fourth for white children; Anger is second for white children, fifth for Navahos. Fear plays a large and important role in Navaho life and much energy is devoted to expelling the presumed sources of it. In white society, by contrast, fear is belittled and scorned and children are taught, "You mustn't be afraid." It is not necessarily that white children have no fear but rather that they would be less inclined to admit it. Similarly the acceptance of anger in the two cultures varies: Navaho children are taught to avoid it or any expression of it, while the English phrase "righteous indignation" indicates that, at least under some circumstances, anger is not only permissible but proper for whites. It is possible, of course, that Navaho culture offers more things to fear and that white culture provides more sources of anger.

SIGNIFICANT THEMES FROM THE EMOTIONAL RESPONSE AND MORAL IDEOLOGY TESTS

1. POSSESSIONS AND PROPERTY

One of the striking findings of these tests is the large part played by property or possessions of various kinds. Having or receiving property is an occasion for happiness or a "best thing that could happen" to a large proportion of the Navaho children; loss of property gives rise to sadness or anger or is a "worst thing that could happen." Acquisition seems more important at Navaho Mountain, and loss at Shiprock.[2] Navaho Mountain children specify sheep or other livestock as the kind of property they are interested in, while manufactured articles compete with livestock in the desires of the Ship-

---

[2] In this chapter findings for Shiprock and Navaho Mountain only will be discussed. The Ramah children did not produce enough responses for satisfactory evaluation. This may have been for the same reasons as their poor performance on the Arthur Test. In a number of cases, the Battery was not attempted because of the child's inarticulateness; in others almost all questions were answered with "I don't know."

rock children. Navaho children far exceed all other tribes tested in this preoccupation with property; they even go beyond the middle-western white children, although the latter approach them rather closely in some respects.

2. IMPORTANCE OF THE FAMILY

Not only do the children say that they are happy when the family is doing things together or when relatives visit, but they recall as sad occasions times when family members go away or are removed by death. This is even more strikingly the case at Navaho Mountain than at Shiprock. While white children associate "happiness" with the family to about the same degree, loss of family members seems to impress them less than it does the Navahos.

It seems likely that this difference may be accounted for by the difference in family structure in the two societies. The Navaho family is large, and each child has not a single but several "mothers" and "fathers" as well as additional "brothers" and "sisters." While emotional ties to a given individual may not be as intense in these circumstances as in the white family, still each child has more than one "father" (for example) that he can lose. Moreover, in Navaho life it is often necessary for wage earners to be away from home entirely for considerable periods of time rather than for the daily eight hours common in white society. Thus "loss of family members" is a usual experience for a Navaho child. Although he may not be as deeply attached to his real father as is a white child, he will be more affected if his father's brother or mother's brother goes away than a white child would be at the departure of an uncle.

If a count is made of all the different people named in connection with the instances of the various "emotions," it shows that about half the list is of family members, which is also the case for the white children. If, however, they are separated into those who stand in a positive relationship to the child (that is, those associated with Happiness and Best Thing), and those who stand in a negative relationship (Fear, Anger, Shame [3]), family members make up more than three quarters of the positive list and only a third of the negative list for Navahos, while they fill slightly more than half of both lists for the white children. Thus the Navaho family appears to be chiefly

[3] Note that Sadness is left out, as not being clearly either "positive" or "negative," and Worst Thing because hardly any persons were mentioned.

a source of security, while the white family has mixed associations for its children.

When the responses are studied for the part played by different family members and non-relatives, the distribution shown in Table 10 appears. A few points worth noting here are: the small part played

TABLE 10

Persons Associated with Various Emotions by Navaho Children, as Indicated by Percentages of Their Test Responses Concerning These Emotions

| | Percentage of Responses Concerning — | | | |
| | Happiness plus Best Thing | | Fear, Anger, Shame | |
	Shiprock	Navaho Mt.	Shiprock	Navaho Mt.
Family (all responses) . .	76	85	26	43
Whole family	13	18	5	5
Father	37	24	2	. . .
Mother	16	14	5	4
Siblings, same sex[a] . . .	8	23	9	17
Siblings, opposite sex . .	2	6	5	17
Nonrelatives	24	15	74	57

[a] Siblings are brothers or sisters.

by parents in Fear, Anger, and Shame at either place and their considerable association with Happiness and Best Thing; the greater difference in importance of father and mother at Shiprock; the more frequent mention of brothers and sisters at Navaho Mountain.

There are some interesting differences between boys' and girls' relationships to family members, as shown in Table 11. The boys appear to associate their fathers with Happiness; the girls, their mothers. The girls seem more aware of both brothers and sisters than do the boys. White children show fewer differences between boys and girls in these respects.

A study of the "praisers" and "blamers" of the Moral Ideology Test shows that family members constitute about three quarters of the list. At Shiprock there are few instances of individual members being named; where they are specified, there is not much difference in their relationship to the boys or girls. At Navaho Mountain, on the other hand, father, mother, and grandparents are mentioned fairly often. For Navaho Mountain boys, the mother and grandparents are equally praisers and blamers, while the father is mostly

a praiser. For the girls, mother and grandparents are equally important and are most often praisers, while the father plays a considerably
smaller part and blames as much as he praises. Thus the role of the
family appears here also to be a large one, and the positive relation
between mother and daughter or father and son is repeated. It is

TABLE 11

PERSONS ASSOCIATED BY NAVAHO BOYS AND GIRLS WITH VARIOUS EMOTIONS,
AS INDICATED BY PERCENTAGES OF THEIR TEST RESPONSES
CONCERNING THESE EMOTIONS

| | Percentage of Response Concerning — | | | |
| | Happiness plus Best Thing | | Fear, Anger, Shame | |
Persons	Boys	Girls	Boys	Girls
Family (all responses) . .	77	75	21	47
Whole family	15	15	3	7
Father	47	14	2	. . .
Mother	5	24	4	4
Siblings, same sex . . .	10	21	8	18
Siblings, opposite sex . .	. . .	. . .	4	18
Nonrelatives	11	12	47	40
Agemates, same sex . .	. . .	. . .	12	10
School and teacher . . .	. . .	. . .	10	6
"They," "somebody" . .	11	12	25	24
Scattered responses	12	14	32	13

of interest that, for the white children tested, family members make
up less than half of the list, and the mother is much more often
named by both boys and girls and as either praiser or blamer than
is the father.

It is surprising that the mother's brother is very rarely mentioned
specifically. Possibly he is lost in translation, or perhaps the child
has him in mind when he speaks of "the family."

3. SICKNESS AND HEALTH

This theme is discussed because of the focusing of Navaho religion upon matters of curing; because of the part "toughening," or
health-building, practices play in traditional child training; and because of the alleged prevalence of illness among the Navahos. As has
been seen, actual physical examinations failed to reveal a startling
health problem, but they told only part of the story.

Health is never named as a reason for happiness or as a Best Thing. It is probably taken too much for granted by all the children to warrant mentioning. Overt references to illness, accident, and death of self or others occur, but not in as large proportion as one might expect. For example, they play no greater part than absence of family members or loss of property among the instances of Sadness; and they make up only a quarter of the dreaded Worst Things.

At the same time it is important to observe that more than a third of things feared and of Worst Things can be categorized as "supernatural." It has been explained in *The Navaho* that the *ch'įįdii*, "witches," and animals of supernatural associations are feared in large part because they are believed either to produce illness or to warn of approaching illness or death. Unquestionably the smaller children have learned to fear only the creatures themselves, but it is quite likely that among older children references to these dangerous supernaturals cloak a concern with illness.

In a study of the sources of uneasiness and fear among Navahos,[4] as found in field notes collected during a four months' residence with them in 1940, it appeared probable that the fears associated verbally with occurrences of supernatural significance, such as breaking the rules of religious behavior, coyotes crossing one's path, or the evil effect of spirits and corpses, implied a fear of the results of these events to health. Sometimes this could be verified by asking, "Well, what harm does it do if a coyote crosses your path?" This might be answered, "It means something bad is going to happen." "What kind of bad thing?" "Somebody is going to get sick, maybe." These data are presented not as proof of the foregoing argument, but as independent evidence which seems to shed some enlightenment on the material of the present study. The tests used did not require finding reasons for the responses offered by the children; if they had, it is questionable whether many of the children would have been able to explain the why's of their feelings.

4. WORK AND PLAY

Play is so generally thought to be a child's prerogative that Navaho attitudes towards work and play as seen in the tests are worth discussing. Various sorts of play, pleasure, or fun are given as about

[4] A. H. Leighton and D. C. Leighton, "Some Sources of Uneasiness and Fear in a Navaho Indian Community," *American Anthropologist*, XLIV (1942), 194–209.

10 per cent of the occasions when the children were happy or as "best things that could happen." Activities of this sort occur as about 4 per cent of the "good things a boy your age could do." Examples of work have a part of approximately the same size in the responses concerning Happiness. They outnumber instances of play at Navaho Mountain and are outnumbered by play at Shiprock. Work is the leading item among "good (or bad) things a boy your age could do." [5] This is common to all but one of the Indian tribes studied, and amounts to at least 50 per cent of the responses, whereas it makes up only about 10 to 20 per cent of the responses of the white children.

Can one conclude from these figures that to Navaho children play is of little moment, and that they are on the whole (with other Indian children) more serious-minded than white children? To do so would probably be to oversimplify the facts. It is doubtless true that Navaho children start "working" younger than white children, but it is not at all sure that they regard this as a hardship or as an interruption of their "play." From the description of Navaho childhood in Part I, it might well be that little distinction is made between work and play. "Play" becomes "work" at times and vice versa. Thus, while the little shepherd works by taking the sheep out in the morning, he spends considerable periods of the time while watching them graze in playing with them or the dog or his fellow shepherd or the sticks and rocks around. Nor is play only for children and work only for adults; all ages do both as it becomes possible or necessary, as a natural and expected matter.

It is a question of attached values, this difference between white and Navaho point of view. The Navaho expects to work, and the little child finds that when he brings in a few pieces of wood he is praised, whereas if he just flings them around outside no one takes any notice of it. The white child expects to play. Too often, when he tries to help his elders, he is told not to meddle or to run outside and keep out of the way. If he is asked to do some work, he feels that his playing time is being taken from him, whereas the Navaho child feels that he is being given an opportunity to participate in the family activity. Naturally there are times and circumstances when what has been said for the Navaho would apply to the white child, and the reverse; yet there seems to be an over-all difference

[5] Work appears as a "good thing to do," and not to work or to neglect one's work as a "bad thing to do."

in emphasis, at least, between white and Navaho attitudes which are reflected in the test results.

5. "GUILT" OR "CONSCIENCE"

Feelings of this sort appear in the responses to Shame in so far as the test material shows them. When this section was analyzed and the instances grouped into categories, the responses were distributed as in Table 12. From this table it can be seen that Shame for

TABLE 12

RESPONSES OF NAVAHO AND WHITE CHILDREN CONCERNING SHAME; PERCENTAGE DISTRIBUTION BY SOURCE OF SHAME

Source of Shame	Percentage of Responses		
	Shiprock	Navaho Mt.	White
Self-consciousness	39	43	12
Making poor personal appearance .	27	22	10
Embarrassment before others	12	21	2
Guilt	20	16	49
Failure or inadequacy	3	11	21
Bad behavior and aggressiveness . .	17	5	28
Other scattered responses	41	41	39

Navaho children is more often a sort of surface sensation related to impressions they make on other people than it is a deep, internalized feeling concerned with how they measure up to abstract standards of behavior. The first might be called "self-consciousness," and the second "guilt," while the standards which give rise to the guilt feelings might be designated "conscience." It is obvious that for white children the emphasis is just the opposite, with more evidence of guilt than self-consciousness.

On the basis of these findings one might expect a white child to feel uncomfortable and "guilty" after stealing an orange whether anyone found out about it or not, whereas a Navaho child would be more likely to enjoy the orange without feeling guilt, but would be "self-conscious" if someone caught him. Of course there are times when a Navaho will feel "guilty" and when a white child will feel "self-conscious" instead, but here only the predominant pattern is being considered. Even white adults tend to act under the restraint of "shame" rather than "conscience" at times, especially in sexual activities.

This difference is a frequent source of misunderstanding on the part of white persons, who are accustomed to associating with people who act from "conscience." When a Navaho culprit gives no evidence of feeling guilty over his misdemeanor, but only shamefaced that he was caught, it is taken as a sign that he is somehow morally deficient. The fact probably is simply that he was trained differently. Had he been taken as an infant by a white family and brought up in a white community, he would have learned a list of actions that were "right" and others that were "wrong," and, furthermore, that there was an all-seeing Power, represented in his own "soul" by his "conscience," that kept account of what he did and held him responsible. He would then feel "guilty" when he misbehaved. If he were brought up by a Navaho family in a Navaho community instead, he would have learned that there are certain things one should not do because "other people" do not approve of them, and there are certain others that are dangerous because, if one does them, supernatural forces will be set to work that may cause illness or death to the offender or his relatives. However, it is implied that if he wishes to take the risk of bringing on himself either sort of hazard, it is up to him. Thus he would have little reason for feeling anything except chagrin that he hadn't been able to "get away with" his deed.

Moreover, it is certain that many of the items on the list of "wrong" deeds in white ideology are the same as those of which "other people" disapprove and even those which offend the supernaturals in Navaho culture. The difference is not one of presence or absence of "moral standards," but rather a different mechanism for enforcing those standards.

The introduction of white notions on the subject has the effect of weakening the force of the Navaho sanctions. The white people teach the Navaho that, if his "conscience" is clear, it does not matter what other people think of him, and the idea that Navaho supernaturals can cause any trouble is ridiculous; but by the time they are doing this the child is probably too old to develop the sort of "conscience" they speak of. Thus he is left without many restraints beyond a desire to maintain the good will of his new teachers. If later he loses interest in them, the restraints are few indeed.

6. AIMS AND AMBITIONS

Some hint of the expectations and hopes of Navaho children can be found in the answers to the question, "What is the best thing that could happen to you?" Responses were distributed as in Table 13.

TABLE 13

Test Responses of Navaho and White Children Concerning "The Best Thing That Could Happen"; Percentage Distribution

	Shiprock	Navaho Mt.	White
Having or obtaining property 44		52	23
Pleasure or fun 16		14	23
Ambitions and achievements 9		7	26
Other scattered responses 31		27	28

There is quite a striking preponderance of interest in property as a "best thing" for Navaho children, and by contrast the concern with achievements of a nonmaterial sort play a small part. The few times such items were named they were usually "to finish my schooling" or "to get an education," which were just the things the white children mentioned. One wonders why they never spoke of becoming a Singer or a good weaver or an expert silversmith. It may be because the testing was done in a white setting, or because being a Singer or a good weaver is something that belongs to older people. Or it may be simply a part of Navaho "informality" and their tendency to let nature take its course, as suggested in earlier chapters, which would make it unlikely for children to plan their futures very definitely.

Whatever its roots, it seems that this lack of drive in the direction of nonmaterial achievement, which leads many white people to undertake the professions, may keep Navahos from entering the teaching, administrative, or medical fields in any numbers. For unless one feels that the intellectual accomplishment is worth while in itself, and unless the surrounding group accords prestige for such accomplishment, there is little incentive to spend long years in school. Particularly is this true if, after spending the long years, one returns to his people to practice what he has learned and finds he cannot earn any more money than a fellow tribesman who spent only a few years at school and then got a job driving a truck. White people are willing to spend the time required, and even to work for years at a low salary in a professional job, because their friends and families admire them for being "intellectual," ask their advice, and in general hold them in high esteem which compensates in some measure for lack of a better income. To a large extent these compensations are lacking to a Navaho who achieves higher education, and in fact he is somewhat suspect for having turned to white men's ways, so that if the salary is low, there is practically no advantage to him at all.

THE NAVAHO CHILD AS PICTURED BY THESE TESTS

SUPPOSING the items discussed in this chapter were the only things known about the Navahos, what could be said of their general characteristics? To begin with, it is quite obvious that The People are not particularly incomprehensible. They have a number of interests and attitudes that are entirely familiar to white people. Beyond that, one might draw the following inferences:

1. The Navahos must be a practical folk to have so much concern for property and for work. One might hazard the guess that livestock is more important at Navaho Mountain than at Shiprock, since it is the sort of property that Navaho Mountain children mention oftenest.

2. There seem to be good feelings among members of the family. Parents particularly have pleasant associations for their children. Sex divisions are fairly definite, the boys aligning themselves with the fathers and the girls with the mothers. Persons beyond the limits of the family are felt to be something of a threat. Thus one might surmise that the family is a warm, affectionate group which keeps a good deal to itself, a situation which would be intensified by the sensitivity of the children to the kind of appearance they make to "other people."

3. Supernatural creatures are both real and dreadful to the children. This goes far beyond the concern of white children with "bogeymen" and corresponds more nearly to the place held by "devils" and "evil spirits" (of spiritual or human form) in European society in bygone centuries and among some European peasants even today. While little is said of the positive, supporting aspects of their religion, the fact that they have such a lively awareness of the negative aspects indicates that religion plays an important part in their lives.

8.

PERSONALITY TRAITS
in NAVAHO CHILDREN

IN THE preceding chapter certain themes were discussed which were
derived from answers of the Navaho children to questions the exam-
iners asked them. In the present chapter attention will be turned to
characteristics that are revealed in tests when the child does not
realize he is talking about himself. These are the Projective Tests
(the Free Drawings, Thematic Apperception, and Rorschach) mentioned in Chapter 5. In the items the child selects to draw and the
way he arranges these items; in the actions, interrelations, and motives he ascribes to the people in the Thematic Apperception pictures;
in the parts of the Rorschach blots he picks out, the form or color or
shading he notices, the sort of objects he sees in the meaningless blot
— in all these, he indicates how the world appears to him and how
he reacts to it.

Because the drawings are the least standardized of these three tests,
they have been less thoroughly analyzed than the others. Study of
them has been limited to investigating what they show regarding
the degree of acculturation as seen in the objects the children include
in their pictures. The reader may see an analysis including other
factors in Appendix II.

The Thematic Apperception Test was considerably modified from
the form in which Murray used it. Line drawings covering a variety
of situations involving people were prepared by an Indian artist.
These were shown to each child, one after the other, with the request
that he tell what the people were doing and saying. Samples of the
"stories" produced as a result are in Appendix I. By studying the
whole series of stories from a single child, much can be learned about
his pattern of reaction and interpersonal relations. By studying the
stories about any one picture from all the Navaho children, the range
of ideas regarding this situation can be determined, as well as the
"average" notion of how the characters would be behaving, and the
reaction patterns of the group can be inferred.

The Rorschach Test was administered, scored, and interpreted according to instructions in Klopfer and Kelley, *The Rorschach Technique*, without any special modifications. Samples of the responses are in Appendix I. Many of the Navaho children said they had sometimes looked at the clouds to see what they resembled, and so they were not greatly baffled by being asked to do the same thing for the blots. Since some aspects of this test can be expressed in figures or percentages, it is the easiest of the three to use for getting an idea of the "average" performance of the whole group, of the boys or girls, or of different age levels. However, since the figures themselves are stated in highly technical terms, they are placed in Appendix I, while their implications will be discussed in this chapter.

Because the drawings have been analyzed from such a different point of view from the other two tests, their results will be discussed separately, while the findings of the Thematic Apperception and Rorschach will be combined.

GENERAL CHARACTERISTICS

THE Navaho drawings blaze with color. In some, considerable artistic skill is shown; in others, very little. Mostly the colors are realistic, but there is little attempt to mix colors to produce a hue to match reality exactly. Generally the children were content to use the prepared paint which most closely resembled the object. Generally, also, they drew the forms with pencil and then colored them. The average number of different items per picture was six. In the pictures drawn by the whole group of children, various items appeared in the following proportions:

Item	Percentage	Item	Percentage
Landscape	38	Transportation	4
Dwellings	17	War and patriotism	3
Humans	14	School	2
Animals	11	Crafts	2
Other buildings	8	Ceremonial items	0

In order to evaluate material acculturation, the objects drawn were separated into Landscape, Native, Early White Derivatives, Recent White Derivatives. For purposes of comparison, landscape and early white derivatives were considered "neutral." Landscape certainly shows nothing about acculturation, and objects derived originally from white culture but so thoroughly integrated into the Navaho way of life that they are thought of as Navaho do not shed much light on the present state of cultural interaction. The proportions were:

Item	*Percentage*	*Item*	*Percentage*
Landscape	38	Recent white	23
Early white	12	Native	27

Thus, for the tribe as a whole there is only a slight preponderance of objects from Navaho culture over objects from recent white culture. From this it might be inferred that although the Navaho children are familiar with white products, so far their own ways have not been displaced by white ways of living.

Both the stories of the Thematic Apperception and the responses of the Rorschach tend to be short, literal, commonplace descriptions with little elaboration or imaginative detail. The reader will notice that this is at variance with what was said of Navaho imagination in Chapter 4. People are identified as individuals rather than simply categorized, and details of personal adornment and attitudes are noticed. While the total environment, both physical and social, seems to be rather limited, within those limits the individual, as he shows himself in these tests, exercises considerable freedom of choice.

Family relations appear from the tests to be fairly smooth. The mother and father divide the responsibilities between them and do not lay duties prematurely upon the children. Parental control is definite but not excessive. Adults in general do not appear domineering, and the children show no generalized hostility toward older people. Rivalry between different children in the family is not especially marked. The first control felt comes from the parents, but later in life this is replaced by pressure from society. Various expressions of aggression are common without evoking a rebuke. The children show a notable lack of guilt feelings over infractions of rules.

Although society demands a considerable degree of conformity, individuality is maintained in a number of ways. One of these is through artistic pursuits, another through variations in clothing and jewelry. Respect for individual differences seems fundamental in Navaho interpersonal relations. Interactions between persons are on an emotional basis and are dependent upon individual motivation rather than upon rules set by the society. Thus, for example, a child

"STAND STILL NOW WHILE I DRY YOU"

VISITORS AT A DAY SCHOOL

AN EXPERIMENT — FREE PLAY WITH ANIMAL TOY

might call all his mother's sisters "mother" and yet might behave much more affectionately towards the one he liked best than towards the others, without censure.

The children's primary concern is with everyday matters. They are essentially practical and matter-of-fact and are not impressed with abstract goals or intellectual achievement for its own sake.

They are very aware of the world about them. On the whole they handle their reactions to it more successfully than they manage the impulses that arise within themselves.

AGE AND SEX DIFFERENCES

As might be expected, the projective tests show certain differences between boys' and girls' personalities and between those of older and younger children. In reading the following sections, it is important to bear in mind that the results reported are for different groups of children of various ages, rather than for a single sample of children as they progress from the age of six to eighteen. In other words some of the differences seen may be the result of unique experiences of a certain age group, such as severe epidemics or economic hard times, rather than of fairly constant molding forces which all children will encounter.

IN FREE DRAWINGS

About the only noteworthy difference in the sorts of things children of different ages draw is the shift from houses and people among the five- to seven-year-olds to landscapes for the older children. The boys tend to draw more animals, structures other than houses, and objects dealing with war and patriotism, while the girls draw more houses. The evidence of acculturation is shown in Table 14.

The preponderance of influence shifts from the white culture

TABLE 14

EVIDENCES OF ACCULTURATION IN ITEMS INCLUDED IN THE FREE DRAWINGS OF NAVAHO CHILDREN, BY AGE AND BY SEX

	Age				Sex	
	5–7 yrs. (per cent)	8–10 yrs. (per cent)	11–13 yrs. (per cent)	14–18 yrs. (per cent)	All Boys (per cent)	All Girls (per cent)
Recent white[a]	32	24	22	20	25	22
Native[a]	30	24	27	26	22	31

[a] For definition of these categories, see p. 175.

to the native culture with age. The girls appear to be more conservative than the boys.

Comparison of the figures of Table 14 with those of Table 17
(p. 181) below indicates that the percentages of recent white and
native objects drawn by the five- to seven-year-old children at Shiprock strongly influence the tribal average for the five- to seven-year
age group, for children of this age at both Ramah and Navaho
Mountain draw more native than recent white items. Whether or
not the percentages in Table 14, or of any of the tables showing tribal
averages, can be taken as representative of the tribal situation depends
upon whether or not the sample of children tested was adequately
representative of Navaho children as a whole. It has already been
indicated that, while the writers feel that the three localities chosen
for testing were representative of the range of variation within the
tribe qualitatively, there is as yet no way of telling what the exact
quantitative proportions of these types of Navaho subcultures are
within the larger group.

Results of the Rorschach and Thematic Apperception Tests can be
stated by ages as follows.

Five to seven years. At this age the children are rather shy and unable to express themselves easily, even in their own language. Their
concepts are often rather vague, and it is impossible to get them to
specify what they mean. They are, on the whole, quite restrained,
and they control their reactions consciously. They are less controlled
in their relations to the outer world than in giving expression to their
inner urges. They are a little anxious in a general way and feel subject to their parents' authority.

Eight to ten years. At this age the children begin to blossom out
in every respect as compared to the younger ones. There is increased
evidence of spontaneity and decrease of conscious control. Their
stories are longer and their ideas for the Rorschach more numerous.
They show more imagination and originality. They are quite sensitive to their social environment and react freely and even impulsively to it. They are less aware of their parents' control over them
than are the younger children. Their inner life, which earlier seemed
either lacking or suppressed, is now seen to be developing and is
given considerable expression. Their primary concern is with matter-

of-fact commonplaces, which shows them to be essentially practical and realistic in their attitudes. All groups of children who have been examined — Indian, white, and others — show such a period of florescence at some time between eight and twelve years.

Eleven to thirteen years. These children are entering adolescence, and there are evidences of the "adolescent withdrawal" at Shiprock, though it is not yet apparent at Ramah and Navaho Mountain. Many physiologic changes are taking place, and "instinctive" urges which the children do not know how to handle are awakening. They are growing up and are big enough to take an almost adult part in economic and social life. Their responsibilities increase, and they can no longer "get away with" a childish performance in their duties.

The two tests reflect the withdrawal both quantitatively and qualitatively. In many respects the performance of the children of this age resembles that of the five- to seven-year-olds. An important difference is that these older children feel themselves being controlled by society, whereas the younger children attribute authority to their parents alone.

Intellectual functions are called upon to control and regulate reactions more frequently than in the younger age-groups. This is much more successful in relation to contacts with the outer world than in relation to their own inner urges. This sort of control is what is called "maturity" in terms of the Rorschach Test, and the concept is based necessarily on what is found in adults in white society, sub-adults being rated more or less mature as they approach the adult pattern more or less closely. In the eleven-to-thirteen age-period, most of the girls have achieved the adult pattern in respect to their behavior toward the outer world, while the number of boys who have done so is much smaller. No doubt this is an expression of the girls' earlier awareness of and conformity to social control. There are more "extroverts" among them, and they show more sensitivity to the social environment than the boys. When one looks at the way in which both boys and girls handle their "instinctual" urges, on the other hand, he finds that they express them with very little intellectual censorship and in a way that would be rated quite "immature" by comparison with white adults. These instinctual urges are probably largely sexual in nature. When it is remembered that Navahos are much less restrained about sexual behavior in most respects than are white people, it seems possible that what looks like immaturity by white standards may be a reasonably mature *Navaho* mode of reacting.

Fourteen to eighteen years. In this period the withdrawal noted previously in Shiprock children becomes more extreme and appears also at Ramah and Navaho Mountain. Spontaneity is even further reduced, the stories are shorter, and the responses to the Rorschach are the fewest of any age-group. There is the greatest awareness of external pressures, and the majority of both the boys and girls have learned to handle their reactions to the outer world in a "mature" way by white standards. As before, relatively few of them (about one third) manage their "instinctual" urges in the controlled manner of white adults. They are at the threshhold of adulthood and will doubtless show further changes in their patterns of reaction when they become more sure of themselves and thus able to loosen the tight hold they have on their behavior at this age.

REGIONAL VARIATIONS

OBJECTS drawn by children in the three communities were classified as shown in Table 15. These items may be grouped into the cate-

TABLE 15

CLASSES OF ITEMS IN THE FREE DRAWINGS OF NAVAHO CHILDREN,
BY COMMUNITY

Item	Shiprock (*per cent*)	Ramah (*per cent*)	Navaho Mt. (*per cent*)
Landscape	38	31	42
Animals	7	20	11
Humans	11	16	16
Dwellings	19	9	19
Other structures	9	5	8
Transportation	4	6	4
War and patriotism	6	3	0
School	5	0	0
Crafts	1	11	0

gories used to study acculturation (see p. 175), as shown in Table 16. From this, one can conclude that, as far as material acculturation is concerned, Shiprock shows the highest degree of white influence and Navaho Mountain the least, with Ramah between.

In the discussion of age and sex differences it was shown that the evidence of white influence is greatest among the smallest children and decreases as the children grow up. Table 17 shows these age changes for each community. From Table 17 it appears that Ship-

TABLE 16

EVIDENCES OF ACCULTURATION IN ITEMS SHOWN IN FREE DRAWINGS
OF NAVAHO CHILDREN, BY COMMUNITY

	Shiprock (per cent)	Ramah (per cent)	Navaho Mt. (per cent)
Recent white[a]	35	22	15
Native[a]	20	30	30

[a] For definition of these categories, see p. 175.

rock and Navaho Mountain stand in rather striking contrast to each other in degree of white influence. It is of further interest that, even at Shiprock, native culture receives more attention from the older children than does white culture. This is presumptive evidence that the social pressure which begins to bear down upon the eleven- to thirteen-year-old children is derived from Navaho rather than white society. Results at Ramah are less clear-cut than at the other locali-

TABLE 17

EVIDENCES OF ACCULTURATION IN ITEMS SHOWN IN FREE DRAWINGS
OF NAVAHO CHILDREN, BY COMMUNITY AND AGE-GROUP

Age group	Shiprock		Ramah		Navaho Mt.	
	Recent White[a] (per cent)	Native[a] (per cent)	Recent White (per cent)	Native (per cent)	Recent White (per cent)	Native (per cent)
5–7 years	51	18	29	36	12	42
8–10 years	40	20	22	32	10	23
11–13 years . . .	31	21	14	36	17	28
14–18 years . . .	15	25	26	25	16	34

[a] For definition of these categories, see p. 175.

ties, very likely because there were fewer drawings to study and also because of the intermediate position of the Ramah Navaho.

Both the Rorschach and Thematic Apperception tests indicate that psychologically Shiprock children are considerably more complex than are those at Navaho Mountain, and that Ramah is much like Navaho Mountain in this respect. Shiprock children seem to have greater sensitivity, a greater range of emotional possibilities, and more different nuances of feeling in response to life experiences. On the other hand, they are under more pressure and more different sorts of pressure at Shiprock, and what they gain in complexity they seem to lose in spontaneity. The complexity, which might be called "sophistication," gives them an appearance of greater "maturity," but at the same time it makes them more self-critical and restrained.

Navaho Mountain children, by contrast, never are under the same degree of pressure as are their Shiprock cousins, and the pressure is a relatively simple one of conformity to Navaho cultural ways. Moreover, they are older when it begins to be felt. While they never attain (up to 18 years) the degree of "maturity" or of emotional subtlety seen at Shiprock, they maintain a larger amount of spontaneity.

In conclusion, it must be emphasized in connection with the findings reported in this chapter and the previous one that they represent an arithmetical average of many individuals, and that the chances are slight that one would be able to find a single individual who would show at the proper ages all the traits that have been outlined. It is justifiable to expect that a ten-year-old child will show more of the characteristics mentioned for children between eight and ten than those for children five to seven or fourteen to eighteen, but no one child can be expected to have all of the "typical" characteristics. Similarly, while in general a girl will show more responsiveness to the outer world than will a boy, a boy and girl could doubtless be picked out who reverse this relationship, with the girl the more restrained. Partly to offset any tendency of the reader to conclude at this point that he now knows just what to expect in a Navaho of either sex and any age, the next chapter introduces a series of children and their families from the groups studied who, in their background and personalities, demonstrate the range of variation among these Indians who are casually thought by some persons to be all alike.

9.

CHILDREN
of THE PEOPLE

IN THE last three chapters the findings of this research project have been reviewed in terms of averages for all the Navaho children, for those of different ages, for boys and girls, and for residents of different areas. The data were necessarily treated in a somewhat statistical way, with little attention paid to what they showed for individuals. In all these chapters the data discussed were derived in the first instance from individuals. Thus it seems fitting that the last chapter of the study should turn to individuals. Moreover, an examination of the life history and test performance of a series of children will furnish an idea of the range of variation included in the preceding averages. It will also show how generally some of the Navaho ways of living described prevail today.

Four children from Shiprock and six each from Ramah and Navaho Mountain have been selected for presentation here. They must not be thought of as "typical" in any sense, but rather as "representative" of various circumstances in their localities, such as good or poor economic and social standing, "progressive" or conservative attitude, degree of acculturation, amount of education in the family, and stable or disorganized family life. In choosing the children to describe, these factors were kept in mind rather than the child's IQ or other personal qualities. In order to preserve the subject's anonymity, pseudonyms have been used, and identifying data have been either suppressed or slightly altered. Cases are presented as of July 1943 because later information was available for only a few of them.

To convey the kind of understanding that will be most helpful in improving matters for The People, it was felt that there were needed as many concrete illustrations as possible of the things that have been said all through this book and *The Navaho*. For this reason, in preparing the cases, attention was directed quite as much to the family background and experience of the child as to the effect of these factors on his character formation and their reflection in the tests. Data from the interviews form a large part of each study.

Table 18 is presented here to remind the reader of the principal distinguishing features of Shiprock, Ramah, and Navaho Mountain, which were more fully discussed in Chapter 5.

SHIPROCK CHILDREN

CASE 1. *This little schoolgirl illustrates the contrast frequently found between acculturation in material things and conservatism in various other spheres. In her case also one sees that an apparently stable, affectionate family is not necessarily a guarantee of a good personal adjustment.*

Susie, seven years of age, is a rather thin and pasty-looking child with badly decayed teeth and dark circles under her eyes. Because her father is a government employee, the family lives in a small cottage on the school campus during the winter. In the summer they usually move to a frame cabin on their irrigated farm. Besides Susie, who is the youngest, these dwellings also shelter the parents, a brother and three sisters, a brother-in-law, an uncle, and a cousin. Perhaps the crowding is partly responsible for the untidy appearance of the house. They live and dress like white people in the neighborhood. All the children have gone to school (Susie for the first time in the year of the study), though the parents did not. Going to the Protestant church takes the place of school on Sundays as something to do. Economically this family is better off than the average; in addition to the father's small salary, they raise salable crops on their ten irrigated acres and own a few sheep and horses.

While in these respects they are much like their white neighbors, in others they are distinctly Navaho. For instance, Susie's mother weaves blankets as far as her rather poor health will permit; Susie's father practices divination, and the grandfather is a Singer. The following incident in their history shows the strength of their belief in Navaho religion; the fact that it was related by Susie's brother, who has spent many years in school, is further evidence of the mixture of Navaho and white ideology in this group.

Susie's mother had been ailing for some time a few years ago, and no one had been able to find the cause or cure her. Finally it was decided that she was being bewitched by a certain Singer of the neighborhood. Several ceremonials were tried in an effort to help her; when they failed, a famous Singer was imported from some distance to perform a rare and costly rite. During the ceremonial, several

TABLE 18

Summary of Principal Characteristics of Shiprock, Ramah, and Navaho Mountain Communities, 1942–43

	SHIPROCK	RAMAH	NAVAHO MOUNTAIN
Area	(District 12) 2,086 sq. mi.	Whites, 225 sq. mi. Navahos, 230 sq. mi.	(District 2) 1,711 sq. mi.
Population density	2.7 per sq. mi.	Navaho, 2.2 per sq. mi.	0.7 per sq. mi.
Type of country	Desert, partly irrigated	Steppe	Steppe
Income			
Source	Wages 20 per cent Agriculture 21 per cent Livestock 46 per cent	Wages unknown Agriculture 10 per cent[a] Livestock 75 per cent[a]	Wages 10 per cent Agriculture 20 per cent Livestock 60 per cent
Per capita, 1940	$82.52	$72.00[b]	$62.81
White influence	Extensive	Considerable but superficial	Slight
Government	Boarding and day schools Hospital Irrigation Court and jail District supervisor	Intermittent services of stockman[c]	Day school Range rider
Other	Many traders White ranchers Missionaries	Traders Mormon, Texan, Spanish ranchers who employ Navahos seasonally Ramah residents	Trader Manager of Rainbow Lodge Occasional "dudes"
Chief characteristics	Populous, prosperous, relatively "acculturated" Many English-speakers Uneasiness as shown in aggression against whites and government, witchcraft, and quarreling among themselves Monogamous single biological family the commonest unit	Crowded by whites and each other Superficial "acculturation," but little fundamental change Suspicion of whites rather than aggression against them All varieties of social units	"Just one big happy family" Live well at extremely simple level No hostility to whites Matrilocal extended families usual; several polygamous

[a] 1942 estimate.
[b] Estimated.
[c] Since 1943 there have been added a day school, a part-time supervisor, and a weekly health clinic.

persons present, including Susie's father, distinctly heard outside the hogan a sound like the gasping of a drowning man. Finishing a prayer, the Singer asked if anyone had heard the sound. When several admitted it, he told them that the witch would drown soon and the patient would then recover. Within a month the man who had been suspected actually did drown. After this, Susie's mother "got well right away."

People's belief in any religion or theory depends upon convincing demonstrations that a theoretical cause produces a visible effect. Even white people's faith in science would falter if they did not see rather often that such-and-such an event is followed in a way which science prescribes by such-and-such a result. Small wonder, then, that Susie's family and tribesmen, faced with not one but many occurrences like that just related, believe in the power of witches and medicine men. It is not surprising, either, that the scientific information acquired during grammar and high school fails to shake confidence in what has been taught and apparently proved to be true since babyhood.

How have these Navaho and white currents affected Susie? To start with, she was born in a hospital, but after that she spent her infancy like a good Navaho baby on a cradleboard. When she became ill with some abdominal trouble at the age of three years, two ceremonials were performed by her grandfather to cure her. She plays with dolls and on the playground apparatus at the school, often with her older sister or with a little girl neighbor. In the home the Navaho pattern of the mother directing the household and being the center of activity holds, even to the extent that the older sister and her husband live with the family. Susie is said to conform to this pattern well and to do as she is told willingly. The group appears to be more important than the individuals who compose it, but relations are harmonious and all seem fond of and permissive toward Susie, who is the baby. To the observer, she seems rather infantile, acting coy and shy with visitors, wriggling about and frequently holding onto the leg, hand, or clothing of her relatives. They often caress her.

Since both English and Navaho are spoken at home by the children, Susie had a slight advantage when she began school at six and a half. Her teacher believes her interested in school and considers her a very good pupil.

Let us see what can be learned of Susie from the tests given her. She made an IQ of only 82 on the Arthur, and 130 on the Goodenough, while the Rorschach and Thematic judge her intellectual capacity "high average," or between 100 and 110. She seems babyish for seven, gives a bland external appearance, and complies blindly with authority; she does not appear to be functioning successfully as an independent individual. She is trying hard to achieve some independence without giving up the emotional support of her family. However, she is quite passive and tries to evade rather than to solve problems. There is considerable restraint upon her spontaneity, as if she distrusted both the world and herself and dared not take any chances with either. That she is anxious about something is shown in two tests. What this might be is not clear in one test although it seems to be related to people; in another, it appears to be fear of older males; on the Battery she says she is afraid of everything and then names "tramps" specifically.[1] There is much evidence of extensive acquaintance with the white world.

Summary and Discussion. How can we understand such a difference in the estimates of Susie's mental ability? Perhaps one of the most important considerations is that the Arthur was the first test she took, and it was given soon after she started school. In addition, she had to take it all alone, from a strange white woman — a situation which was probably quite difficult for such a shy, immature child. The Goodenough came several months later, was done in a group, and required only the carrying out of instructions. Although the Thematic and Rorschach Tests were given also by a stranger, a Navaho girl was present and Susie could speak in Navaho. Moreover, she had been in school four or five months by this time. It seems obvious, at least, that 82 is too low, and it is likely that she shares the tribal advantage on the Goodenough (see Chapter 6), so that here perhaps the Rorschach-Thematic estimate is closer to her real ability than either of the others.

In Susie's family we find a veneer of white living habits, which probably gets thicker every year but has not yet fundamentally disturbed the deeply rooted values which are the tribal heritage. For the parents this underlying faith is undoubtedly a great support, giving them a sense of security in whatever fortunes life brings

---

[1] A number of Shiprock children spoke of tramps. Evidently they come through the neighborhood along the highway.

them. For Susie, who knows more about white ways of living than the Navaho belief, there is no such support. She can be scared by the "tramp" bogeyman and also feel uneasy because she hears a "witch" is making her mother sick. She is too young to have any perspective; she is unable to make a choice for herself; so she stops trying to a certain extent, gives in to the various influences, and feels anxious without knowing what bothers her.

Thus, although the family appears to be getting along all right both internally and externally, and although they not only are fond of Susie but show their affection in many ways, they have not been able to give her a feeling of security. They do not seem to feel the conflict between white and Navaho cultures so strongly as she does. Susie will be happier if she can acquire either white beliefs or the firm belief that has guided her parents, and most unhappy if she falls between the two cultures, disbelieving Navaho teachings and not grasping those of the white world.

CASE II. *Instead of a cultural contrast, one sees here how items from white culture can be amalgamated with an essentially Navaho way of life.*

Harriet is an energetic, neatly dressed, eight-year-old schoolgirl with a determined expression on her face. She and her family occupy a well-built log house perched on the edge of the mesa above the river valley, two or three miles from the school. Below the mesa lies their twenty-acre irrigated farm, part of which is a peach, apricot, and apple orchard where they camp during the summer. Surrounding their farm on three sides are the farms of several Navaho neighbors. Harriet's father knows these people quite well and is somewhat a leader among them. Besides his good farm, which he manages intelligently, the father owns a small coal mine from which he digs $200 to $300 worth of coal a month in the winter. He has a half-ton truck for hauling the coal.

The father never went to school, but he has picked up a little English and keeps on talking it until his hearer finally understands him. In Navaho too he likes to talk, often making long speeches at meetings. He has independent views on many topics and lost much of his following when he became an advocate of an unpopular measure.

In spite of their prosperity, the family lives in a simple Navaho manner, their chief luxury being a double bed. The mother dresses and keeps house in the Indian style. Harriet helps her mother with housework or herds the family flock of sheep. The boys help their father. Of the nine children, four including Harriet have gone to school, but only she and her older brother attend currently. The father knows and frequently performs the Blessing Way ceremonial, and both grandfathers are well-known Singers.

Harriet is the second girl and seventh child in the family and the most active of all the children. She prefers herding sheep to housework, but she does whichever her mother tells her. She has had good health except for an illness when she was two and a half years old. On this occasion a diviner said she needed a certain ceremonial, and her grandfather performed it. Her symptoms persisted throughout, and at its end her parents were just about to take her to the hospital when she improved rather suddenly.

She began school at about six and a half, going there by bus fairly regularly. She seems to like school. She tries hard in her classes, is a little slow, but persists until she finishes. During recess she plays mostly on the swings and slides. She is more of an independent worker than either a leader or a follower. While in the hospital waiting to have her tonsils removed, she had such a good time with her neighbor, laughing, singing, and jumping on the beds that she had to be reprimanded by the nurses.

The tests given Harriet confirm a good deal of what has already been said about her. She made an IQ of 96 on the Arthur and 109 on the Goodenough. Both the Rorschach and Thematic judged her superior (IQ 110-120) in intelligence. Perhaps her slowness penalized her on the Arthur. The tests also show that she becomes a little anxious when faced with a new task, so that she cannot use her full ability; this would interfere with her best performance. She has a high energy level, reacts strongly and rather impulsively to her environment, and seems to be somewhat concerned about this. She feels her independence to be especially important and is ready to defend it, but if that is not questioned she is quite compliant. All of these things give her a superficial appearance of aggressiveness, which really is not deeply rooted in her character. Once she makes sure that no one is trying to push her around she can form very good emotional relationships. She is evidently on good terms with her parents. Her father appears to be the real authority, while the mother is perhaps more important in her affections. She does not like girls' as much as boys' occupations. She gets along well in white-culture situations but does not feel an intimate part of them.

Summary and Discussion. This seems to be a relaxed sort of family which continues its accustomed Navaho existence. It has accepted modern irrigation, coal mining, and education without feeling under any necessity to behave like the white people who teach these things. There thus seems to be a minimum of conflict for its members between white ways and Navaho ways; they merely take what they want from the white world and let the rest go. Perhaps this is partly also a reflection of the father's spirit of independence, which Harriet shares. The general atmosphere here seems sounder and easier for children than the two-sided situation in which little Susie finds herself.

CASE III. *In this case we see how the extended family functions and also how much effect three generations of schooling has had on a way of life.*

Our subject is George, a friendly, husky-looking boy of ten. George may be found either at his mother's irrigated farm on the mesa, a few miles from the school or at his grandparents's hogan several miles farther away. While his immediate (biological) family contains only his mother and five children, the "family" he thinks of is the extended family; it includes his mother's parents, several unmarried uncles, a married aunt with her husband and daughter, and occasionally other relatives. Sometimes these people all live together; at other times they are scattered, farming, working for wages, or caring for their combined flock of sheep. George's father is living, but he is rarely at home and contributes little in either support or influence to his children. When George's mother was asked about her son's childhood, she rarely had a chance to answer the questions, sitting quietly while her mother, father, and sister did the talking. Only when her sister accused George of being naughty did she fire up and say that *he* was never naughty, it was her other son. It may be partly because of this family dominance that George's father does not remain at home.

George was born at home, a cradle board was used, and he was nursed for "about a year." [2] When his mother started to wean him

---

[2] Any estimates of such periods are very approximate. As stated earlier, measurement of time is of little interest to The People.

by leaving him with his grandmother, he cried all night long. His grandfather undertook to "raise" him, so George has spent much time with the old man. The maternal uncles have also played a part, either as older brothers or substitute fathers, and he evidently admires them greatly, except for the youngest (fifteen years old) whom he fears. When one uncle was drafted, the others taught George the sweathouse songs so that he could join them in the sweatbath before the uncle went off to war. Now he takes sweatbaths with his grandfather and taunts his youngest uncle with being afraid to try it. The maternal relatives have taken the father's place further in that they farm George's mother's place for her. Although George is the oldest boy, and old enough to help with the work, neither he nor his brother seem to do much except play. The youngest uncle says they are both lazy.

Beginning with the grandparents, the whole family has been to school, most members for five or six years. At home, Navaho interspersed with English is the language used, and the children have considerable acquaintance with English before they come to school. The mother went away to Catholic boarding schools for part of her education. The grandparents' home is more Indian than white in its furnishings, but the mother's might almost be a white rancher's cabin. The chief difference is that it has only a dirt floor. The whole family is listed as Catholic. However, when George fell off a fence at the age of a year and a half and hurt his head, the family called in a Singer.

The grandfather has served as a tribal official for the past twelve years. He and his family make a better-than-average income from their farming and their sheep, yet they are always hard up and often need relief supplies, probably because of the large number of dependents. They dress George and his brother and sister in good clothes for school.

George calls his grandmother "mama" and his mother by her first name (in English). He seems to regard his mother more as an older sister than as a parent. He and his younger brother used to fight so much that they were kept apart, but they have outgrown this and now play together, though they do not seem especially fond of each other. The younger boy is much more active and quick than George and is frequently compared to him by the family to George's disparagement. George likes to tease his sister and cousin by eavesdropping on their conversations and later repeating what they say.

In school everyone thinks George is a "fine boy." He causes no trouble, is responsive, and, if sufficiently praised and encouraged, does rather good work. Otherwise he tends to idle instead of study.

On the tests George appears to be quite bright. He makes an IQ of 116 on the Arthur and 130 on the Goodenough. The other tests also show that he has better-than-average mental capacity but indicate that this is of limited usefulness, and that he is entirely occupied with observing details without attempting to synthesize them into concepts with larger meaning. He seems both passive and submissive and very dependent on the affection and encouragement of the people around him for a sense of security. He assures this affection by being a good boy, behaving in a very conventional manner, and holding himself tightly in check except for a limited amount of childish impulsiveness and liveliness which probably makes people think he is cute. He is quite sensitive to other people, but he is too anxious to please them and seems unable to form really satisfactory emotional relations with them. He is very immature for his age and lacks techniques for getting along in an appropriate fashion.

Summary and Discussion. How much difference has all the schooling of this family made? They earn their living like Navahos and live in the traditional matrilocal way. They call in the "medicine man" when they are sick rather than go to the hospital. On the other hand, the grandparents have few modern conveniences, but the parents have more; perhaps when George has a house it will have a wooden floor and a radio and running water. They can use English fairly readily, the grandfather fits into the tribal governmental scheme, and the boys are free to play instead of having to help with the family work.

The acculturation problem does not seem to trouble George much, but having such an extensive family with someone always to run to for praise and comfort if someone else exerts a little discipline has probably made it easier for him to stay rather a baby and has kept him from the necessity of finding more satisfactory ways of adjusting himself. The grown-ups have probably felt sorry for him because his father takes no part in his family and have petted him and excused him too often from working. He seems to lack either an internal or an external stimulus to grow up, and he may wake up some day to find himself a man physically without having ceased to be a little boy emotionally.

CASE IV. *In this boy's family the acculturation process is going forward rather smoothly and penetrating more deeply than in any of the other families.*

Tom, our focus in this family, is a tall, slender, shy but friendly boy of eighteen, now in the ninth grade of school, who affects rather flashy cowboy outfits for dress occasions like other boys of his age. Because he is the oldest of six children, he is kept out of school in the spring and fall to help farm their thirty acres. Farming has always been his job rather than sheepherding, which has fallen to the younger members of the family. He is a good worker and now can manage the planting, irrigating, or harvesting without instruction. He carries much of the responsibility for the crops because his father is busy as a government employee a large part of the time.

Tom's father (who is Susie's father's brother) had six years of schooling. He is said to be the most capable Navaho in his line of work. He has acquired several different farm plots, which he manages well with Tom's help. He has built a very attractive house on one of these, and his unschooled wife (who is Susie's mother's sister) takes good care of it. Many flowers are planted outside, and the rooms are decorated with well-arranged photographs and paintings made by one of the children. All these things point to the facts that they make a better-than-average income and have an unusual appreciation for the refinements of the white way of living. The wife's lack of schooling has not made her less ready to utilize white comforts, as happens in some cases.

When Tom was about eight years old he was taken to the hospital for some contagious disease, and there was found to have tuberculosis. The parents accepted the advice of the doctor that he needed sanatorium care, and the boy spent two years at Albuquerque. He has remained well ever since. He insists that he never had a ceremonial performed for this illness, which is the more remarkable because his maternal grandfather is a Singer. On Tom's return from the hospital he went to school, as have all the other children. As a group they are very attractive, bright, well-mannered children, but Tom comes at the bottom of the list in these qualities; moreover, he is rather quick to lose his temper or get stubborn.

In addition to this extensive contact with the white world and acceptance of its material improvements, Tom, at least, claims not to believe in Navaho witches and ghosts. If he were not fairly skeptical about them it seems unlikely that he would spend nights alone in one of the family homes as he does during the winter when the others are in school and his parents away at sheep camp or working. All the children are listed as Protestant, but how much this means is open to some question.

On the other hand, both parents are thought to be very distrustful of the government and of the white people who work for it. The mother said as much when asked to tell about her children and refused to give any information. The father sent the children to the public school first and then wanted them to go to a mission; but finally he had to put them in the government school which he thinks is "no good." He is quite a leader in the area and would probably oppose the government vigorously if he were not employed by it and more interested in keeping his job than in carrying out abstract principles.

The tests underline many of the qualities we have heard of in Tom. He is about average in intelligence, getting an IQ of 96 on the Arthur and a similar rating from the other tests. His attitude throughout was one of lack of interest in exerting himself and of not "giving out" much on many of the tests. Creativity and imagination are low, and he is concerned almost exclusively with commonplace, practical matters. He is inefficient in the use of what capacities he has, in that he makes so little effort. He is shy of emotional relationships and of anything that suggests sex, though he seems to be very aware of the latter. His relations with people are not bad, but he has relatively little to do with them. He evidently feels freer out of his home than in it, probably because he compares himself unfavorably to his more gifted brothers and sisters. He would rather get along quietly and undramatically than assert himself in competition with them. He is quite well adjusted on this level, but he is not making much of himself.

Summary and Discussion. Here is a family as little Navaho and as much white in their way of living as one is likely to find among The People. They seem to have tried their best to do what the government told them was advisable, from farming by modern irrigation methods and building a good house to sending their son to the sanatorium. As far as is known, they do not make much use of Navaho ceremonials, and Tom for one appears to have abandoned Navaho fears as well as Navaho beliefs. Yet something has gone sour, and they hate the source of the change. One wonders if this is the result of "going white" too quickly and thoroughly and thus losing the support of traditional beliefs that seems to have helped Susie's family. Susie's parents do not exhibit the same hatred. Perhaps, in spite of doing everything they were told in order to attain the promises held out to them, Tom's parents still find themselves regarded as "just Indians."

Tom himself does not seem troubled by his family's attitude, perhaps because he does not yet function independently of them. He gets along with them and with white people about equally well, chiefly by keeping his own counsel and doing as he is told. His wish "to go some place else besides the Reservation" may, however, reflect the family feeling of frustration in the present situation. His personality is a rather uncomplicated one which should get along well within its limitations unless he attempts something beyond his powers. He shows little tendency toward doing this.

RAMAH CHILDREN

CASE 1. *This boy is a member of a large, moderately well-to-do, socially and politically inconspicuous family where the wife is a local woman and the husband comes from outside the community. Two children have been sent away to school, but in general they are a rather conservative group, though living fairly near the white settlement.*

Bill, six and a half years old, is the eighth child and third boy of ten children. All the older children work, but Bill and the younger ones have no regular responsibilities. He is thus the oldest of the little ones and leads their play. Although he should be quite carefree, he usually wears a little frown as if he were worried about something. He alternates between rough and noisy play, with more show of aggressiveness than the others, and withdrawn, daydreaming behavior.

The family live in a group of hogans and square log cabins on the edge of the pinyon and cedar trees near their cornfield. On the other side of the cornfield can be seen the hogan of the oldest daughter and her husband. They do not live with the rest of the family because the mother and son-in-law should not look at one another according to the rules of mother-in-law avoidance. The daughter and her little girl stay much of the time in Bill's home, however, while the husband is away working.

When they were visited, Bill's father was helping one of the traders. His mother spent most of her time weaving. The three oldest sisters carded, spun, and dyed wool from their sheep, which they either gave to their mother to weave or made into blankets themselves. The oldest son was away from home. The next three children, a boy and two girls, were a mile or so away with the sheep, herding all day and sleeping at the sheep camp at night. It took the combined efforts of all members of the family except the three youngest to provide for the needs of the group.

The mother is definitely the center of the family and does most of the planning of the children's activity, even though she is aided in household work by her many assistants. The second girl, who has been to school, is her lieutenant. Orders originating with the mother will often be issued by this daughter. There is very little idle sitting around. When it becomes too dark to work, the family go to sleep.

The three youngest children — all boys — are often joined by their niece in play. The baby is the pet of the whole family and receives much attention and caressing from all the older ones. Bill and the brother just younger keep him amused and tolerate him in their games but are less enthusiastic in their attitude toward him than are other members of the family. He is the only child whom the mother pets. Doubtless Bill and the younger boy had their turn, but their places have been usurped — Bill's twice, the other boy's once. As pointed out in Part I, this is the usual situation in Navaho families.

Almost the only special notice Bill and his brother receive comes in the form of directions to run some errand. When Bill is in his daydreaming mood and does not pay prompt attention, angry shouts spur him on. When the father comes home in the evening, the little boys crowd around him and push each other for the privilege of sitting closest to him. He permits this and even seems pleased by it, chatting with them, and comforting them if they get into trouble with the rest of the family.

Bill's performance on the Arthur Test earned him an IQ of 106.

This is the level estimated by the other tests also. The Rorschach and Thematic Tests suggest that he accomplishes less than his ability warrants because he is very cautious, does not want to take a chance on anything, and is not sure of himself. He holds his reactions to the outer world strictly in check, but gives in to his imagination more freely and seems to retire into the world of fantasy when the situation gets too complicated for him. He is quite anxious in a diffuse way, especially in his relations with people. He would like to have warm ties with other people, most particularly with his mother, but is unable to achieve them. He does not express directly his resentment of being rejected and pushed around, but is instead passively resistant or aggressive against others than those who mistreat him. Both emotional and intellectual capacities are sufficient for a good adjustment.

Summary and Discussion. In this family, life is a sober affair, and only the baby is judged to need affectionate demonstrations. If one is old enough to work, he deserves a certain amount of recognition, but between babyhood and the age of participation in the family economy one scarcely exists. In many such groups, one of the older children would have furnished the emotional tie that Bill seeks, but here they all seem to be too busy. He will probably get along better when he is older and more important in the family, but obviously he would develop best in an atmosphere of more encouragement and affection.

CASE II. *This family lives some distance from Ramah, is poor, and has had more dealings with Mexicans than with other white people. The father is a diviner and a sheepherder. The child is one of the two survivors of eight pregnancies.*

Carlotta, not quite six when tested, is a winsome, active little girl who is coy and shy until she becomes acquainted, but is then quite friendly. She lives with her parents and eight-month-old brother in a well-built hogan among the pinyons that border a broad valley south of Ramah. Somewhat closer than Ramah is a small Mexican settlement, and several ranchers own land among the Indian allotments. Most of the other Navaho families in the neighborhood are near relatives of Carlotta's father, but none live closer than two or three miles, so that Carlotta has no playmates and sees few visitors.

The home is simple but is beginning to have added to it such conveniences as bedsteads. The family seem to be frequently out of groceries. Once the mother excused herself from conversation with visitors so that she could continue to weave the blanket that was to reopen their credit with the trader. Recently they have begun to build up a flock of sheep, a number of which have been paid to the father for his divinations. Formerly these animals were kept with the flock of a relative, but since Carlotta has grown big enough to help with the herding, they take care of the little flock themselves. Her first experience of lambing was in the spring before she was tested. Her mother said she was greatly astonished to see the lambs born and couldn't get over it.

Four babies died before Carlotta was born, and two have died since. Only one of these children survived as long as two years. All the rest were born dead or lived only a few months. It is small wonder, then, that Carlotta is cherished and that the baby also is closely watched. The little girl must have been well aware of the two deaths after her, because she was four years old or more at the time. She had been quite jealous of the sister who came just after her, often trying to push her out of her mother's lap when she was nursing and crying angrily when in turn her mother would push her away. Her father, to whom she seems quite close, would take Carlotta and play with her and comfort her on these occasions. She likes him to teach her Spanish words and Navaho songs; perhaps she likes caring for the sheep better because that is his specialty. Besides herding, she is expected to fetch wood, help care for the baby, and run errands. Sometimes she does these things willingly; sometimes she refuses. She is not under strong compulsion to do them, but her mother is usually the one who tries to get her to help.

The father is a mild, somewhat shy and timid, but rather stubborn man, with curly hair, who spent several years in his teens herding sheep for Mexican ranchers.[3] Through them he learned good methods and picked up some Spanish, and he has continued to work for them at times for wages. His mother was partly Apache, his father a recluse who is known for rarely speaking and having little to do with his fellows. Carlotta's father and a large number of his maternal relatives practice divination. After being so long with Mexicans, he regained his place among his tribesmen by teaching

[3] His life story may be found in A. H. and D. C. Leighton, *The Navaho Door* (Cambridge: Harvard University Press, 1944), pp. 95–108.

them what he had learned of animal husbandry and by earning a reputation for successful divination. He is more considerate and helpful with his wife than is the average Navaho man and spends more time playing with his children.

The mother is a stolid, probably not too bright woman, who is a fair weaver and seems interested in her home and children. Her only complaint of her husband is that she gets lonesome when he is away on trips to the trader or for divination. They seem a very congenial and well-suited pair.

When Carlotta was four years old the family spent a few months with the mother's sister where there were many children. Up to that time the little girl had not talked much, but her speech developed greatly with this stimulus. She still uses a sort of baby talk.

Carlotta's test results were confusing. They showed throughout immaturity and lack of discipline to such an extent that it was difficult to tell just what her ability was. She rated an IQ of only 53 on the Arthur, for instance, but on the Rorschach and Thematic seemed less defective than this would imply, though no one was willing to estimate her mental capacity definitely. She went at the tests in a confused, unorganized way. Although the evidence is not conclusive, she appears to have been rather crudely shocked by something, probably of sexual nature, which has caused her to withdraw into a shell, and although she is strongly affected by stimulation from outside, she evades reacting to it. She is afraid of the world and does not find enough support in her emotional ties to solve her problems.

Summary and Discussion. It seems possible that the birth and death of younger children, together with her experience of seeing the lambs born, may have combined somehow to frighten this child who, through her father, comes of a family with many members who show signs of instability. She is probably not very bright and has taken a longer time than usual to grow up even to the six-year standard. The affection of her parents for her and for each other, and their gradually improving economic status, may contribute enough security to permit her to find a way of recovering from the effects of the shock which now interferes with her normal functioning. It is possible that she may never cope with life very successfully. Like her father, however, she may well learn to live with her liabilities without ever ridding herself of them and may even be able to capitalize on some of them as he has.

CASE III. *This boy belongs to one of the most prosperous extended families of the region. Although no one in the group has been to school, it is rather "progressive" in its attitude. There are two wives who manage the home and flocks, aided by their large number of relatives and descendants, and by their gay, romantic, and at times industrious husband.*

Jose is the oldest child of his mother, who is the older of the two wives and the boss of the family. He is a pleasant, friendly, energetic boy of about twelve, who likes to wear good clothes and ride a fine horse and go to ceremonials with his father and the other men. When the men are away, he is his mother's companion and the leader of his brothers and young cousins. He is kind to the little ones and helpful to his mother, sometimes even doing the cooking for her.

The family fortune was begun by the wives' parents, who built up a large flock of sheep. When the parents died they left instructions that the sheep should be kept together and that Jose's mother should supervise them, even though many of them belonged to her sisters, brothers, and cousins. This is doubtless one reason why so many of the relatives live together. At the time Jose was tested there were the husband and two wives, their seven children, two of the wives' younger brothers, two cousins, and a niece.

The father (of Yaqui-Zuni-Navaho derivation) had previously married Jose's mother's older sister. When this woman died, he married Jose's mother and later also her younger sister. He has been "married" briefly to a surprising number of other women in the area and has begotten at least twenty children. Jose's mother has provided him with six and her younger sister with one. The father owned a few sheep when he joined the family and has increased his flock as well as helping with that of his wife and her relatives. He holds a dominant position in the family, by virtue of his force of character, physical strength, and dashing appearance. He is rather strict with the children but plays with them a good deal and takes pleasure in bringing them good clothes and toys and candy from the trading post. Jose appears to admire him and at the same time to be a little afraid of him. The father's philosophy is that it is foolish to work hard to make money unless you spend it for things you want and have a good time. He has bought a half-ton truck in which he spends much time driving around the country, sometimes to haul wood or help with ceremonials, at other times to visit his friends or buy a drink. Another of the modern improvements he invested in was a gasoline sheepshearing machine. While he does not work continuously, he is very strong and works hard at such times as harvest. He sees to it that the work is done at all times. He speaks a little Spanish and understands a little English, though he never speaks it.

The family lives quite simply, the chief signs of affluence being the truck, the gasoline shearer, and a good amount of silver and turquoise jewelry. The quality of clothing and the amount and variety of food bought are also considerably above the average. They have a hogan, a tent, a shade, and a small shack made of milled lumber which contains a double bed and kitchen cabinet. In their living habits they show little white influence, though they flavor their food more than is common among Navahos. They are very proud of their large flock of sheep and their good horses, their Shetland pony, and fancy saddles.

Jose had some sort of illness when he was small, for which a Singer was employed. A few years ago, when a horse kicked him in the face, his father took him to a government hospital to be sewed up. They believe in the "medicine man," but at the same time have no hesitation in going to the hospital. When a day school is built they look forward to sending some of the children to it, but they do not want to send them far away to boarding school.

The two wives seem to get along quite well, but there is no question that Jose's mother is the "lady of the house." While this is partly because she is older and because of Navaho custom, it is even more a result of difference in character and the final instructions of their parents. The two sets of children also are on good terms.

Jose went at the tests willingly, apparently wanted to do his best, and yet did not seem to care greatly whether he knew what he was supposed to do or not. He was willing to take a chance on this new task. A good deal of the time his mother watched, scolding him if he hesitated too long. In spite of this, he made an IQ of only 64 on the Arthur; a generally below-average level was confirmed by the other tests, though not quite so low as the IQ figure. He seems to be quite free and unafraid in his reactions, held back only by his limited ability. He appears to be trying hard to grow up and achieve adult status. He shows good feeling for people and is evidently getting along well in a sound home environment. He is a little afraid of incurring his father's criticism and would like to become more closely attached to him than he has been able to do.

Summary and Discussion. Lack of schooling certainly has not held this family back economically, nor have their interpersonal relations suffered as far as we can see. This is one child whose lack of school experience cannot very well be held responsible for his low IQ, for his performance throughout the tests was somewhat below average. Moreover, his father considers him a little dull, saying, "He's like a a burro — he doesn't hardly think." White people might think that the fact that there are two wives would cause difficulty, but it has not done so in this case. Here, as in many families where there is more than one wife, the work seems to be made much easier, for one can care for the home while the other supervises the flock. If their husband is away much, as often happens, they can keep each other company.

Jose, too, is not bothered by having a rival for his mother in the family. His position is good and it seems probable that a person with the qualities of his father would help him to make use of what abilities he has, even though they are limited. He has been spared any problems that might have arisen from his intellectual limitations if there had been a school and he had been sent to it. As it is, he has been trained, in a way suited to his capacities, for a life he would probably lead whether he had gone to school or not.

CASE IV. *Betsy's family lives near the white settlement. Her mother went to school, and her father worked for white men at distant places long enough to learn their ways. The family's slightly above-average income is due partly to wage work by both parents. The children are sent away to school as they become old enough.*

This case is the same Betsy whose life story appears in the Introduction. Supplementary data will be presented here to fill in the picture. Betsy is an attractive, lively child of eleven, on the go most of the time, laughing and talking. At times she is moody and sulky, but this does not last long. She much prefers herding sheep and taking the horses to water, as she writes, to doing household chores. These she leaves mostly to her younger sister.

When Betsy was tested, the family were living in a hogan and log cabin in a little valley leading into a high hill, all but the center of the valley forested with pinyons and cedars. They have a bedstead, two mattresses which her mother made, a small iron heating stove which is also used for cooking, and a sewing machine. The two older girls wear "American" clothes, but the mother and youngest girl prefer Navaho dresses. They almost never grind corn, and the mother does not weave. They buy most of their food from the store, with the exception of meat, which comes from their flock or from other Indians in payment for services of various kinds.

The schoolteachers taught the mother how to cook and keep house in the white style, and she follows some of their instructions in a modified fashion. She keeps her children much cleaner than the average and spends much time washing out their clothes. Sometimes she takes the wash down to an irrigation ditch about half a mile away, at other times her husband hauls water for her from a well a little farther off. Like most Navahos who have been to school, she supplements the family income from time to time by interpreting.

The father lost his parents at an early age and was educated in the Navaho way by various relatives, especially his wise old maternal grandfather. He was thus familiar with the classical Navaho tradition, but before he married he went away from Ramah to work, once traveling as far as California. He learned enough English to understand simple conversations and can read and write a little. He farms a patch of corn, squash, and melons but makes his living chiefly by craft work, at which he is quite skillful. His wife also learned the craft and often helps him.

Betsy's parents are a congenial and very devoted pair. Her mother handles contacts with the white world and can be quite persistent on behalf of her family or for other Indians. The father deals mostly with Navahos, to many of whom he is related. Both are very much interested in their children, and, while they instruct and direct them, they also take pleasure in their companionship and play with them. Indians in the neighborhood seem to be seeking their advice and services increasingly, and it is likely that as they grow older their influence will become much greater than it is now.

Betsy is the only child of the seven in the family who was not laced to a cradle board in her infancy. Probably her mother thought at first that the teachers knew best but later found that a cradle board has advantages in a hogan. Betsy writes that she received both Navaho and white medical treatments for different illnesses. In general, the family seem to use Navaho medicine as white people use a medicine chest and go to the hospital for anything they think serious.

In addition to the father, his sister, Betsy's aunt, exerts Navaho influences on Betsy. The two families live close by, and the children play together. Betsy is lent to the aunt as sheepherder in the summer in return for the aunt's care of the flock at other times. Through her Betsy learns something of the old Navaho ways of cooking and raising children.

The school to which Betsy and her sister and brother go is about fifty miles from their home. It is not "progressive" in its method but emphasizes English and the things white children get in school. Betsy has now reached the third grade and writes quite well for a third-grader. She started with an advantage in that she was familiar with English words at home, though it is doubtful if she spoke English there.

On the tests [4] Betsy made an IQ of 126 on the Arthur and 111 on the Goodenough. The other tests estimated her ability "superior" or "very superior." She appears to be direct, energetic, and friendly, needing and liking warm, affectionate relationships. On the surface she seems to be very confident that the world will give her what she wants, but underneath she is a little less sure of this. She is more interested in the sort of things that boys do than in girls' work. Her family life is sound, and there is abundant evidence of experience with the white world. There is something bothering her, apparently in the sexual sphere. It may be that this is due to her adolescence; or possibly she has just come face to face with the fact that, even though she likes things boys do, she is a girl, and she has not yet adjusted herself to the idea. This problem has not upset her seriously, and on the whole she seems well adjusted and headed towards a satisfactory solution of her conflict.

Summary and Discussion. Here is seen the meeting of two currents almost as different as in the case of Susie from Shiprock, yet Betsy's family have achieved more of an intermingling of the two; the material side is less completely white, and the spiritual and value system less completely Navaho. They are tolerant of both cultures, the father feeling more at home in the Navaho world, the mother in the white. They probably get much less support and security from

[4] The analyses of Betsy's test results are reproduced in Appendix II.

Navaho religion than do Susie's family, but they may also be a little less fearful of the witchcraft possibilities. Betsy, with her intelligence, liveliness, Navaho background, and school experience, might well take a successful part in the next stage in the acculturation process.

CASE V. *The family of this boy have Laguna Indian blood as well as Navaho. They are poorer than the average and suffer from a reputation for witchcraft and also for drinking, stealing, and sexual license.*

Our subject in this group is a good-sized, well-built boy of about fourteen named Comas. His behavior depends on what is going on around him. If there is excitement of some sort, or if his mother pays attention to him, he is fairly lively and boisterous, showing off and seeming to enjoy what he is doing. If left to himself in the absence of stimulation, he lapses into a quiescent state. He is somewhat awkward and clumsy and likes to tease his mother with rather crude threats which he does not carry out.

During the testing it happened that there were always a number of relatives staying at his place, so that he was in the active phase of his behavior. At first he made excuses to avoid taking the tests, but finally he agreed to do them and threw himself into the task.

He and his sister and mother, a married uncle and brother and their wives, and at times other relatives live with his maternal grandfather. His father, who was half Laguna, died when Comas was a baby. The grandfather achieved the reputation for being a witch by learning a ceremonial from a man generally believed to be one; and his daughter, Comas' mother, is also somewhat suspect. The grandfather gave up singing some years ago, partly because of advancing old age, and since that time the family have lived on their farming and flock, with some weaving and pinyon-nut gathering. They have about the same amount of possessions as Carlotta's family, but these have to be shared by eight adults here instead of only two.

A maternal aunt was one of the few recognized prostitutes in this area, an activity which some of her descendants have continued. Comas' brother and maternal uncle get drunk frequently. Comas himself, with a young companion, once stole and ate two sheep and spent twenty days in jail as punishment. Comas stayed in jail without complaint, although the companion ran away several times.

The grandfather is the focus of family life in spite of age and feebleness. He is watched over and waited on with more of an appearance of affection than is accorded to anyone else. Although he is a Singer, he submitted to a medical examination and expressed gratitude for medicine given him.

His daughter, Comas' mother, has a severe, humorless face which occasionally breaks into a grotesque smile. She was gracious to visitors but nagging to her children. Comas is her chief mainstay since his brother took to drinking and then got married, but she seems to do little to make the work more attractive, merely prodding him when he fails to do it. She did not remarry after her husband's death, and she looks disappointed in life.

The sister is a lumpish sort of girl, if anything even more inert than Comas. She seems amused at his foolishness when he is showing off but goes no further than that in furnishing companionship. She weaves a little, herds the sheep occasionally, and helps in gathering pinyons.

There is less bustle and industry in this household than in any Navaho home we visited. Their poverty does not seem sufficient incentive to spur them into persistent and productive activity. They do what work they cannot avoid and get along as best they can. They usually attend the annual fiesta at Laguna, where they visit Comas' father's people and exchange gifts. Comas himself has been there ten times.

Comas' life has been quite limited, consisting chiefly in tending the sheep and otherwise helping his family. Sometimes he has worked for neighboring white ranchers. His chief complaint is that he has no opportunity to know other boys; when observed with others of his age, he appears friendly and agreeable. He does not seem to pay much attention to girls. When his brother and uncle are around, they boss him a good deal but get small response from him. He says that he has never had a drink and doesn't intend to because he "sees too much of that around this place."

The results of the tests emphasized a number of these points. He is at least of "average intelligence," scoring an IQ of 104 on the Arthur even though he has never been to school. The other tests indicate that he does not use his ability consistently nor efficiently, and that he is neither realistic nor practical. He seems to be very much disturbed by his environment. He is so disappointed in it, in fact, that he tries to blot it out of his mind instead of either rebelling against it or giving in to it. The chief trouble is a lack of affectional ties. He has a good capacity for forming affectionate relations with people but little opportunity for it in his family. He disapproves of the behavior he sees and wants no part of it. He says he is ashamed of his stealing. He seems to do best when stimulated moderately from outside himself, or before an audience. He is aware of his sexuality but suppresses it.

Summary and Discussion. In this family we find behavior that is considered bad by both Navahos and whites, plus some that is bad only by Navaho standards. One wonders if the accusation of witchcraft was made more readily because of the blood of different tribes in the family and the feeling by "100 percent Navahos" that they are "foreigners." Has the accusation broken their spirit, so that they do not feel it worth while to try very hard?

Comas appears to have good potentialities, but they have been stifled by an environment which has starved him emotionally, kept his horizons narrow, and disgusted him in addition. Had there been a school near by, perhaps he would have found there what his family failed to provide, and such an outlet would have helped him to develop some of his abilities. As it is, there seems to be little to keep him from following his brother's footsteps or at least drifting into shiftlessness. He might still improve over his present performance if, for instance, he should marry a girl in a more energetic family than his own, where the stimulation of that environment would supply the impetus that he lacks.

CASE VI. *This girl's family is about average in every respect and represents the kind of people who are the pillars of Navaho society. Two daughters went to school briefly. Here again are examples of men with more than one wife.*

Bianca, our subject here, is a pretty girl of about sixteen, the fifth daughter in a family with six girls and one boy. When we gave tests in this family, Bianca, her parents, her brother, a younger sister, a niece, and a nephew were living in a well-built hogan on the edge of their corn and bean field. This is situated a few miles from the home of Carlotta and is thus a considerable distance from Ramah. About fifty yards from their hogan stood another with its back to Bianca's, in which lived two older sisters and their husband. About a mile away lived two more sisters and their husband. The husbands rarely appeared because of their practice of mother-in-law avoidance, but the sisters and their many children were constant visitors.

The family make their living from raising corn, beans, and sheep. The ewes and lambs are kept by the two sisters a mile away, while Bianca's parents are responsible for the rams. They herd rams and goats belonging to other relatives and friends as well as their own. Until eight or nine years ago this family had no regular abode and moved frequently from place to place as other pieces of land seemed more desirable. Finally a government agent suggested that they file a claim to some land and showed them the piece they now use. It has proved a good choice; even in dry years the father is able to raise a small crop, and in good years he grows more than the family can eat. He harvested over twenty-five hundred-pound sacks of beans the year of the testing program.

They are in modest circumstances and tend to spend their money on useful things rather than on adornments. They own a good wagon and an iron cookstove that is used for heating as well as cooking. They frequently bake their Indian bread as biscuits in the oven instead of cooking it in big flat tortillas on top of the stove. They have little good jewelry, but the girls who went to school learned to do beading and have presented the family with several elaborately beaded belts, sleeve garters, and hat bands.

Bianca is a hard-working, pleasant girl who is rather shy with strangers, but after this has worn off she is friendly and even vivacious. She seems to enjoy working and rarely stops long from morning to night. While her mother [5] directs activities in general, Bianca does not wait to be told what to do but goes ahead on her own initiative. In this she is different from her younger sister who never works if she can avoid it, and when she works does it sloppily. Bianca often rebukes her for this. Her mother considers Bianca the brightest and the second most industrious of her daughters.

Bianca helps her father or her mother or herds the sheep or cares for the niece and nephew, whatever needs to be done. She works either with others or alone. She does not seem to resent adult directions and is respectful to her parents. She appears to be fond of them, but not especially close to them or to most of the others in the

[5] For life story of Bianca's mother, see *The Navaho Door*, pp. 109–119.

A SHAMPOOED CHILD SHAMPOOS HER DOLL

ENCOURAGING THE FIRST STEPS

family. An exception is the sister immediately above her in age who is the second wife in the near-by hogan. Relationships in the family in general seem to be cordial but not close. Even the parents have not become especially devoted to each other through the years they have spent together. They get along very well in a matter-of-fact, unemotional way, each managing his own sphere and helping the other as need arises; and both are interested in making their common living and raising their family.

Two anecdotes about them are typically Navaho. The mother was asked why only two of the children had been to school. She replied that the rest had not wanted to go. Asked why she had not insisted, she said, "I listen to my children, and I have to take their word." (The two remained at school two years each. They learned a little English which they have mostly forgotten and are too shy to use.)

The other illustrates the Navaho (and general Indian) attitude toward ages. Dr. Leighton first saw Bianca in 1940, when she looked, and was said to be, about thirteen. In 1942 the parents insisted she was sixteen or seventeen.

Of the two households with more than one wife, one evidently gets along well, and the other not so well. In the group a mile away the two sisters supplement each other in the work of cooking, cleaning, caring for the children, and tending the sheep. The visitor gets the impression that the smoothness is due principally to the submission of the younger sister to the older. In the hogan near Bianca's home a good deal of friction exists. This had really started before the second sister joined the group, for it was felt that she alienated the husband's affections for his first wife. Matters were made worse when, after her marriage, she did not take the secondary place, as the first wife expected. At the time of the testing, the husband and second wife had gone away to sheep camp and left the first wife behind. Apparently this was practically a separation, and the first wife's temper was very bad, especially after brief visits from the husband to see their two little girls. The younger wife, it will be remembered, was Bianca's favorite sister.

Later we heard that Bianca also had married this man. Since she and the second wife were on good terms, and doubtless the wife had consented to the arrangement, it is likely that this combination will work better than the first one. Perhaps Bianca would prefer living with this sister and sharing her husband to either staying at home unmarried or marrying and having to live alone with her husband.

The tests gave Bianca an IQ of only 57 on the Arthur. Her general behavior and her performance on the other tests makes this evaluation seem very much too low, for she does better than average elsewhere. She shows the expected Navaho interests and attitudes and is well aware of the sort of behavior that is expected of her. She seems to be in the midst of an active adjustment both to being an adult and to being a woman. She goes at the problem vigorously, depending more on her intellect than her emotions to guide her actions. She has not yet achieved a really mature status, but she shows no serious difficulty of adjustment and will probably reach her goal successfully.

Summary and Discussion. This family lives by the techniques and in the manner that have been described as the way of The People, yet they, like most others, have been touched to some extent by the encroaching white world. For this family it has not raised any particular problem as yet and has mostly served to make their life a little easier than that of their forbears. Even the girls who went to school did not stay there long enough to become dissatisfied with their parents' way of living.

Bianca has been thoroughly educated to fit into this same kind of life and can be expected to be an adequate Navaho housewife. Since she seems to take pleasure in working, holds the attitudes that her tribe has developed, and knows no other way of living, she will probably find her life reasonably satisfactory.

NAVAHO MOUNTAIN CHILDREN [6]

CASE 1. *Light Boy's family is in the "younger married set." In twelve years they have built up a nice flock of sheep from a small beginning and have made themselves a good place in the community, although the husband is an outsider. Their little son has the best assortment of personal and environmental assets of any of the sixteen cases.*

Light Boy at seven is a bright-eyed, lively little boy who, with his nine-year-old brother, represents the family at the day school. An older brother stays at home to herd the flocks of his parents and grandparents, and two other brothers and a sister are too young for school. Two children have died. Light Boy, thus, is in about as

---

[6] Figure 1 on p. 142 is an abbreviated family tree of the Navaho Mountain children.

undistinguished a position in his family as was Bill (of Ramah) in his, too young to take an important part and too old to be a baby.

From a very early time in his life this boy has seemed to be "growing up" faster than most children. For example, he is said to have ceased to nurse of his own accord a little before he was a year old, preferring goat's milk flavored with coffee in a cup; and, very soon after he learned to walk, he is said to have always gone outside to urinate like the men instead of wetting himself as had his brothers. While it is likely that his precociousness is somewhat exaggerated, these reports show the impression he made on his family. He learned to talk early and tried to sing Navaho songs when men came around to practice with his father. After he went to school he liked to show the children at home pictures in magazines, making up English names for things he saw if he didn't know the right one. Everything new that he heard about he wanted to try, especially if it was something the men or older boys were doing.

In all of these things Light Boy is unique in the family, and they represent his spontaneous imagination and activity, since no one has urged him to do them. His family is much amused by him and shows no tendency to suppress him, though he is expected to conform like the other children to good Navaho manners.

Although his mother must have been very busy with bearing and rearing eight children in twelve years, as well as supervising the sheep, she had time to notice Light Boy and to remember his doings. On the other hand, he could not be said to be her favorite. She made more of a pet of his next older brother, who was sickly as a baby and has always stayed around the hogan more than the others. The mother is an attractive woman, a good housekeeper, and definitely the mistress of the home but not at all domineering. She and her husband get along well together and take much interest in their children.

Since the family lives close to the mother's parents, Light Boy has his grandfather and a half-grown uncle as well as his father to admire and imitate. The grandfather has a reputation for being lazy, and the fact that he does not do much work gives him plenty of time to spend with his grandsons and nephews, whom he teaches to ride, hunt, and perform other manly occupations. They are all very fond of him.

As might be expected from what has been said, Light Boy was anxious to go to school. He was allowed to do so before he was six, and he took part enthusiastically to the best of his ability. Although he did not accomplish much scholastically, he enjoyed himself and became the school pet. He goes around the school grounds counting to himself sometimes, will stay after school is dismissed to finish reading a page he has started, and likes to sing before the class, sometimes even persuading other little boys to sing with him. He is not a show-off, just greatly interested in everything that is going on and not afraid of being laughed at. He tags around after the bigger boys when he is not busy playing. At home he is the leader even if his older brothers are present, but at school he defers to the older boys.

On the tests, too, Light Boy was eager and successful. He made an IQ of 136 on the Arthur, and the other tests show him to have superior mental ability. He seems to be nearer to maturity than one would expect for his seven years, but he still is hampered to some extent by babyish tendencies, so that it is difficult to tell just how well he can use his intellectual gifts. He seems very spontaneous and free in his activity and very successful in his personal relations. He should get along well with both his agemates and older people, and he gives evidence of a very sound personal adjustment himself.

Summary and Discussion. Here is a child who has qualities that are prized in white society as well as his own; intelligence, for instance, and a free-and-easy way with people. In spite of being something of a pet wherever he finds himself, he has not been spoiled by it but, perhaps, further encouraged to develop the friendly tendencies he possesses. Life has treated him kindly and given him no reason to distrust it or to build defenses against it.

All this has happened in a quite average family, no better and no worse than many others. Perhaps his parents' chief contribution, besides the chance combination of characteristics which he inherited from them, has been to let him alone to develop at his own speed. It is possible, too, that the attention and instruction of an adult like his grandfather has helped to give him a self-confidence that makes him able to mobilize his capacities. In that case, one might well ask, "Why is Light Boy the only one in the family like this?" To that we do not know the answer, and it is probable that chance, both in his inheritance and his life experience, played a large part.

In any case, Light Boy is an outstanding child, with qualities which may well make him a leader in his community when he grows up.

CASE II. *The mother of this child died when the little girl was two years old, since which time her paternal grandmother and stepmother have taken care of her. Her father is an elderly and much respected Singer.*

Little Runner is now seven years old. She is an attractive brighteyed little girl, who seemed quite unabashed to be at the school to be tested and dashed around the place when not working on tests. However she showed little tendency to play with the other children and seemed rather self-willed and headstrong.

Her mother was a young girl from another locality. She was visiting at Navaho Mountain when she died in giving birth to a second child, who also died. As her family did not claim the living child, her husband's mother took care of her. Little Runner, then two years old, had been nursing until this happened and is said to have had no idea how to eat solid food. Her father found her a bottle for goat's milk, and her grandmother chewed up food for her. In about six months, her father married again and left the grandmother's place. Little Runner was evidently something of a companion for the old lady and was taught to card wool and do other things which are unusual for a child of that age. On the other hand, she received even less than the usual amount of training in cleanliness and conformity to Navaho social customs. When she was three the grandmother tired of keeping her, and the father, who had reached the conclusion that she needed more supervision than she was getting, took her to his wife.

This woman, Little Runner's stepmother, had two children, seven and nine, but because she had at one time been very ill her father had insisted that she have the ceremony and take the medicine that are believed to confer sterility. Since that time she had never become pregnant, and she was happy to have a small child added to the family. Because Little Runner was not her own child, however, she hesitated to discipline her as she really needed, but she accomplished a certain amount by persuasion and encouragement. A problem arose when she took a small nephew into the family for the winter. Little Runner was very jealous of this child and unkind to him at first; but, when urged to "act like a good relative" to him, she gradually got over this, behavior. Although the grandmother did not want the little girl any longer herself, she kept a close eye on what the stepmother did, and frequently spread gossip that the child was being mistreated. This does not seem to have any basis in fact and is belied by Little Runner's freedom of action and attitude toward her stepmother.

The father is a Singer who is in considerable demand. He is a kindly person of about sixty, fond of all children, and especially fond of this small daughter. In addition to his ceremonial work he farms for his family. Although he has been well paid for his singing, he has never managed to accumulate a fortune, perhaps because he has had to pay for the treatment of illnesses of his four previous wives. He has several children living in different places with their maternal relatives, and Little Runner is the only one with him. One of his sons went to school for many years and worked for missionaries. In spite of the difference in viewpoint that this may have caused between them, he and his father are very cordial to each other.

The family live near the stepmother's mother. Little Runner was the only small child in the group for some time and played mostly with her stepsister, who was five years older.

On the tests, the child's lack of discipline was very evident. It seemed to interfere greatly with her making a good showing, although on the Arthur she earned an IQ of 95 in spite of it. Elsewhere she showed momentary evidence of better-than-average intellectual capacity, but such impulsiveness and babyish tendencies that she was not consistently good. She is very aware of the world around her, but she has not found a satisfactory way of dealing with it and is rather concerned over this. (It is probably for this reason that she did not play with the schoolchildren.) She views adults as people who make her do some things or won't let her do others.

Summary and Discussion. This is an active little girl, probably quite bright, whose life experience has not yet helped her to exercise the control over her activity which she needs to make it most effective. Her mother's youth and early death, the grandmother's age, and the stepmother's reluctance to seem to discipline her have all contributed to this lack of control, which is partly due also to the fact that she was the youngest child for so long and her father's favorite. The relationship between stepmother and grandmother reminds one of that between divorced parents in white society where the child soon learns to play one against the other for his own ends.

Although Little Runner is willful and undisciplined, she is teachable, and the very fact that she is concerned about her relations with others may be an indication that her self-control will increase. It seems as if she would be benefited by going soon to school, where she will be with more children of her own age and will not be able to manipulate people because of emotional ties but will have to do the adjusting herself.

CASE III. *In this boy's well-to-do family the mother is very conservative and perfectionistic, the father more "progressive" and lenient. Our subject, though intelligent, has difficulties with his interpersonal relations.*

At the time of the testing, Teasing Boy, a freckle-faced lad of fourteen, had been coming to the day school from the time it was built six years earlier. An older brother also came until he grew too old for day school and decided he did not want to go away to boarding school. Teasing Boy has always been a tease. When he played tricks on the other children in school one of his teachers thought he was doing it "for meanness" and used to punish him. In this atmosphere he made a very poor showing and had almost decided to quit school when the teacher was replaced by one who encouraged him and overlooked his mischief. This sort of handling brought out the boy's better qualities to such an extent that he has become one of the best pupils in school and a leader of the children instead of a nuisance to them.

Both Teasing Boy's parents belong to the "Navaho Mountain Family." The mother has never allowed her husband to buy her any household aids such as beds, a cookstove, or a sewing machine, because "that wasn't the Navaho way" and "it would make them lazy." She is the best weaver in the area but is said to weave her rugs always in the same pattern, varying only the colors. She is a very particular housekeeper. As her health has become poor, she has had to depend more and more upon her mother, who lives in a near-by hogan, and her daughters to help her maintain her standards. There is a hint that one daughter feels rather overworked.

Though the mother has never played favorites among her children, she admits to a special feeling for Teasing Boy and the rest of the family think she spoils him. She can do more with him than can the rest.

The father is a kindly, hard-working man who is devoted to his wife and anxious to make her life easier. He is interested in community affairs to the extent of coming often to the school and making presents of food when supplies seem low. He is generous to his children also and bought one of his sons the first Indian-owned truck in the region when he wanted one. The family is rated as the most prosperous at the Mountain, which is due in part to the whole group's labors, in part to the father's shrewd management. Teasing Boy has done his share of the work, mostly sheep herding and farming, and is said to be a good worker; but because of his teasing no one wants to work with him.

Our subject is fifth of seven children who range in age from thirty years to four. He was the baby of the family for seven years and had started to school when his next youngest brother was born. He was hard to wean and slow to walk and talk. He is thought to be shy by his family because he never talks very much. He remembers liking to try to make the baby laugh when he came home from school in the afternoon, and he is now proud of his little brother for the things he can do but very impatient with him when he shows any babyish traits. In spite of his affection, he makes the smaller boy's life miserable with playing tricks on him. The youngest child is a girl, and she is the only one in the family toward whom Teasing Boy seems to feel free to show his affection.

On the intelligence tests this boy's rating of best pupil in the school is justified when he attains an IQ of 120. On all the other tests also his intellectual capacities seem to be superior. However, he does not make as much use of them as he might because he is over-cautious and over-critical and does not want to do anything unless he knows he can do it right. He is shy of any sort of emotional relationship with other people, and because he cannot deal with them on this basis, he maintains a contact of a sort with them by directing them. Evidently he feels quite attracted to people but dares not admit it; he works out the frustration he feels in petty acts of aggression, like teasing. He must feel very insecure, and the only defense he relies on beside teasing is his intellect. This means that he is very restrained in his reactions and controls the expression of his imagination as well as of his emotions.

Summary and Discussions. In the light of the test results, one can understand many things in Teasing Boy's life story that seemed rather incongruous otherwise. For instance, why should a boy with a superior mental endowment be slow in walking and talking? It is commonly thought that such a child is subnormal mentally, but this certainly is not the case here. Rather, it seems that his cautiousness and need for being sure of his ability stood in his way, so that he didn't try to talk until he really knew how. Perhaps if one questioned his parents carefully, it would be found that he spoke his first words more correctly than most babies do.

Many readers will have known some person who acted in the "contrary" way this boy does with his teasing. Like him, many of these persons behave thus because they want to carry on relationships with other people but are not able to do it in a more direct and satisfactory manner. When a teacher punishes such a child for his clumsy efforts at friendliness, it cuts off his only contact with his fellows. The more skillful act of turning the aggressive impulses into channels of leadership eliminates the feeling of frustration the punishment roused, and also opens new and more productive possibilities to him.

CASE IV. *The father of this child spent ten years in boarding school, then came home and became a Singer. Both parents have decided characters and ideas; this has created a problem for this daughter, who is a nonconformist to Navaho ways.*

Slim Schoolgirl, thirteen years old, is a rather shy and self-contained girl who has been coming to the day school for five years. She is the only child in a family of seven to attend school and was sent partly because she wanted to go, partly because she was not much use around the home and disliked women's work. From the time she was a little girl Slim Schoolgirl has been something of a lone wolf in the family. The other children all liked to care for the sheep or do their other work in pairs, but this one preferred to herd with only the dog for company. She showed no aptitude for cooking, carding wool, spinning, or weaving, and actively resisted learning these arts. A good deal of pressure was put on her to do them "like a good Navaho," especially by her maternal grandmother, and she was frequently compared to her older sister who did everything she was supposed to do. She rather enjoyed herding the sheep and looking after her little brothers and sisters, but not the other work. Her family hoped that she would like school better.

Actually she does get along well in school and has become the best student of the girls. But her ability is chiefly along lines of learning by memory, and she does not show much tendency to develop her own ideas on the basis of facts she learns. Although she reads well, she is not good as an interpreter. She does not like to be called on and often refuses to answer, but she will frequently volunteer. If the class is acting out a little story from the book, Slim Schoolgirl likes to read it for them and pays close attention to see that they do just as the book says. As at home she does not like cooking and sewing and is not good at them. This is not just because they are manual, for she does very good art work. She does not seem to have any close friends among the girls, nor does she establish close relations with the teacher or the Navaho assistants. In school quarrels she always takes the part of her mother's brothers, who are about her age.

When the whole school was taken to Tuba City to be X rayed to see if there were any cases of tuberculosis, Slim Schoolgirl acted almost terrified by the unfamiliar situation, stuck very close to the group, and seemed greatly relieved when she got back to the Mountain. When she developed mumps with most of the rest of the pupils, she ran away from school so that her father could treat her. He scolded her roundly for running away.

Slim Schoolgirl's father is one of the few of his generation at the Mountain who went away to boarding school. He was told to stay there until the family sent him word to come back, which they did after ten years. On his return he married and settled down in the community as if he had never been away. He even learned to be a Singer, which occupation has become an important source of income to him. Partly because of his schooling he has represented his people politically, and because of this and his native force of character and intelligence, he is often called in to settle local disputes. One might speculate that his becoming a Singer after ten years in school was a repudiation of white people's ways, but we do not know enough about this man to do more than guess. It may mean that, like his daughter, he knows what he wants and gets it.

His wife is quite conservative, especially when they are living near her mother. Both she and her husband recognize that they get along better by themselves than with her mother, who is inclined to make trouble between them, but at times they come "home" in spite of this. Both parents are interested in their children and try to treat them impartially. From the interview in which they describe them, however, it is plain to see that they do not know just what to do with Slim Schoolgirl. She is headstrong, rather than pliable like their other children, and if she will not learn the duties of a Navaho woman, the only alternative is to send her to school. The father has more influence with her than the mother.

On the Arthur Test Slim Schoolgirl achieved an IQ of 100, so that she has good average ability. This was confirmed by the other tests and is probably in keeping with her school standing. The most striking thing about her performance is the great degree of reserve and restraint that she showed. She has very little originality or creative powers and can use her intellectual ability only in set, routine ways. She is very shy of any kind of emotional contacts with other people, as is Teasing Boy, but she does not show the desire to make contacts that he does. She is immature emotionally for her age, has not become independent of her parents as yet, and on the whole has a rather rigid, unyielding pattern of reacting. There is a hint that she resents adult authority; but, instead of fighting it, she resists it passively. It seems probable, also, that there is more to her than appears in the tests, for she was more reluctant to "give forth" than most children. This unverbalized part of her personality may find expression in such things as art or craft work.

Summary and Discussion. Slim Schoolgirl is a child who does not appear to have found her proper niche in either home or school setting, though she gets along better at school than at home. Her difficulty seems to be a combination of being unique in her family (see first paragraph of this case) and being born into an environment that does not give her many chances to choose activities that she likes and can perform. Even if her family had wanted to provide her with outlets she could utilize, there was little they could offer except work around their home or going to school. Perhaps if she had fitted into the family life better, she would have had less trouble with her interpersonal relations, for she would have felt some approval and security simply from being a good girl. As it is, she cannot get close to people easily; she knows besides that she is not doing what is expected of her and is disappointing her family, which makes it even harder for her.

Speculations as to Slim Schoolgirl's Prospects. What of her future? We could paint it very black, with Slim Schoolgirl not getting along well anywhere, and we might be right. Another possibility is that she may go away to boarding school for a time when she finishes the day-school grades. If she could bring herself to do this in spite of the sort of feelings she showed when she went to be X rayed, she might benefit greatly from the broader experience and could probably be trained to do routine work that would keep her from having to live as a Navaho housewife. However, wherever she goes, she will probably marry sooner or later and become a Navaho housewife of some sort. Since she expects this, she will very likely accept it with fair grace and do the work better for herself than she does for her mother and grandmother.

She may never be very enthusiastic about this nor radiantly happy, but she will probably not be acutely miserable either, since she has lived already for several years in a way that was not ideally suited to her, and yet she has not been by any means unable to bear it.

CASE V. *This boy's family was founded by a man from a distant region who came to Navaho Mountain and married two sisters, who bore him twenty-three children. Many of them are now grown and married. The father's affections were necessarily spread rather thinly, so that the chief ties of the children have been with their respective mothers. Tabaha's Son, our subject, is the seventh of nine children of one of the wives and at sixteen is the oldest one left at home.*

This family furnishes one example of why the Navaho population has increased so much in seventy years. Here it has taken only about forty years for three individuals to multiply seven times in the first generation; if grandchildren were counted, the increase would be closer to fifteen-fold in the same period. It is rather unusual that so many of the children should have survived.

Whereas in white society to have so many children would probably spell poverty and public assistance, in Navaho life the children frequently improve the economic status of the family by their help in herding, farming, and weaving. Occasionally, of course, illness or bad luck intervenes and the extra numbers become only a burden, but in general the children easily "pay for their keep," and it has evidently been so in this family. Even though six children of our subject's mother are already married and so no longer helping at home, the standing of the father and mother is still better than average. This has happened, moreover, in spite of their having sent three of the children away to school for several years. Undoubtedly the parents are good managers and the children good workers. Perhaps they were unusually fortunate in their selection of a farming place deep in a canyon where there is more moisture and less danger of frost than on the higher ground.

A child so far down the list as this son might well have become lost among so many full and half brothers and sisters. However, Tabaha's Son was spared this by two factors. In the first place, he was the baby for four years, so that his mother could devote more time to him and also become much attached to him. In the second place, the older children, including the three boys, married and left home before this boy was very old, so that he became the "man of the house" in his father's absence. Since the two wives maintained separate establishments, even though they were not far apart, the father must have been away from each hogan more than where there is only one wife. This gave Tabaha's Son more responsibility and also more feeling of being important than one might expect in such a family.

It is not known whether this boy ever wanted to go to school, but in any case he did not do so. Instead he stayed home and learned to be a good farmer. He never had a chance to go away from the Mountain until the year of the study, when his brother-in-law took him out to work. The report came back that Tabaha's Son "sure caught on quick." He was something of a favorite of his maternal grandfather, who thought he would make a good Singer. This grandfather used to take him up into the Mountain looking for plant medicines for different ceremonials, and since the old man's death he goes by himself to find them.

He is said to be a steady, dependable worker and the one of the family on whom his mother and sisters can count for help when they need it. He has always been quiet and easy to handle and seems to want to do as he should without being told. When seen once in a group of white strangers, he appeared interested and willing to participate but usually waited for the others to make the first move.

Tabaha's Son was willing to walk nine miles to the school to take the tests. He did quite well on them for a boy without school experience, earning an IQ of 99. His performance throughout was consistent and solid at a good average level, with great emphasis on the practical commonplaces and little evidence of originality or imagination. He has a good feeling for other people but avoids emotional relations with them, preferring rather to treat them as an adult does a child. This attitude seems to have arisen from his having had to assume an adult position rather suddenly and before he was really ready for it. He feels a little "on the spot" and uneasy about his ability to fulfill people's expectations. He is in full accord with "typical" Navaho attitudes and beliefs, which he seems to have accepted without much question, as his mother tacitly assumed he would. He admires strength, industry, and the acquisition of property, but he is not aggressive or competitive in regard to these things himself, content to do as well as he can and be satisfied with that.

Summary and Discussion. Tabaha's Son is a "good Navaho" of a plain and uninspired but quite substantial sort. It is likely that he will go through life in a thoroughly creditable way, causing no one any trouble, and enjoying himself quietly.

CASE VI. *The case of this girl's family is an example of how lack of parental harmony and balance creates problems for the children.*

The mother of seventeen-year-old Round Girl is a talkative, goodhearted, but "bossy" woman who dominates the family scene. She is married to a man from another district who has never made much of a place for himself among his wife's relatives. He is not much concerned with making a living for his family, leaving it up to his wife and children, nor does he take much responsibility otherwise. It is hard to say whether he acts like this because of his wife's domineering ways or whether his wife became bossy because she had to take charge of the family affairs.

The family consists of six children. The first is a boy who took over his father's functions to a large extent, giving advice and teaching and controlling the younger children, as well as helping with the work. Round Girl comes next. She has always been a quiet, hard-working girl, completely under her mother's thumb and very dependent upon her. The next girl revolted somewhat and has caused the family great concern by "running around" too much. Of the three younger boys, the oldest was backward in developing, is extremely shy, and has bad nightmares. The middle one runs away from both home and school, depending on where he is supposed to be staying, and, although a bright little chap, he is very hard to control. The baby of the family, at six years, is still unduly dependent on his mother. Thus none of these children, except possibly the two oldest, could be called well adjusted.

There was an opportunity to see the mother in action when she brought the youngest boy to take his tests. She stayed with him while he took the Arthur, and although it was explained to her before starting and she was reminded throughout, that it was a test for him and not her, she insisted on telling him what to do. Instead of looking at the examiner or the interpreter, as was common in other children who were uncertain of what they were suposed to do, this child kept looking at his mother. She would give him advice, which was often wrong because she knew nothing about the tests herself. The testers' impression of the performance was that she confused the little boy, and he did not do so well as if he had trusted his own judgment. She was excluded from the room during the other tests, and the child seemed quite able to function adequately.

What of the two oldest? There is not a great deal of information on the boy as he had left the community, first to go to boarding school and then to a defense job. Perhaps he had the best chance by being the eldest because he stepped into a position which permitted self-expression without any competition. Evidently he shared enough of his mother's executive qualities to carry this off well.

Round Girl has never caused anyone any concern on account of her behavior. She started to herd sheep as soon as she was big enough, cared for the family flock until one of the younger boys could take charge, and since then has been her mother's mainstay in the hogan. She was always very shy and rarely went anywhere, not even to the trading post or day school often, in spite of the fact that her sister and two brothers attended the school and her mother was its most frequent visitor.

When Round Girl was sixteen, her mother decided it was time for her to marry and looked about for a husband for her. She

settled on a schoolboy who planned to make his future among white
people. When he finally told the mother that he did not think
Round Girl would fit into his scheme, she was furious. Round
Girl's own reaction was profound shame, which made her want to
hide from everyone for several months, but before long another husband was found. Within three weeks after her marriage Round
Girl's shame had disappeared, and even her shy manner was quite
changed. It was as if she had been behaving as she thought she
was supposed to: when she was a young girl, she was supposed to
be shy; but when she was a married woman she must hold up her
head and look the world in the eye. There was no corresponding
alteration in her character otherwise. Her life is almost exactly the
same as it was before; she does not even have a separate hogan, and
her mother still directs her every move.

Her experience has been very limited, for the family did not live
very close to any other as a rule, and she had no playmates but the
sheep. Even when she was little, she did not have any playthings
except for an old bone that she used to pretend was a baby or an
animal. When her brothers and sisters came along, she was busy
with the sheep most of the time and did not have a chance to play
even with them. Thus her natural disposition and her lack of opportunity have worked together to limit her human associations. One
feels that the schoolboy perhaps did her a favor when he refused
to subject her to the need for getting used to many people of a sort
she knew little about. If she had the right qualities, even with her
limited background, such an experience would be very developing,
but under the circumstances it would probably hold much misery.

Round Girl came to do the tests with apparent willingness but
with little self-confidence. She achieved an IQ of only 69 on the
Arthur. The other tests make it seem that this is almost surely too
low to measure her ability. She is probably about "low average"
(around 90). It is clear that she has spent much time near a forceful person, and that she gets along by retiring from a challenging
situation rather than reacting directly to it. She is passive and dependent, naïve, and rather immature inwardly, though her outer
reactions are conventional and adult. She is aware of the demands
of the world but not at all sure that she can meet them satisfactorily; nor is she sure of her adequacy as a woman. It is plain that
she has been disappointed in her relations with men and feels a

little anxiety about her sexual role, as if she had had sexual activity forced upon her before she was ready for it psychologically.

Summary and Discussion. What is wrong with this family? We have seen dominating mothers before but none so blatantly domineering as this mother. Here, moreover, the father does not contribute much to offset the mother's effect on the children. Round Girl "gets along" well enough, but it has hampered her development to have her mother make all decisions and tell her exactly what to do. Her personality has been "dwarfed" in a sense, and her maturing delayed. In other words, she is not the person she would have been if she had grown up in a family where she was encouraged to take responsibility and make decisions.

Of the children younger than Round Girl, all seem to be reacting in an undesirable way to their situation, but whether it can all be blamed on the mother is hard to say. Some of them may be too much like their mother and thus be in conflict with her. Others may feel the lack of help from the father or too much overshadowing by the older brother. The details would be different for each child, just as the sort of behavior difficulty is different, depending partly on the child's own personality, partly on his position in the family and relations to other family members.

One often thinks that problem behavior in children is a product of the complexity and strains of "civilized" ways of living, but we can see plainly here that complexity has nothing to do with this case. One can hardly imagine people living more simply or with less social complexity than at Navaho Mountain, yet the same difficulties occur that are found in children of both rich and poor in white society. As one often finds when he carefully examines problems in white children, here also the trouble seems to lie in the interpersonal relations of the group of which the child is a member.

DISCUSSION

One of the striking things about these sixteen children is their variability. Some of the qualities are mentioned frequently, yet always in a different combination. Some children seem a good deal alike fundamentally, yet their life experiences have caused them to develop differently. There are features common to several families, yet none is exactly like another.

Most readers will have exclaimed to themselves for at least one of the cases, "Why, he's just like the boy I know down the street here!" or "Cousin Mary's oldest daughter is just like this girl." Readers who have had occasion to do case work may think, "The Joneses are just like Round Girl's family. Mrs. Jones is the most awful boss, Mr. Jones doesn't amount to much, and there is something the matter with most of the children there, too." However, if it were possible to gather in the same place the boy down the street, Cousin Mary's oldest daughter, the Joneses, and their Navaho counterparts, the chances are that the differences between them would be more apparent than the similarities. Much of their social behavior would set them apart into white people and Navahos, and things that pleased and interested one group would leave the other cold or even annoyed. Left together long enough, Cousin Mary's daughter and Slim Schoolgirl might discover that they had much the same assortment of assets and liabilities and that they liked to work in much the same way, but it would be a long time indeed before a present of a war bond to Slim Schoolgirl and a sheep to Cousin Mary's daughter would be equally satisfactory to each girl. No matter how alike they are fundamentally, they have grown up in different worlds, and the superstructure of habits, tastes, and goals erected upon the underlying character sets them far apart.

In conclusion it it worth pointing out that the tests provided indications of many of the social and psychological characteristics of Navahos which had been described or inferred by previous observers.

This would seem to have important implications for future research. In the case of the Navaho, perhaps, one might argue that the research program was not really entirely necessary because there were adequate data from other sources. But suppose one wished these data for a group that had been less extensively studied. By applying these methods, or better ones, could the main characteristics be supplied? The picture would be incomplete in some respects, and many of the finer details might be missing, but the principal outlines, sufficient for general forecasting and planning, could be expected to appear. The writers are by no means willing to assert that tests alone will show everything about a group of people. In the present experience, they seemed to supply useful material with relatively little time and energy. But it is important to point out that success in analyzing them seemed to depend upon at least a minimum acquaintance with the culture of the people tested. Had it been done entirely "blind," the conclusions might have been markedly skewed. Thus the net impression is that tests are useful and hold considerable promise for quicker means of reaching an understanding of people than the usual anthropological techniques. However, in their present state of imperfection the tests cannot be trusted implicitly to give the information desired but must be checked against, and used in conjunction with, material obtained by the time-honored methods of observation and interview.

CONCLUSION

THE PROJECT AND THE PEOPLE

THE PROJECT
and THE PEOPLE

IN THIS final chapter three questions will be discussed briefly: What did the Research Project contribute to an understanding of Navahos? What was actually learned? What is the general implication for administration and planning?

CONTRIBUTIONS OF THE PROJECT

To begin with, this was a coöperative venture in which many people took part, as can be seen from the list in the front of the book. No one interpreter, tester, interviewer, or analyst dominated the material. If one person skewed the conclusions a little in one direction because of his personal biases, another probably offset the error by skewing them in the opposite direction. At the least, the inescapable selective effect of any single worker on any body of data was counterbalanced to some extent. Thus assertions and opinions in this book are a consensus, not the notions of one individual or even of a few persons.

Largely because the investigations were coöperative, it was possible to work in widely separated areas, where the geographic, social, economic, and intercultural conditions varied considerably. This provided an opportunity to see what the range of variation was in response to standard techniques, what local characteristics emerged from the tests and interviews, whether or not there were common characteristics that would set all of the areas apart from a white community or a group of other Indians.

It was found that The People do share certain common traits and attitudes even though these are modified somewhat in the three areas studied. The common traits become even more apparent when one compares them with those found for Hopi, Sioux, Papago, and Zuni in the present project.[1] It is obvious that the variation between Shiprock, Ramah, and Navaho Mountain is less than the difference between Navahos and white men or any of the other tribes studied.

---

[1] See the volumes listed in the Preface and articles noted in the Bibliography.

General "plans for Indians," then, must be especially tailored to fit the Navaho situation, and even a "Navaho plan" will have to be modified further according to where it is being put into effect.

The government has failed to achieve all it hoped for partly because it did not take enough account of psychological and cultural factors in its work with The People. Although many persons who had worked with Navahos had their ideas as to "Navaho psychology" and the Navaho view of life, few had been willing to state them. Something could be gathered from hints and inferences in their writings, but there was no systematic effort to set the matter forth. This was due somewhat to hesitancy on the part of the various individuals to attribute to Navahos generally what they had found to be true of the limited number they themselves knew; somewhat also to the fact that few of the workers considered themselves competent to discuss psychological questions.

One is now able to state these psychological characteristics with a conviction that they are valid because they appear in data collected and interpreted by so many people (including those not working in this project) and in such diverse areas as Shiprock, Ramah, and Navaho Mountain.

WHAT WAS LEARNED

MANKIND everywhere is faced with certain basic problems of existence. The way in which these problems are dealt with (together with the social usages, sentiments, and attitudes that develop around both the problems and their solutions) has been spoken of as "culture" or "way of life." This is by no means a simple, unitary affair. Nor is it static and unchanging. What has been said of it in this book and *The Navaho* is already out of date in some respects owing to subtle or more drastic alterations which are continually taking place.

One might say that the way of life or culture of any group of people is created by three principal interacting sets of factors — the physical environment, the "personalities" [2] of members of the group, and the historical accidents (including contacts with other peoples) which the group experiences.

At the same time, one is forced to recognize that each of these three sets of factors is also greatly influenced by the group's way of

[2] Used as defined in Chapter 6.

life. For example, a young Navaho becomes "characteristically Navaho" only if he grows up in the Navaho social environment. If he is brought up by white people in New York City, or even if his own parents take him far from the tribe to grow up, he will differ in both obvious and subtle ways from his cousin who stayed on the Reservation. The traces left by historical experience become a part of the cultural tradition. Even the physical environment is subject to being changed in some respects by the way of life of the people who occupy a given part of it. These interactions could be diagramed thus:

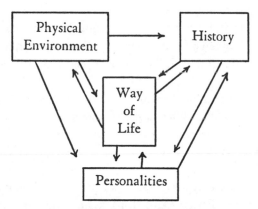

While the diagram is greatly oversimplified, if each box were enlarged to itemize all the factors it includes, it would present a fairly adequate picture. Certain features of the outer three boxes are comparatively independent, owing to inherent or accidental factors, but the central box is utterly dependent upon the rest even though at the same time it may strongly influence the others.

In the most general sense the outer boxes could be elaborated as follows: The physical environment of The People consists in high, dry, brilliantly colored, fantastically sculptured country where the climate and vegetation vary from "desert" at the lower altitudes to "steppe" at intermediate heights and even to "sub-humid" on the mountain tops. The natural progression of an "erosion cycle" in this easily eroded soil and the considerable overstocking of the range have combined to eliminate much of the formerly abundant grass and have led to the formation of innumerable gullies where once were productive fields and meadows. In addition population has increased greatly, and hence there are more horse trails and wagon and automobile tracks to channel the flow of surface water and cut more gullies. Although the weather in most regions is pleasant, unpredictability and violence of temperature change and rain or snowfall are characteristic.

As to their history, The People emerged from the mists of the unknown into the southwestern regions as bands of hunters of wild animals and gatherers of wild plants, with probably a very simple culture of bare subsistence. They appear to have admired what they found among the Pueblo Indians and gradually to have taken over many of their customs and methods. Possibly they became farmers, living in small compact villages on mesa tops like the Pueblos. Then came the Spaniards, bringing to the Pueblos sheep, horses, and cattle. By the time the Spaniards first saw The People, some, at least, had acquired domestic animals in addition to their even more important farming.

As to the chief personality traits to be found among The People, one might say first that Navahos are preëminently a practical folk. This has become apparent in so many connections that it seems almost axiomatic. A second striking trait is their respect for individuality, which allows each person a measure of free choice of action within the limits set by society and assigns a nearly equal place to men and women. Perhaps the third quality that should be mentioned is their activity, freedom of movement, and general air of alertness and interest in the world around them. White strangers might miss this because of the Navaho capacity for control of behavior in a strange situation, but those who know them well have a strong impression of their energy, vitality, and curiosity. Even their language emphasizes varieties of action rather than more static values. Although they maintain an outward poise and control under most circumstances, inwardly they may be in turmoil. They are sensitive to criticism and ridicule by other people, but not prone to feel guilty over undiscovered misdeeds. Their imaginative capacities seem to find expression in adapting the inventions and methods of others to their way of living, in the artistic embellishment of themselves, their horses, and the designs of their jewelry and weaving, and in the music and poetry of their ceremonials. Although they are moody at times, they seem, on the whole, to enjoy life and have a keen sense of humor which delights in subtle puns and the frailties of human nature.

It is worth noting that this entire description of personality is in terms of culture. This is by no means accidental, for the principal way in which one assesses personality is to study how it shows itself in action, either physical, "mental," or "emotional." This fact serves to highlight the interdependence between "personality" and the "way of life" by which it is molded and in which its qualities become apparent. Yet it is equally important to bear in mind the probability that some personality characteristics are independent of culture to a degree; that Navahos are born with certain temperamental potentialities which may differ from those of other groups of people. These potentialities are as necessary to the development of a particular life-way as are the cultural forces in shaping individuals to a pattern.

In order to see further how culture is affected by, and in turn affects, the three factors already described, let us consider certain items from The People's way of life and contrast them at times with corresponding items in the culture of the Pueblo Indians to see what is peculiarly Navaho about them.

One could say of both Pueblos and Navahos that their adaptation to southwestern conditions of climate and geography had been subsistence farming with sheep raising as a commercial crop, and he would be quite correct. However, there have been important differences between the two groups which seem to emphasize contrasts both in personality and in history. In some Navaho regions, farming remains the principal occupation as it does with the Pueblos, while in other regions sheep raising surpasses it; yet, even where sheep raising has become important to a Pueblo tribe economically, farming still maintains a central place with greater emotional weight than herding ever acquires. Another interesting difference is that the Pueblo Indians rarely "follow the sheep" but prefer to take turns at leaving the village to stay with the herd or even to hire a herder; Navahos deserted their villages entirely and took to living in scattered family groups that moved to summer and winter pastures or from water source to water source according to the needs of their animals. Moreover the Pueblo Indians did not utilize the horse to rove far and wide as did the Navahos.

It seems probable that these differences are in part an expression of the greater fluidity of Navaho ways, of their greater freedom of mind and body, of their curiosity, and also of a difference in historical background. It would undoubtedly be a much more drastic move for Pueblo Indians, sedentary for hundreds of generations, to start camping about with their flocks than it would for the comparatively recently roving hunters who had, to be sure, been sedentary at the time they acquired sheep, but only for a few generations. Perhaps it seemed like a welcome return to "the good old ways"; perhaps the Navaho character had begun to feel somewhat cramped by the exigencies and restrictions of village life and was glad of a change. It is as important to bear in mind that some Navahos remained primarily farmers as to take note of the fact that others became primarily herders, for it underlines the ability of Navaho society to allow more than one way of life. However, even the Navaho farmers left the Pueblo-like villages, and now throughout the tribe prestige comes from fine flocks and many horses rather than from good crops.

Another interesting subject to consider is the way in which Navahos shaped Pueblo ritual forms and myths to their own purposes. It seems likely that whatever The People had in the way of religion when they arrived in the Southwest was very simple compared to what they found among the Pueblos and what they themselves have developed since. The restoration of universal harmony is a main endeavor of Pueblo religion, and one expected result of this is that the supernaturals will bring rain to water the crops and assure survival in a dry land. The Navahos borrowed many things from Pueblo agriculture and Pueblo religion but never amalgamated the two in the same way. Instead they spent much of their religious energy in trying to restore harmony for one individual at a time, in the expectation that thus he would be relieved of ills of mind or body. To be sure, Pueblo religion is used for curing to some extent, and Navahos pray for rain and good crops in connection with their curing ceremonials.

The reasons we might suggest for the difference in emphasis are, of course, in the realm of speculation. From what we have seen of present-day Navaho personality, it is not hard to understand the emphasis on individuals. It is possible that in their previous wandering existence illness was a major calamity because it interfered seriously with their means of getting food. Probably also poor hunting or meager yields of wild plants sometimes did not suffice for their nutrition, with consequent illness or even death. There would have been little reason for them to develop interest in improving crops, since they simply gathered what nature provided. Very likely agriculture of any sort seemed to hold so much promise of relief from hunger by contrast with picking wild foods that supernatural assistance did not at first appear necessary. At the same time it is remarkable that they did not take the Pueblo rituals to be a necessary condition of agriculture. Possibly they learned how to farm from observation before the Pueblos admitted them to ritual performances. Fundamentally, however, the changes they made in the aim of religious rites seem to indicate strongly a preoccupation with illness, for whatever reason, and that that was the area in which they felt the greatest uneasiness and need for supernatural help.

Navaho social organization is known only for the historic period. One cannot say whether it, too, was greatly modified by contact with the Pueblos or whether it remained essentially unchanged. Since many of the clans are named for southwestern localities, it seems likely that they, at least, are new since the arrival of The People in their present habitat, but the pattern may have been in the culture before. It does not seem strange that they should have felt the strongest bond to the mother, because her relationship with the children was probably more stable than that of the father. At the same time, Navaho social structure as seen today does not give an undue amount of importance to the mother. She and the children are the closest, perhaps, but her sphere has its limits, and she shares with her husband in many matters, while outside the hogan the husband's prerogatives are greater. Although this is the "typical" situation, one must never lose sight of the fact that it has many variations, and that it is not very much commoner, probably, than the family where the woman "runs the show" or where the man is the head. The way it works out in any given case depends chiefly upon the personalities of the individuals involved, and Navaho custom permits much more latitude here than does the custom of the neighboring Pueblos. The same thing could be said of choosing a place of residence — it depends on personalities and practical considerations of all sorts which are permitted to modify the general framework.

Another aspect of social organization which is affected both by the looseness of form and by the tendency to individuality is group coöperation. Families coöperate closely, and so do larger related groups periodically, as has been described in *The Navaho*. However, when it comes to a "community" where a number of families and clans are involved, it is sometimes very difficult to get any sort of concerted activity. No one present has any inherent conviction that his opinion or plan is better than that of his neighbor, and the rest of the group are of the same mind. Moreover, if it is a matter of one family having to make concessions or sacrifices that either will not benefit them at all or will chiefly benefit unrelated families, they do not show much enthusiasm for submerging their interest in that of the larger group. Here again is contrast with Pueblo peoples, where the good of the group takes precedence over almost all individual considerations.

Contacts with white men have, of course, been strongly influenced by the same factors that shaped the Navaho way of life. The characteristics of the white people themselves and of the way of life they had developed were also of tremendous importance. The first white men to appear, the Spanish, had little effect upon The People by direct contact or intention. Their principal contribution was domestic livestock, which produced profound changes in Navaho economy and ways of living, as we have seen. Next came a few pioneers from white American society, and then the soldiers. From the very first, white men misinterpreted Navahos because they took it for granted that "Indians are Indians" and that, since eastern tribes had chiefs whose word bound the tribe, Navahos would have them also. Perhaps this idea came partly from white custom, too, where political or military leaders were expected to take charge of inter-national matters and speak for their people. In any case, it led to serious misunderstanding and finally exasperated the military so much that "the Long Walk" resulted (see *The Navaho*, Chapter 1).

Probably the first real impact of "civilization" came at Fort Sumner where, under duress and from dire necessity, The People learned to eat the foods and to wear the dress of white men. There and subsequently they also became acquainted with many of the tools and techniques of white society. Characteristically they picked and chose, adopting only those which fitted their manner of living — silver-making tools, for example, but not the spinning wheel.

Soon after their return to "Navaho country" a school was started and missionaries began to make an appearance. Traders also came and set up posts in many remote spots. By these means knowledge of white culture and white people continued and increased. Again, characteristically, the white men were judged on an individual basis, some respected and beloved, others detested. At the same time all the bad deeds, disappointments, and broken promises of these white people, of government agents, and of the increasing number of white settlers became rolled into a stereotype of white character which was as mistaken as the white idea that "an Indian is an Indian." There was a tendency, also, to attribute to the whole group, whether white or Navaho, the motives and deeds of the various evil-doers who appear in all societies. There was lack of recognition on both sides that what looked like evil intentions, untrustworthiness, or utter unpredictability was really only a matter of the natural consequences of acting according to different fundamental premises. Each side took its own views so much for granted and felt them to be so "natural" that it could not grasp the possibility that other views might be "natural" to other people. This same attitude has persisted throughout Navaho-white dealings and has done, probably, the greatest damage of any single factor. There was again a contrast between Pueblo and Navaho Indians in their way of meeting white encroachments and pressures of all kinds. The Pueblos consolidated themselves in every way against the invaders, while the Navahos scattered and protected themselves by making it difficult for the whites to deal with more than a family or two at a time.

Finally, let us consider briefly the Christian missions to the Navaho. Many churches have established missions in the Navaho country. Missionaries of the various denominations have worked long and earnestly among The People. Some have become fluent in the language and acquired many close Navaho friends; others have offered school or hospital services; all have done their best to make Christianity attractive to the Indians by various means. Yet only a handful of converts resulted from all this effort. One might blame the failure on the missionaries because they demanded that converts give up their previous beliefs and rites. While this doubtless played a part, it seems probable that no matter how presented or what the inducements, the fundamentals of Christianity are too frequently contrary to basic Navaho premises for Navahos to grasp them clearly, let alone accept them. For example, the practical, literal People could subscribe more wholeheartedly to "Carpe diem" than to "Lay up for yourselves treasures in heaven where neither moth nor rust doth corrupt and where thieves do not break through nor steal." The concept of an "immortal soul" might well horrify the Navaho as being a sort of super-ghost that could never be considered safely disposed of. While much of Christian ethics, such as doing good to one's neighbor, might be acceptable, the reason behind it — of storing up credit for the life after death or of being impelled by conscience to good deeds — would be neither understandable nor acceptable. Most of Christian theology is much too abstract to interest The People.

This is, of course, not the whole story. Other, and perhaps more important, considerations are the feeling their own ceremonials give Navahos that The People are of supreme importance in the world, the social and dramatic aspects of the ceremonial performances, and preëminently the fact that Navaho religion developed out of the needs and ways of the Navahos rather than out of those of Hebrews and Europeans. It is interesting to consider whether Christian Science, with its healing aims closer to those of the Navaho than most other Christian sects and its rationale also more similar, might have "caught on" more successfully than the other denominations.

If we return now to our diagram and fit into it one of the less complicated cultural items discussed, namely the introduction of sheep and horses, the interdependencies become quite striking.

Here it is apparent that what looked at first like a relatively simple, uncomplicated matter of "improving" the native economy had a number of far-reaching effects which were unforeseen and, in part, undesirable. The same sort of result may be expected with any new scheme that is introduced. Thus, in advocating any change, one must try to see all the effects it will have upon the total Navaho picture. Suppose, for example, the Spanish or the early white American administrators had thought of the results to the land of innumerable sheep and goats and had forestalled these results by limiting the number of animals any family could have. Many years later the depleted condition of the land forced this measure, but by that time Navahos had formed definite attitudes and sentiments about their large flocks, which engendered the greatest reluctance to reduce their numbers. Sufficient foresight might have mitigated slightly the serious effect of the erosion cycle, to say nothing of sparing both Navahos and the government many difficulties.

GENERAL IMPLICATIONS

ENOUGH has been said in the preceding section to indicate that those who undertake to administer Navaho affairs wisely have no easy task. The point is that any change that is introduced, unless carefully considered beforehand in all its ramifications, is bound to have results not intended and often not helpful. Change will inevitably occur even if it is not willfully brought about by The People themselves or their administrators. It will be less upsetting if it occurs spontaneously and gradually than if narrow-visioned local leaders or planners from afar, not well acquainted with Navahos and their ways, try to impose "improvements." Large-scale introductions can be expected to meet uneven success because of the very diversity and individuality of The People. What suits a group on the eastern

INTRODUCTION OF SHEEP AND HORSES

Physical Environment
Permitted livestock

There resulted:
    Overgrazing
    Serious erosion
    Destruction of farm land

History
The People, originally hunters and gatherers, but
More recently sedentary farmers,
Received animals from Spanish via Pueblos and
Became herders and weavers

Way of Life
Before livestock Navahos were:
    Village dwellers
    Farmers
    Sedentary people

After livestock Navahos lived as:
    Scattered families
    Herders and farmers
    Widely traveling people

Personality Factors
Individualism
Activity
Curiosity
Elasticity
Practicality

Permitted the change and were fostered by it.

border of the Reservation may go greatly against the grain of a central or western community.

Take as an example the compulsory education currently demanded by Navahos. One could expect that this would not greatly disturb a group where there was little sheepherding and much farming. With relatively little upheaval the families might even move closer to the school to facilitate transportation. The schedule could easily be adjusted to allow the students to help in the planting, cultivation, and harvesting of the fields. In a herding community, on the other hand, either drastic changes in current techniques would have to be made or the children would have to be provided with living quarters at the school. If these families and their flocks were to converge on the school, as might be feasible in the farming community, a huge, bare, grassless patch would soon develop over the entire school area as it has already done around so many hogans and watering places where the sheep come and go over the same land day after day.

Each day the flocks will have to go farther away from the school. Who is to herd them? If the father does it, who will get the wood and water? If all school-age children are away from home, who will help care for the little ones while the mother weaves? Will diseases increase greatly when space between families is reduced? Will social tensions grow, or will a willingness to coöperate in a common interest develop?

These are only a few of the more obvious problems that the suggestion of compulsory education raises. They are not insoluble, and they do not of themselves indicate that compulsory education is inadvisable. Rather they point out that, if it was decreed today that all Navaho children must go to school, Navaho families, educators, and administrators would find that the matter involved a good deal besides putting up and equipping more buildings and recruiting teachers. An alternative scheme, not without difficulties of its own, would be to investigate different Reservation districts and provide and enforce compulsory education where conditions were suitable, gradually extending it to the whole Reservation when the necessary preliminary changes had taken place.

Who should determine where, how, and what sort of changes are to take place? Should that be the duty of a kind and fatherly Navajo Service? No, because this would keep The People forever dependent and dissatisfied. Should it be the Navahos themselves exclusively? Again no, but they should certainly play the major role. Although the extent to which changes in life-ways are "determined" consciously by anybody is limited, eventually whatever is done must be done by the Navahos; but for a time they will need white counselors to interpret white culture to them and to intermediate in various ways. Gradual self-management should begin as soon and proceed as rapidly as possible. The soundest, though not the easiest, way to accomplish this will be to discuss the facts of any given situation with The People involved, let them decide upon ways and means, and let them do the carrying out. Only in this way will The People finally take an independent place in the nation and add their contribution to the American cultural heritage.

SAMPLE RESPONSES, BETSY'S TESTS

I.

SAMPLES

of TEST RESPONSES

A. STEWART EMOTIONAL RESPONSE TEST

THESE responses were elicited by the question to each child, "Have you ever been very happy (sad, afraid, angry, ashamed)?" If the child answered, "Yes," the examiner would say, "Can you remember when you were very happy (sad, afraid, angry, ashamed)? Tell me about it."

For happiness, a Shiprock girl of seven (Child A) gave these instances:

1. When my father buys me a new shoes.
2. When I get a new doll.
3. When I get hair pins or combs.

A Shiprock boy of twelve (Child B) responded:

1. If your father buy something for you.
2. If you're going to town.
3. If you are going to a Squaw Dance.

A Navaho Mountain girl of ten (Child C) answered:

1. When my sister takes me to herd with her.
2. When I have a lamb to play with.
3. When my father brings me candy from the trading post.

A Navaho Mountain boy of seventeen (Child D) said:

1. I can't remember, but whenever I hear good news or get new clothes I am happy.
2. I am happy most of the time.
3. When my father and I go to the Sing.

For sadness, these same children gave the following examples:

Child A. 1. When my big sister goes away.
          2. When someone kills my goat.
          3. When my sheep gets sick and die.

Child B. 1. I am never sad.

Child C. 1. I am never sad.

Child D. 1. When I lost my beautiful bracelet — I'll never get another like it.

2. When someone stole my money a few years ago. I never did find out who did it.

3. Not many other times.

Things which arouse fear in these children are:

Child A. 1. Man that goes around. They catch you, my mother told me.

2. That is all.

Child B. 1. I'm afraid of Santa Claus.

2. I'm afraid of tramps.

3. If a car is running fast.

Child C. 1. I am afraid to go outside in the dark — the *ch'įįdii* might get me.

2. I am afraid of the wild cattle in Navaho Canyon — they scare me.

3. I am afraid of snakes — soon they will be out.

Child D. 1. Maybe, but I don't remember. When I was small, but not now.

2. Only of Navaho witches, but I always look out for them.

3. Nothing else.

All of these children disclaimed anger. Responses of others ran like this:

A Shiprock boy of fourteen:

1. I get angry about Farmington when I don't go over there.

2. Sometime I am about candy if I don't get it.

3. Sometime my cat steal the thing — I get angry.

A Shiprock girl of eleven:

1. I make myself angry.

2. When someone treats me mean.

3. That's all.

A Navaho Mountain boy of fifteen, away in boarding school:

1. The boys here at school make me angry — then I fight them.

2. I get angry when my teachers scold me — I'm not dumb, but they make me mad.

3. I hate to herd sheep — they are so dumb — they won't go anywhere.

An unschooled Navaho Mountain girl of ten:

1. I don't get angry — I just feel bad and cry.

It was difficult in many cases to get the children to relate instances
when they had felt ashamed. Here are a few samples:

A Navaho Mountain boy of seventeen:

1. Only when I need new clothes.

A Navaho Mountain girl of ten:

1. I let the goats eat the needles of the pinyon trees. Then the
needles stick in the stomach and they die.
2. Now, because I don't have any shoes.

A Shiprock girl of seventeen:

1. When I am late to school.
2. When my sister is angry to my classmates, it makes me
ashamed.
3. When I don't tell my mother I'm going to town, I'm ashamed
when I come back.

A Shiprock boy of fourteen:

1. I'm ashamed to dance.
2. I get ashamed when I spoil something and my mother punish.

When asked, "What is the best thing that could happen to you?"
the original four subjects, answered as follows:

Child A. To get a new dress.
Child B. Get some horse.
Child C. Have lots of new clothes and candy.
Child D. If I could have a lot of money I would work for it.

The examiner also inquired, "What is the worst thing that could
happen to you?" with these results:

Child A. To move from where we live.
Child B. Cough [means tuberculosis, perhaps?]
Child C. Be struck by lightning — maybe.
Child D. To be with a girl of my own clan.

Needless to say, the above material would not be sufficient to provide a clear picture of all the attitudes and reactions of Shiprock and Navaho Mountain people, but it is a fair sample of the sort of data gathered by means of this part of the Psychological Battery.

B. BAVELAS MORAL IDEOLOGY TEST

WHEN the question was asked, "What could a boy (girl) of your age do that would be a good thing, so that someone would praise him (her) or be pleased?" replies of this sort were obtained.

Child X (Ramah boy of ten):

1. I hardly know. People don't praise me much.
2. [On being pressed] Doing different kinds of work. [Who would praise you?] My mother.
3. Doing the cooking sometimes. My mother would praise me.

Child Y (Ramah boy of six):

1. Herd sheep and feed them well. My mother would praise me.
2. Make a hogan. My mother would praise me.
3. Haul in water and bring it to the hogan. My mother would praise me.

Child Z (Ramah girl of seventeen):

1. Weaving and carding. Mother and father would praise me.
2. Taking good care of sheep and lambs. Father or mother or sister or husband would praise me.
3. Doing all the work I am supposed to do and not doing anything wrong. Sister or husband would praise me.

When asked, "What could a boy (girl) of your age do that would be a bad thing, so that someone would blame him (her) or think badly of him (her)?" these children replied as follows:

Child X:

1. Some of them steal. [Who will blame him or think badly of him?] Different ones — other people.
2. I don't know what else they do.

Child Y:

1. Stealing sheep. [Who will blame him?] Somebody.
2. Being lazy. Father will blame him.

3. When his father tells him to bring wood and he doesn't do it. Father will blame him.

4. If his father sent him to the trading post to get something and he wouldn't get it. Father would blame.

Child Z:

1. Stealing sheep out of a corral. [Who would blame?] Anyone who saw it.

2. Stealing wool. All my relatives would blame.

3. Fornication. My husband and also my mother and all my relatives would blame.

Other tests from the Psychological Battery are not reproduced because they were not utilized in this book in evaluating Navaho attitudes and interests.

C. THEMATIC APPERCEPTION TEST

THE Thematic Apperception Test is a little difficult to discuss without a set of the pictures which were shown to the children, but it may interest readers to see the kinds of stories the children produced. Twelve pictures were used, some of which turned out to be more revealing than others. They are on file with the Committee on Human Development at the University of Chicago. As a rule, if a child would tell a story for one picture, he would invent one for each, or at least most, of the others. Sample stories follow.

Picture I. (Two male figures stand facing another male figure, who is apparently older.)

Child M (Ramah boy of fourteen): The three of them come together and talk about something. One of the two asks the other man, "Where do you come from?" The man by himself tells a story to the other two. They ask him, "Where are you going?" That's all.

Child N (Shiprock girl, ten): This man looks like he's saying that he's going someplace. And these two are going someplace too. Looks like these two are saying that they're going to the trading post.

Child O (Ramah boy, eight): This man is telling these fellows that he is going to put them in jail for stealing a horse from him.

Child P (Navaho Mountain boy, fourteen): The old man is talking to these two boys. Maybe he's saying they stole something.

Child Q (Ramah girl, eighteen): This man is telling these boys that he wants them to go hunting for rabbits. The one in front says it's all right with him and the other one doesn't say anything.

Picture II. (A woman with baby on lap sits looking at two children and turtle on ground in front of her.)

Child M: The mother is holding the baby and nursing it and the other two kids are just playing.

Child N: Looks like the baby is going to sleep. Looks like the boy is saying that the turtle's going to bite him. Looks like the girl's saying, "The turtle's going to bite you." (What does the mother say?) "The baby is asleep, don't make too much noise."

Child O: This woman is telling her kids not to play with the turtle and to go ahead and take the sheep out. She's holding the baby.

Picture III. (Two men face each other, one leading a horse, the other with his hand up.)

Child O: This man wanted that horse in three days, to be sure to bring it in three days. And this other fellow isn't so sure about it.

Child Q: These men can't understand each other, they're just making motion. And it seems like this white man is telling the Indian to come see him in four days.

Child R: (Ramah girl, ten): This man is buying this horse. At first he said he was going to give this other fellow $4.00, then he said four head of sheep.

Picture VI. (An old man in ancient costume sits on a rock with stick in hand and head bowed.)

Child N: Looks like that man is hungry and he's sitting down. Looks like he was herding the sheep. He was herding the sheep someplace far away from his home.

Child O: This man's name is Nabeho. He is just thinking about getting married again at a different place.

Child M: That man is sitting there and looking at the plants, wondering what kind of plants they are. He thinks they are very pretty plants. This is a place quite close to a cornfield. He had been doing many things before he found the plants, but after he saw them he sat down. He had not finished his work but had decided to return home. On the way he found these plants. After he had studied out the plants he thought he would like to go and hunt some more like those. He thought, "Perhaps there are some around my home too, but I have never seen them." That's all.

D. RORSCHACH TEST

THIS test has been fully described by a number of writers, one of whom is listed in the Bibliography. The only attempt here will be to give an idea of the fullness or scantiness of the records obtained by tabulating the original responses of three children: one who had little to say, one who gave a fairly "average" number of answers, and one who produced considerably more than "average." (See Table 19.)

Even to a person who knows little about such a test, it would be obvious that more can be discovered about the individual who responded with the full record than with the other two, and much more than about the one whose record is so scanty. However, it must be pointed out that even scanty records on two children are quite different and give some information about the subjects. There are all degrees of variation in fullness and other aspects among the 110 children who took the Rorschach test, but these samples will be sufficient to indicate the type of data collected. Of the three, the first two were obtained through an interpreter and the third directly in English. However there are a few equally full records where an interpreter was used, so that familiarity with English does not seem to be the sole explanation for the amount said.

Quantitative analysis of the Navaho Rorschach protocols is shown in Table 20. These data will be of interest chiefly to persons who have had technical experience with the Rorschach Test.

TABLE 19
ORIGINAL REPONSES TO RORSCHACH CARDS BY THREE NAVAHO CHILDREN

Rorschach Card	Child I (Scanty responses)	Child II ("Average" responses)	Child III (Full responses)
I	Nothing	Doesn't look like anything.	1. Mask. 2. Look like two fox. 3. Look like a fox, his head.
II	Bear, two	This looks like a bear. The head is mostly this way, and he's got his back turned the other side.	1. Looks like old man. 2. Looks like one lady, one man dance. 3. Monkey, this part. 4. Lady dancing right here. 5. Whole thing looks like a sheepskin burning right here. 6. Looks like a light.
III	1. Duck 2. Water	This looks like two men standing towards each other. Here's their arms and legs.	1. Looks like these two men are going to get the water. 2. Looks like butterfly. 3. Looks like monkey fell down. 4. His neck is long one (man's).
IV	Frog	Whole thing looks like a frog.	1. Looks like a big giant. 2. One dragon going into hole. 3. Look like turkey's head. 4. Look like one man, right here. 5. Big giant riding the dragon.

TABLE 19 — (continued)

V	Butterfly	I don't know what it is.	1. Looks like a butterfly. 2. Looks like a rabbit flying! 3. Those two rabbits going in here. 4. Like rabbit hanging down. 5. Like man going under the water.
VI	Nothing	This looks like the hide of the skunk, just the hide.	1. Like Indian chief standing right here. 2. Here looks like girls' hair. 3. Look like sheepskin too. 4. Look like grass around lotta rock. 5. Look like there's a ditch. 6. Look like statue.
VII	Girl	Looks like sky, but the bottom doesn't look like it.	1. Looks like George Washington's hat. 2. Looks like boy roller skating. 3. Looks like house. 4. Looks like water coming down here. 5. Looks like that ugly witch walk. 6. Look like you go like this (pointing finger). 7. Head of old man — he was under the water. 8. Elephant's head. 9. Looks like they shut the river and here's a lot of water.

TABLE 19 — (continued)

Rorschach Card	Child I (Scanty responses)	Child II ("Average" responses)	Child III (Full responses)
VIII	1. Lamb 2. Water 3. Rock	Those are wild cats. They're both climbing on a tree.	1. Look like two prairie dogs. 2. Look like old witch walking. 3. Look like one tent, right here a hill. 4. Look like big fire right here. 5. Look like one man hiding behind rock. 6. Look like this thing (prairie dog) sort of climbing the rock.
IX	Nothing	This looks like a little child, two of them, lying under something.	1. Look like cloudy. 2. Look like one cowboy coming. 3. Look like one woman coming to him. 4. Look like a moon coming up. 5. Look like one lizard standing up. 6. Look like two kings fighting.
X	Nothing	I can't imagine what that is.	1. Look like two deer. 2. One man is sitting down. 3. Here are two men trying to go across these two rocks. 4. Look like lady. 5. Look like man. 6. Look like spider. 7. Look like king.

TABLE 20

QUANTITATIVE RESULTS OF THE RORSCHACH TEST ADMINISTERED TO 110 NAVAHO CHILDREN

Item	Shiprock			Ramah			Navaho Mountain			Tribal		
	Boys	Girls	Total	Boys	Girls	Total	Boys	Girls	Total	Boys	Girls	Total
Number of subjects	15	28	43	13	15	28	25	14	39	53	57	110
5–7 years	1	9	10	2	1	3	5	2	7	8	12	20
8–10 years	4	8	12	3	5	8	6	2	8	13	15	28
11–13 years	7	6	13	6	3	9	8	4	12	21	13	34
14–18 years	3	5	8	2	6	8	6	6	12	11	17	28
Average number of responses [a]	20	22	21	8	12	10	16	12	14	15	17	16
5–7 years [b]	:	:	:	:	:	:	:	:	:	14	19	16
8–10 years	:	:	:	:	:	:	:	:	:	24	22	23
11–13 years	:	:	:	:	:	:	:	:	:	13	15	14
14–18 years	:	:	:	:	:	:	:	:	:	9	12	10
	(Per cent)			(Per cent)			(Per cent)			(Per cent)		
Percentage of subjects rejecting one or more blots [c]	53	54	54	85	60	71	52	64	56	60	58	59
5–7 years [b]	:	:	:	:	:	:	:	:	:	62	25	40
8–10 years	:	:	:	:	:	:	:	:	:	31	62	50
11–13 years	:	:	:	:	:	:	:	:	:	52	46	50
14–18 years	:	:	:	:	:	:	:	:	:	91	76	82
	(Per cent)			(Per cent)			(Per cent)			(Per cent)		
Manner of approach [d]												
W	19	18	18	30	34	32	23	27	25	24	26	25
D	62	58	60	64	51	58	66	69	67	64	59	62
d	7	7	7	1	3	2	5	3	4	4	4	4
Dd and/or S	12	12	12	5	11	8	6	4	5	8	9	8

TABLE 20 — (continued)

Item	Shiprock Boys	Girls	Total	Ramah Boys	Girls	Total	Navaho Mountain Boys	Girls	Total	Tribal Boys	Girls	Total
"Inner maturity" [e] (M greater than FM) [d]	*(Per cent)*			*(Per cent)*			*(Per cent)*			*(Per cent)*		
5–7 years [b]	65	60	..	50	17	..	0	18	..	38	32	..
8–10 years	..	..	..	..	..	..	..	..	..	25	21	..
11–13 years	..	..	..	..	..	..	..	..	..	35	21	..
14–18 years	..	..	..	..	..	..	..	..	..	20	36	..
										38	32	..
"Outer maturity" [e] (FC greater than CF) [d]	*(Per cent)*			*(Per cent)*			*(Per cent)*			*(Per cent)*		
5–7 years [b]	..	..	..	..	..	..	..	..	..	20	50	..
8–10 years	..	..	..	..	..	..	..	..	..	80	21	..
11–13 years	..	..	..	..	..	..	..	..	..	29	83	..
14–18 years	..	..	..	..	..	..	..	..	..	80	85	..

Tribal averages, P per cent and O per cent [d]	P per cent Boys	Girls	O per cent Boys	Girls
5–7 years	11	10	8	3
8–10 years	21	22	7	3
11–13 years	24	25	3	9
14–18 years	32	30	2	6

[a] White adults average 20–40 responses; white children under ten years average less than 20. (Bruno Klopfer and Douglas McG. Kelley, *The Rorschach Technique*, Yonkers-on-Hudson, N. Y.: World Book Co., 1942).
[b] Percentages were not calculated for the age-grades in the communities because the number of subjects in each was so small.
[c] There were 3 total rejections, all from Shiprock.
[d] For meaning of symbols, see Klopfer and Kelley, *op. cit.*
[e] For explanation of this term, see Chapter 8 above.

FULL ANALYSES

of BETSY'S TESTS

IN ORDER to show what the various tests contributed to the whole picture of the child's personality and how each test supplemented the others, analyses of all the tests taken by one child are shown here. The subject is Betsy, the child whose autobiography is given in the Introduction; she is also Case 4 of the Ramah children described in Chapter 9.

All of these analyses were made by people who had never met Betsy and knew nothing about her except what they could learn from the test itself. Only after each had made his analysis independently were the results compared. This same procedure was followed with all of the sixteen cases described in Chapter 9, and the results checked with or supplemented each other to about the same extent as in this instance.

FREE DRAWINGS (ANALYSIS BY LISBETH EUBANK)

THAT Betsy produces fourteen pictures instead of the usual eight may indicate high energy output. She seems to be direct and purposeful in the handling of content and shows an intelligent approach with a great mind for detail. She is one of the few girls to show the sex of the animals. From her drawings it seems possible that she may feel some anxiety in her home, or perhaps it is just that she does not like some relationships there or the tasks she has to perform. She is at her best in a picture of a Navaho lady at a sheep camp. She is evidently stimulated by this atmosphere, or by the security and happiness she finds there. In this one picture she shows high creativity, and matter-of-factness gives way to imaginative powers. She certainly does not shrink from people and attempts coherence, organization, and balance when she treats them.

She seems most responsive to the outside world, has good intelligence, no unusual creativity. She shows slight anxiety and hesitancy in the matter of line and form elements, but she is responsive to color and achieves balance by this means. Except for the one picture showing buildings at the school, her content is wholly concerned with her immediate home environment and Navaho culture.

PSYCHOLOGICAL BATTERY (ANALYSIS BY ROBERT J. HAVIGHURST AND LISBETH EUBANK)

BETSY is fairly self-confident, somewhat impulsive, friendly, and socially responsive. She has average intelligence and makes effective use of it; but she is not overly creative. She is more overtly aggressive than most of the Navaho girls. She seems to be trying hard to incorporate white ways into her own philosophy and way of living; she shows some anxiety about it but apparently feels secure in the Navaho pattern.

THEMATIC APPERCEPTION (ANALYSIS BY WILLIAM E. HENRY)

A. *Summary*

THIS is the record of a girl whose general adjustment both to self and to her environment is good. She is a rather pampered child who approaches the outer world with strength, vigor, and confidence. Her adjustment, however, is somewhat uncertain, and her appearance of excellent social relations is based more on her high conscious control than on an adequate balance between her inner life and her reactions to the environment. She is a somewhat masculine girl whose rejection of some of the feminine role leads her to boys' interests and tasks. Raised in a very genial family, her general outlook on life and her techniques for adaptation are constructive and suggest an excellent prognosis. There is, however, evidence of specific sexual anxiety which arises largely from her mother's own uncertainty in this area. The father is an adequate Navaho man and presents no specific problems to his daughter. The family seems to have had considerable contact with white men and have not rejected this contact in any way.

Betsy is a girl of a very facile impulse life who has developed her fantasy to a usable degree but seldom avoids problems by escaping into fantasy. Her first approach to new situations is vigorous and direct, though not without some anxiety. She may retire once she has tackled a problem and finds it too difficult, but her first reaction is somewhat of a challenge rather than either complete acceptance or rejection.

B. *Details of the Record*

1. Mental Approach. She has superior or very superior intelligence. The efficiency of her intellectual functioning should be excellent. She shows energy and directness. At times, if she should become unsure of herself, it seems probable that her efficiency would be reduced because of her tendency to lose her organizing capacities. There is a suggestion that the directness of her approach is modified by some slight anxiety and a tendency to overact.

Her organizing capacities are good and she is able to utilize them in both routine and creative areas, but they are subject to the influence of emotional factors and are occasionally disrupted.

2. Creativity. She produces creative ideas readily and with ease. Her imaginative capacities are good and are used frequently as an attack upon emotional problems.

3. Behavioral Approach. An active, vigorous girl who approaches the outer world in a direct and slightly demanding fashion. Her handling of daily events suggests a certain superficial confidence in the outer world, both in her ability to handle it and in its eventually giving in to her. This is the picture of a somewhat "spoiled" child who, because she is basically somewhat afraid of real contact with the outer world, denies this fact by affirming complete confidence in it. She has a rather playful contact with reality which suggests that the first impression she makes upon people is uniformly good, and which also betrays her real doubt as to the stability of her grasp upon reality.

Her relationships with her agemates should all be excellent, and she should be a constructive member of any group. She is somewhat more masculine than feminine in her interests and orientation towards her mates. She seems to try to avoid the usual feminine household tasks and prefers masculine diversions and duties. She does not appear to be avoiding girls but would seem more readily identified with boys.

With adults she is able to recognize their potential control and authority but is not unduly impressed by it. This suggests good confident relations with parents and ability to work well with adults in general.

School work should be very good in all areas. Intellectually she should make a superior student, and her drives toward action and superiority should serve her well in classwork. Relationships with teachers and students should be satisfactory and coöperative.

While there seems to be no real difficulty at present in the area of behavior, there are suggestions that she may have tendencies toward overactive aggression when she does not get her own way or when her superiority is questioned; and toward periods of depression or moodiness, perhaps, when someone's affection is removed, or she thinks that it is.

4. Family Dynamics. Betsy's feelings for her mother are good and she has adequately handled any external control which her mother may enforce. The mother seems, however, to be rather lenient and not to have unduly dominated her daughter. As mentioned above, Betsy has rejected somewhat the usual household feminine role, and while she feels a little guilty about this, she may still refuse, or at least protest against, household duties. This makes her not quite at ease with her mother, and there is also another reason for uneasiness which will have a more far-reaching influence upon her development. This is the problem of her sexual adjustment. Since there seems to be little hostility to her mother, it is possible that Betsy's orientation in the feminine sexual role has been communicated fairly directly to her by her mother, whose own sexual adjustment must have some elements of rejection.

There are no data on other family members except that the relation to the father is sound, and, considering her masculine trends, may imply closer feeling for him than for the mother. The family atmosphere is generally good and there seem to be no specific hostilities nor undue domination of one member by another.

5. Inner Adjustment and Defense Mechanisms. Her basic emotional attitude is slightly aggressive. She has a good acceptance of her inner life, seems quite vital and intense, and is on her way to a very sound mature adjustment. Inner life is quite fluid and active and is used fairly well in solving emotional problems. There is a hint, however, that she does not get quite enough support from her inner life to enable her to handle her problems. While her solutions are generally forceful and direct, she is aware of her more tender side; she would like to relax and be compliant for once, but is unable to do so.

She is especially aware of other people and generally dependent upon them for stimulation and support. She must have them in her environment in order to feel safe. She is actively concerned with problems of her relations to them and has not reached any adequate solution. She is genuinely driven towards contact with them, but is not able to completely accept them emotionally.

One cannot say that she is mature or immature. She is in a state of adolescent change and concerned with problems typical of that period: worry over the future and her relation to it.

6. Emotional Reactivity. Her drive towards the outer world is strong, though she is not able to accept everything she meets in it. Occasionally she retreats from outer world contact. She always puts her best foot forward, but she is actually a little wary of the world. She is in general spontaneous and vital except for some restraint in the sexual area, but she has not yet reached sufficient maturity to be completely free in her dealings with reality.

7. Sexual Adjustment. There is some specific sexual anxiety and consequent rejection of the usual feminine role. She is very sex-conscious, yet confused over the significance of her sexual life. She has difficulty accepting herself as feminine, though she is aware of herself as a person to be loved.

RORSCHACH TEST (ANALYSIS BY ALICE JOSEPH) [1]

A. *Summary*

BETSY is a very intelligent, spirited girl, evidently just blossoming into adolescence and not yet master of the new impulses this has given her. In her contacts with people she will probably appear still rather egocentric, with vivid alternating moods of enthusiasm, aggression, opposition, and withdrawal into herself. There may also be a slight display of self-consciousness.

B. *Details of the Record*

This girl's intellectual capacities are superior, as shown by good form quality, originality, variety of content, and good organization. Her intellectual efficiency, however, is below her potentialities. It is affected by the emotional conflict which seems to occupy her mind and leads her to overplay her imagination and take refuge in tiny details instead of making more meaningful whole concepts. She has remarkable imaginative capacities, perceiving 12 original concepts in 30 responses. She uses both imagination and creative powers to aid

[1] All other Rorschach analyses were made by Dr. Leighton.

her in solving the emotional conflict with which she seems to be struggling.

Her basic emotional attitude includes aggression, impulsiveness, and passion. There is a need and appreciation for warm, affectionate feelings. It appears that suddenly for some reason her ready and passionate responsiveness has become questionable to her, and much of her energy is called upon to solve this problem, which affects her with the force of a fresh trauma. She gives no evidence of anxiety, but she appears to be definitely aware of the conflict within her.

Her way of reacting is exceedingly complex and intricate for a girl of her age. There is a first immediate violent reaction of desire and fear that she cannot master externally. So her imaginative abilities are called into play, used effectively, and to an unusually high degree for her age. There are certain very disturbing emotions which do not yield to this treatment, which she then tries to inhibit. This disturbance is superimposed on an originally natural and spontaneous acceptance of the outer world, which, apart from this one side, appears to her very friendly and serene. It is this fact mainly that suggests the existence of a fresh trauma. From the content of the answers in which the conflict is apparent, it seems probable that the drives she cannot accept are of sexual nature. Her conscious control is good, neither too much nor too little, and is refined by a rather strong tendency to introspection.

The present conflict has no neurotic quality and does not affect deeply her basic personality structure. It is probably temporary, and to some extent connected with her physiological and inner maturation. Her imaginative and creative capacities seem sufficient to achieve a solution in time.

She is an introvert and her tendencies are also introversial.

Her maturity is rather more than would be expected from her years but still not excessive nor such as would indicate over-adjustment.

REFERENCES AND BIBLIOGRAPHY

REFERENCES and BIBLIOGRAPHY

CHAPTER 1

Dennis, Wayne, "Does Culture Appreciably Affect Patterns of Infant Behavior?" *The Journal of Social Psychology*, XII (1940), 305–317.

———— *The Hopi Child* (New York: D. Appleton-Century Co., 1940). The cradle-board study referred to on p. 30 above is described in Chapter V of this book.

Hill, Willard W., *The Agricultural and Hunting Methods of the Navaho Indians*, Yale University Publications in Anthropology, No. 18 (New Haven: Yale University Press, 1938). Section quoted on p. 36 above is from p. 56 of this monograph.

A more detailed and technical account of some features of the first few years of life will be found in Clyde Kluckhohn, "Some Aspects of Navaho Infancy and Early Childhood," *Psychoanalysis and the Social Sciences*, edited by G. Róheim (New York: International Universities Press, 1947). See also: "Personality Formation among the Navaho Indians," *Sociometry* IX (1946).

CHAPTER 2

Dyk, Walter, editor, *Son of Old Man Hat; a Navaho Autobiography* (New York: Harcourt, Brace and Company, 1938). Sections quoted on pp. 50 and 63 above are from pp. 6–7 and 9–10 of this book.

CHAPTER 3

Wyman, Leland C., and Flora L. Bailey, "Navaho Girl's Puberty Rite," *New Mexico Anthropologist*, VI–VII (1943), 3–12.

CHAPTER 4

Kluckhohn, Clyde, *Navaho Witchcraft*, Papers of the Peabody Museum of American Archaeology and Ethnology, Harvard University, XXII (Cambridge, Mass.: The Museum, 1944).

Leighton, Alexander H., and Dorothea C. Leighton, *The Navaho Door* (Cambridge, Mass.: Harvard University Press, 1944).

———— "Some Types of Uneasiness and Fear in a Navaho Indian Community," *American Anthropologist*, XLIV (1942), 194–210.

Wyman, Leland C., and Betty Thorne, "Notes on Navaho Suicide," *American Anthropologist*, XLVII (1945), 278–288.

CHAPTER 5

General

Anonymous, "1940 Statistical Summary, Human Dependency Survey, Navajo Reservation and Grazing District 7" (Mimeographed, Window Rock, Arizona: Navajo Reservation, 1941).

Navaho Mountain

Collier, Malcolm Carr, "Preliminary Report on the Navajo Mountain Navajo." Manuscript.

Kluckhohn, Clyde, *Beyond the Rainbow* (Boston: The Christopher Publishing House, 1933).

Ramah

Bailey, Flora L., "Navaho Foods and Cooking Methods," *American Anthropologist*, XLII (1940), 270–290.

Kluckhohn, Clyde, "Participation in Ceremonials in a Navaho Community," *American Anthropologist*, XL (1938), 359–369.

—— "Navaho Women's Knowledge of their Song Ceremonials," *El Palacio*, XLV (1938), 87–92.

—— "Some Personal and Social Aspects of Navaho Ceremonial Practice," *Harvard Theological Review*, XXXII (1939), 57–82.

—— "Theoretical Bases for an Empirical Method of Studying the Acquisition of Culture by Individuals," *Man*, XXXIX (1939), 98–103.

—— "Notes on Navaho Eagle Way," *New Mexico Anthropologist*, V (1941), 6–14.

—— "A Navaho Personal Document with a Brief Paretian Analysis," *Southwestern Journal of Anthropology*, I (1945), 260–283.

Leighton, Alexander H., and Dorothea C. Leighton, "Elements of Psychotherapy in Navaho Religion," *Psychiatry*, IV (1941), 515–524.

—— *The Navaho Door* (Cambridge, Mass.: Harvard University Press, 1944).

—— "Some Types of Uneasiness and Fear in a Navaho Indian Community," *American Anthropologist*, XLIV (1942), 194–210.

Tschopik, Harry, Jr., "Navaho Basketry" (Manuscript, 1939).

—— "Navaho Basketry: A Study of Culture Change," *American Anthropologist*, XLII (1940), 444–462.

—— *Navaho Pottery Making*, Papers of the Peabody Museum of American Archaeology and Ethnology, Harvard University, XVII (Cambridge, Mass.: The Museum, 1941).

—— "Taboo as a Possible Factor Involved in the Obsolescence of Navaho Pottery and Basketry," *American Anthropologist*, XL (1938), 257–262.

Shiprock

There is no published material which relates solely and specifically to the Shiprock area.

BIBLIOGRAPHY FOR THE TESTING PROGRAM

The following books and articles may be consulted for information on the tests used in this study.

Arthur Test

Arthur, Mary Grace, *A Point Scale of Performance Tests* (New York: The Commonwealth Fund, 1933). 2 vols.

Goodenough Test

Goodenough, Florence L., *Measurements of Intelligence by Drawings*, (Yonkers-on-Hudson, N. Y.: World Book Company, 1926).

Psychological Battery

Bavelas, Alex, "A Method for Investigating Individual and Group Ideology," *Sociometry*, V (1942), 371–377.

Stewart, Kilton R. Personal Correspondence.

Projective Techniques in General

Frank, Lawrence K., "Projective Methods for the Study of Personality," *The Journal of Psychology*, VIII (1939), 389–413.

Thematic Apperception Test

Morgan, C. D., and H. A. Murray, "A Method for Investigating Phantasies: The Thematic Apperception Test," *Archives of Neurology and Psychiatry*, XXXIV (1935), 289–306.

Murray, Henry A., "Techniques for a Systematic Investigation of Fantasy," *The Journal of Psychology*, III (1937), 115–143.

—— *Thematic Apperception Test Manual* (Cambridge, Mass.: Harvard University Press, 1943).

Rorschach Test

Klopfer, Bruno, and Douglas McG. Kelley, *The Rorschach Technique*, (Yonkers-on-Hudson, N. Y.: World Book Company, 1942).

Results of the Indian Education Research Project are reported in the following papers. Those completed but not published are on file with the Committee on Human Development, University of Chicago. Tribal monographs resulting from the project are listed in the Preface.

Hallowell, A. Irving, Royal B. Hassrick, Alice Joseph, Bruno Klopfer, and Dorothea C. Leighton, "American Indian Rorschach Studies." In preparation.

Havighurst, Robert J., "Belief in Immanent Justice and Animism among Indian Children of the Southwest and Sioux." Manuscript.

———— "Comparison of American Indian Children and White Children by Means of the Emotional Response Test." Manuscript.

———— "The Comparison of Indian Children and White Children by Means of the Moral Ideology Test." Manuscript.

Havighurst, Robert J., and Lisbeth Eubank, "The Attitudes of Navaho, Zuni, and Sioux Children toward Rules of Games." Manuscript.

Havighurst, Robert J., Minna K. Gunther, and Inez E. Pratt, "Environment and the Draw-A-Man Test: The Performance of Indian Children," *Journal of Abnormal and Social Psychology*, XXXIX (1946), 50–63.

Havighurst, Robert J., and Rhea R. Hilkevitch, "The Intelligence of Indian Children as Measured by a Performance Scale," *Journal of Abnormal and Social Psychology*, XXXIV (1944), 419–433.

Henry, William E., "The thematic apperception technique in the study of culture-personality relations," *Genetic Psychology Monographs*, Jan.–June 1947, vol. 35, no. 1.

Joseph, Alice, and Dorothea C. Leighton, "Results of Physical Examinations of Indian Children." In preparation.

INDEX

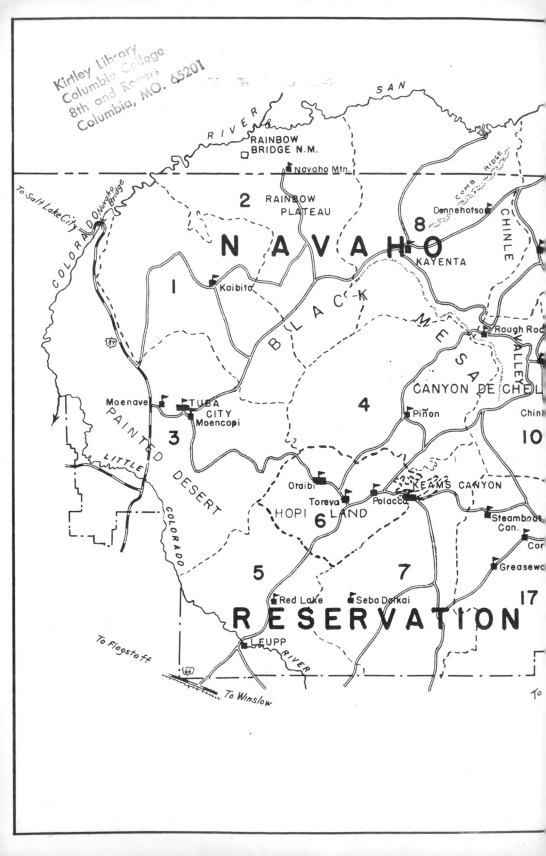